# THE

# NAVAJOS

## THE PAST AND PRESENT
## OF A GREAT PEOPLE

# John Upton Terrell

WEYBRIGHT AND TALLEY
New York

# 204801

Published in the United States by
WEYBRIGHT AND TALLEY
750 Third Avenue
New York, New York 10017

Published simultaneously in Canada by
CLARKE, IRWIN & COMPANY LIMITED
Toronto and Vancouver

LIBRARY OF CONGRESS CATALOG CARD NUMBER: 70-112033

Printed in the United States of America

BOOK DESIGN BY BENTE HAMANN

MAPS BY VAUGHN GRAY

# Author's Note

specified. It is a conglomerate of greed, bias, religious humbug, intellectual snobbishness, and self-righteousness held together by the mortar of racial prejudice.

Some Navajo publications display the words THE NAVAJO NATION. It is a futile slogan. The Navajos are not, and never will be, a nation. They are, and always will be, an American minority group. And that is one of their greatest misfortunes. They know the same travails, frustrations, and rejections experienced by other minorities. Opportunities are denied them because of their skin color. Housing is not generally available to them in cities, except in the poorest neighborhoods or the ghettos.

A hundred years ago there were fewer than ten thousand Navajos. By 1970 there were approximately 125,000. Their population is still increasing at a rate twice that of the nation as a whole.

For centuries, before the United States occupied the Southwest, the Navajos had been embroiled in perpetual warfare with other Indian tribes and had built up a strong economy based on banditry. Since the treaty of 1868 they have undergone the most amazing transition of any Indian people in history. Brigandage and armed conflict long ago were supplanted by orderly progress, unstinting drab labor, and commendable ideals. The Navajos have forcefully demonstrated that they are as intelligent, as adaptable, as industrious, as law-abiding, as competent as any people on earth.

Why, then, does one seldom meet a Navajo doctor, lawyer, professor, or business executive in the white world? The answer is simple. Very few Navajos have been accorded the opportunity to reach such heights. The government's program of Navajo education has always been geared to turning out laborers, mechanics, and other craftsmen—for most of whom there is no work in the Navajo country. Government

# The Navajos

# OTHER BOOKS

# BY

# JOHN UPTON TERRELL

LA SALLE
*The Life and Times of an Explorer*

ZEBULON PIKE
*The Life and Times of an Adventurer*

JOURNEY INTO DARKNESS
*The Story of Cabeza de Vaca*

FURS BY ASTOR
*A History of John Jacob Astor and the American Fur Trade*

BLACK ROBE
*Pierre-Jean deSmet, First Missionary in the
Rocky Mountain Region*

FAINT THE TRUMPET SOUNDS
*The Life and Trial of Major Reno*

ESTEVANICO THE BLACK
*Discoverer of Arizona and New Mexico*

THE MAN WHO REDISCOVERED AMERICA
*A Biography of John Wesley Powell*

teachers, social planners, and indifferent, if not dishonest, political appointees have insisted that the only method by which the Indian burden can be removed from the backs of taxpayers is to destroy the Indian's way of thinking, destroy his beliefs, his religion, his customs, and force him to forget his own language and history.

The contention that Navajos can be absorbed into American society is a myth. Every instinct, every attribute, every desire the Navajos possess, makes that an unreachable goal. The Navajos are Indian-Americans, and they cannot be changed, by themselves or anyone else, into Anglo-Americans.

Many other shadows darken the view from the Navajo capital of Window Rock. The great majority of Navajos begin life speaking only their own tongue. They must become fluent in English before they can find a place for themselves in the outside world. Thousands of Navajos who have migrated to industrial areas speak no more than a few words of English. The handicap not only limits the number of jobs they can obtain, but makes them lonely strangers among the urban masses. They cling to one another for a time, and then many give up and go home to become welfare problems or drunks in the honky-tonks of Gallup and other towns.

Poverty is rampant in numerous sections of the gigantic Navajo reservation. Eighty percent of all Navajo homes have only one room, and in many rooms eight or more people dwell in frightful squalor. Hundreds live in noxious slums, and the insanitary conditions create distressing health problems with which the limited medical services cannot effectively cope. The Navajo labor force so greatly exceeds available jobs that the entire Navajo country remains in the throes of a serious depression.

The dilemma of the Navajos is not insuperable, but the

only hope of combating it is through the development of industry and the establishment of schools of higher learning *in the Navajo country.*

As well as being fully capable of progressing and supporting themselves, the Navajos are eager to do it, but only without the loss of their self-respect, their dignity, and their identity. That happy day, however, will remain beyond their reach until a great many more white Americans support, and abide by, the guarantees embodied in the Constitution and civil rights statutes. Judging by existing attitudes, that will be a transition more difficult to achieve than modifications in Navajo culture.

JOHN UPTON TERRELL

# The Navajos

# 1

THE NAVAJOS SPEAK OF IT AS DINETAH, "Old Navajo Land."
It is a region of pastel canyons, juniper-covered mesas, and
saffron washes in northwestern New Mexico. East and south
of it high hogbacks jag the Continental Divide. To the
north, in southwestern Colorado, rise the peaks of the San
Juan and La Plata mountains. And to the west the Carrizo,
Lukachukai, and Chuska ranges lift blue pine-clad barriers
against the Arizona sky. The San Juan River enters Dinetah
in the northeast, transects it in a slow southerly bend, and
leaves it near the guarding sentinel of Winged Rock (Shiprock to Americans), beyond its northwest corner.

The Navajos call themselves Dineh, "the people." In their
language the name "Navajo" is not to be found. They use it
only when speaking Spanish or English, for it was applied to
them by the early Spaniards and adopted by Americans.
Before the time of written history they did not know it.

In the Navajo origin myths, man evolved through four

underworlds before reaching the surface of the earth. Most emerged in the mountains of southern Colorado, and others beside the western sea. And all of them moved to live together in Dinetah.

In the Navajo Genesis the four underworlds and the surface world are portrayed as superimposed hemispheres, the skies of which are supported by deities. All events that occurred in the four underworlds were evolutionary steps toward the birth of mankind in the surface world. In the first underworld there were four clouds, which embodied the prototypes of males and females. First Man was created, along with an ear of white corn, when two of the clouds met in the east. In the west two clouds met and created First Woman and an ear of yellow corn. Although First Man and First Woman lived together, they did not produce mankind. They were merely prototypes, not in themselves human beings. But in this darkness it was predestined that man would be, for First Man and First Woman planned his creation and, with the cooperation of Coyote Beings, Spider Beings, and other animate creatures among whom they dwelt, also planned all other developments for the surface world of man.

In the second underworld the prototypes fought with Bird Beings, and moved up to the third underworld. There they encountered Holy People and various other kinds of beings. In the third underworld many miraculous things came to pass. There the emerging people, the Dineh, found the prototype of Changing Woman, who represented fertility and life, "its regeneration and recession with the seasons." There agricultural seeds were obtained. There were found the prototypes of the four sacred mountains that would mark the boundaries of the Dineh's world on earth.

But the third underworld was not without misfortunes. There the sexes were temporarily separated, with the result that monsters were born. The Water Monster produced a great flood that drove all the beings upward to the fourth underworld. At last the sexes were reunited, but the monsters made the fourth underworld a fearful place, and First Man and First Woman led everyone up to the fifth world, the surface.

All the prototypes of mountains, rivers, and other geographical features, which were both male and female, were also brought up to the fifth world, and there the animate and the inanimate took the forms in which they would forever remain. According to the cosmic plan formulated in the lower worlds, the sun, the moon, and the stars were assigned their places, and so night and day and the seasons were established. The Holy People, the spiritual deities, went to live on the four sacred mountains—Big Sheep Peak, in the La Plata Range on the north; Mount Taylor, near Grants, New Mexico, on the south; San Francisco Peaks, near Flagstaff, Arizona, on the west; and Pelado Mountain, in the Jémez Range, on the east—which were adorned, respectively, with jet, turquoise, abalone shells, and white shells.* Ever since, when the Holy People have wished to make a journey, they have traveled on sunbeams, rainbows, and lightning. And Changing Woman, who is blessed with eternal youth and beauty, lives in a great house beside the western ocean.

Archaeology, ethnology, and linguistics, of course, provide a different account of Navajo beginnings. The directions of their migrations as given in the Navajo origin myths are correct, that is, southward from Colorado and eastward from the Pacific, and the evidence is clear that the first permanent homeland of the Navajos in the Southwest was Dinetah.

The Navajos came into the United States from northern

* Some Navajo singers say the eastern sacred mountain is Sierra Blanca Peak in Colorado. Thus the names of both mountains are contained in Navajo legends.

Canada. Their tongue unmistakably belongs to the Athapascan linguistic family, which was at one time the largest
and most widely distributed linguistic family in North
America, extending from the Arctic to northern Mexico and
from the Pacific coast to the mouth of the Rio Grande. The
languages of Indian peoples who live, or formerly lived, in
Alberta, British Columbia, Alaska, and along the Pacific in
Oregon and northern California are similar in innumerable
respects to the Navajo tongue. However, when or how the
Athapascans who would come to be known as Navajos, as
well as the Apaches, who belong to the same family, moved
to the Southwest remains a mystery.

But some evidence has been found that throws pinpoints
of light into the dark vaults of time.

These Mongoloid peoples who would later be mistakenly
called Indians came from many climates and from many
kinds of country. They spoke many dialects, and their ways
of life, their legends, spiritual beliefs, and deities, varied
greatly. Their physical characteristics showed wide vari-
ances, for men of different bloods moved through the land
mass of Asia long before any peoples migrated to the Western
Hemisphere. It is not known how many entered Asia proper
from Africa and the eastern Mediterranean, but even a few
would have been enough to leave telltale marks of their
different origins. The peoples who eventually moved on to
North America would bear those marks, though they would
be minimal and Mongoloid features would be dominant.

There was only one way they could have reached North
America: from the far north. They began to reach it at a time
when much of the world's water was locked in glaciers. But
the water passage called Bering Strait was then a land
bridge. Even afterward, when the oceans rose with melted
glacial water, it was narrow.

People crossed the land bridge long before the end of

the Ice Age, probably much more than forty thousand years ago. Crude stone tools of this age have been found by archaeologists in the California desert.

The migrants advanced southward with the slowness of glaciers. There was no mass migration then or in later centuries toward the south. The great mammals of the Ice Age—the giant bison, mammoth, and others—did not become extinct in the region of what is now the United States until between seven and eight thousand years ago. Also, other types of animals crossed over the land bridge from Asia, and man and beast trickled down into Canada, along the Pacific coast, into the northern Rocky Mountains, and through the millennia continued southward until they had reached the southernmost tip of South America. The animals found the best grazing grounds, and the people followed them, depending upon them and wild plant foods for their subsistence.

The search for more bountiful hunting grounds was the most significant factor in the prehistoric migrations. When northern Europe was glaciated, the animals moved southward and eastward to areas that were free of ice. As the ice retreated, the animals moved northward and eastward through Asia, and the people, who were dependent upon them for a steady supply of meat and furs, moved with them. They followed them into Siberia, and then across to North America.

In North America the migrants found two avenues of travel to be the most feasible as well as the most rewarding. One ran along the Pacific, and the other along the eastern slope of the Rocky Mountains. Over these two great natural thoroughfares most of the people moved. Over them passed culture after culture, each distributing its own mores and economic and social systems. The hunters, the scavengers, the carvers, the weavers, the builders, the destroyers, the planters came each in their turn, and the meteorological disturbances, the disasters of the heavens and the earth, pestilence, hunger, and warfare were not powerful enough, singly or together, to obliterate any one culture completely. Some vestiges of each one were perpetuated by successors.

The pace of the southward movement of the Athapascans is unknown. They were hunters, trappers, fishermen, and food gatherers. They brought with them to the vast region of the American Southwest the culture of a northern forest people. They lived entirely on game and wild fowl, and the nuts and fruits of the great forests, mountains, plains, and deserts through which they passed in their long slow journeys. The bounty of nature guided their movements. Adverse weather and food scarcities forced them to take meandering routes in search of sustenance. In areas where food supplies were stable, bands may have remained through several lifetimes.

They made their clothing from the furs and hides of animals, their temporary shelters from leaves and brush-wood, and they carried their small supplies in parfleches. They used wooden and clay utensils, and their crude tools were wood or bone. They knew nothing of weaving or metal-working, and very little, if anything, of masonry. They hunted with short sinew-backed bows—powerful weapons that may have been of Turkish origin—and with pointed sticks and snares made of vegetal fibers. They did not till the soil. Living on the land, they were as much a part of the wilderness as the lower creatures they consumed.

Most of the Athapascan Navajos traveled along the west-ern edge of the Great Plains. Certainly the Athapascan Apaches came that way. Some of the Navajos may have wandered eastward from the mountains for considerable distances before turning once more to the southwest, for their Shooting Chant relates how a Navajo traveled to a buffalo hunting village, and the Enemy Way Ceremony requires that the rattle used must be made from a buffalo scrotum. There were no buffalo in Dinetah. Some of the first Navajos may have penetrated the mountains—there is no archaeological proof that they migrated by way of the Great Basin—and circled southward through them, on the way living for many years among Paiutes.

However, wherever they wandered, whatever circuitous routes they took, the Navajos found that other peoples had preceded them. A number of important cultures had flourished and had been absorbed in the Southwest before the Navajos arrived—the Folsom, the Cochise, the Hohokam, the Salado, and others, in what is now Colorado, New Mexico, Arizona, and western Texas. Indians inhabited parts of this region as early as 30,000 B.C., and perhaps long before that date. However, it was the Anasazi, or Basket Maker–Pueblo, civilization that more than any other influenced the lives of the Navajos and shaped their history. This fact would indicate that the Navajos were relative latecomers to the New Mexico region.

Toward the southern end of the Rocky Mountains, in Colorado or northeastern New Mexico, the main trail of the migrating Athapascans branched. One fork continued southward, and over it traveled the Apaches. The other fork turned southwestward from the high plains, but there is no certainty as to where it entered the mountains. Some investigators believe it passed through the San Luis Valley of Colorado, crossed the Continental Divide, and descended the San Juan River into New Mexico. Other scholars believe it left the plains in northeastern New Mexico, ran through one or perhaps several passes in that area, crossed the Rio Grande in the vicinity of Taos, and continued west over the Jémez

Range and the Continental Divide and into the valley of the San Juan River. On it, whichever way it took, traveled the Navajos.

The Apaches also identify themselves by the name of Dineh. They would find their first permanent southwestern homeland in eastern New Mexico and western Texas, far to the south of the point where the trail branched. But unlike their Navajo relatives, who merged into a single tribe, the Apaches would develop into several tribal groups and would steadily expand until they dominated enormous parts of New Mexico, Arizona, and northern Mexico. They would reject the cultures of the sedentary peoples they encountered, and would maintain (even well into the American period) a hunting, food-gathering, raiding way of life.

The Anasazi culture was flourishing in the Four Corners region—southwestern Colorado, southeastern Utah, northeastern Arizona, and northwestern New Mexico—when Christianity was born. Many of the Anasazi beliefs, customs, and ceremonials have been preserved and are practiced today by the Pueblos and, significantly, by the Navajos.*

The period of Anasazi culture called Pueblo III was the "golden age" of the Pueblo Indians. It covered nearly three centuries, ending about A.D. 1300, and it is in the earlier part of this period that the first bands of Navajos may have reached Dinetah. The qualification is required.

Most of the great Pueblo cliff houses, some of them in caves high on immense canyon walls, and the large pueblos on mesa tops were constructed during this golden age. Population centers were located in the Kayenta, Chaco, Mesa Verde, and La Plata areas. Their ruins, protected today

---

* *The overall name "Anasazi" which anthropologists have given to this ancient civilization is an anglicized form of a Navajo word indicating "old peoples."*

in national parks and monuments, provide a glimpse into the past for thousands of tourists each year.

Before the big cliff apartments and mesa towns were built, the Pueblos lived in small independent villages, each containing no more than several score persons and each dominated by a social clan, all members of which were blood relatives. There are several theories as to why the people of these little towns decided to amalgamate and build large urban-type communities: easier defense, pooling of agricultural labor, more efficient use of water supplies, manufacture of improved types of utensils because of the greater variety of skills available. The caves were desirable locations; facing south, they were warm and sunny in winter, and protected from rains and snows.

By the beginning of the fourteenth century, or soon thereafter, the cliff houses and community pueblos were abandoned. No single force but a combination of factors brought about the end of this amazing human experiment.

Attack by raiders was the least of the pressures that caused the Pueblos to leave the big houses and towns, move south and east in clans, and resume their former way of life in independent and scattered communities. There were no Indian adversaries in the region strong enough to sack and destroy the easily defended cliff houses and large towns. The Navajos were in the region, but they were few in number. Their presence is indicated by the Navajo Flintway legend, which tells of a sun temple. This building was located in what is now Mesa Verde National Park. It was inhabited from about 1250 until a short time after 1300.

The Navajos, and possibly small bands of Paiutes, Comanches, and Apaches, drifting in from the mountains to the north and the plains to the east, might have made incursions, pilfering corn and carrying off unguarded women and children. That such raids took place during this period against smaller pueblos there is no question. The ruins of isolated villages show that they were destroyed by fire, and in some of them arrow points have been found in skeletons, both male and female, indicating that the Pueblos died defending their homes.

This is not the case in the great cliff dwellings and the larger pueblos. Yet it does not seem logical that people would construct these fortress-like buildings half way up towering cliffs, necessitating the hauling of water and provisions up a series of ladders, if not to safeguard themselves. The fear of invaders must have had some influence on their actions, but the fact remains that the cliff houses and large urban pueblos were not destroyed by enemy attackers, and their inhabitants were not involved in large-scale warfare. Some burned rooms have been found in them, but doubtlessly these fires were accidental. In a few places charred bones and crushed skulls have been discovered, but it is reasonable to assume that violent rows, especially between members of different clans or with visitors, occasionally occurred with tragic results.

The main causes of the great exodus from the cliff houses and big mesa towns appear to be drought and internal dissension.

The science of dendrochronology—dating based on the nature of annual rings in cross sections in trees—provides support for the first premise. It has shown that a severe drought persisted in the Pueblo region between the years 1276 and 1299. Water supplies would have been inadequate, and might have failed completely in some places, game animals would have abandoned the stricken area, and crops would have failed to mature. Reserve food supplies would have been consumed long before the catastrophe ended, and the people would have been confronted with the specter of starvation. Their only alternative would have been to leave and rejoin relatives or take up residence among friendly tribes where water was available. Members of a clan would have remained together, and thus the united peoples of the large towns once more would have separated.

Archaeology, and especially ethnology, lend support to the second premise as the cause of the extensive movement. The people who amalgamated to build the large towns came from many small pueblos, each one with its own social and religious customs and ceremonies. Although the people adjusted the material aspects of their cultures to existence in the big towns and cliff houses, they refused to abandon their respective social and religious practices.

For example, four towns, each containing fifty people related to each other, gathered together and built a big cliff house. The four groups helped each other in various ways, but each group insisted on maintaining its social and ceremonial structures, which were well adapted to a small town but not to a large one. Therefore, mores, marriage regulations, methods of reckoning blood descent, and various ceremonies prevented the development of a strong central administration to act for the whole group. Actually, the big town consisted of four independent towns, each functioning differently from the others. The result was that the big town was constantly disturbed by internal feuds. Amicable relationships between clans were impossible. The big town was a sociological disaster. Finally it collapsed. The clans moved out, going their separate ways, and eventually the big town was left to the ghosts.

The Pueblos' exodus had a marked influence on all Indians of the Southwest, forcing many of them to shift to new locations. Peoples moved at various times, and in varying numbers, into the Hopi country, into the valleys of the Rio

Grande, Little Colorado, Puerco, Verde, San Francisco, Pecos, and even as far south as the upper Gila and Salt rivers.

Into the abandoned land of the spectacular cliff houses, multistoried mesa-top towns, and sprawling communal dwellings in the deep canyons moved the Navajos. And there they stayed.

The Navajos did not take over the deserted big towns. They built their homes as they had built them from time immemorial, but lack of materials did force them to make some changes. In the far north their hogans had been constructed of forked sticks and covered with bark, leaves, and the skins of large animals. Through all the centuries of their long migrations they had constructed them in this manner whenever possible. If they remained for a time in an area where timber was easily obtained they sometimes used logs for the base. In the plains region they covered poles with buffalo hides. As they moved into the drier regions they were forced to use earth. In Dinetah they built the low walls using both poles and stone, and covered them with dried mud. But the traditional forked-stick hogan was preferred, and it is still found on the Navajo reservation, sometimes standing near newer-type, larger hogans built of logs, rocks, and earth, sometimes beside the ruin of an ancient pueblo, sometimes beside a modern cracker-box house.

Regrettably the forked-stick, brush-covered hogans were particularly vulnerable to the ravages of time and the elements. Were it possible to find the remains of those built early in pre-Columbian times, much more could be known of the migrations of the Navajos. Some hogan-type ruins found in western Colorado appear to date from A.D. 1000, and may have been Navajo dwellings. The ruins of other hogan-type structures having walls of stone have been found in the same general area and are believed to have been constructed as early as 1100. People living in the Largo and Galina canyons of New Mexico between the years 1100 and 1250 had pottery very similar to the gray type known to have been made by early Navajos. This evidence is insufficient to be accepted as conclusive, but that is not the case with three sites found in the Gobernador Canyon of New Mexico. They are unquestionably early Navajo, and they range in dates—determined by tree rings—from 1491 to 1521. Two decades after the latter year the period of recorded history opened in the Southwest.

The hunting, food-gathering Navajos practiced a shamanistic-individualistic religion that was dramatized chiefly in rites by which they hoped to cure physical ills and obtain greater supplies of game. Their political structure was the loosely knit band. They knew little or nothing of farming. They maintained a patrilineal descent. All these customs were to be supplanted or drastically transformed.

The Navajos' arrival, first in Dinetah and later in areas farther south and west, was accomplished with little difficulty, for they occupied an unoccupied land. It was a country of strange and surpassing beauty, of great canyons with sheer walls of many hues, of sprawling angular tablelands, of flat treeless reaches carpeted by desert grasses and sagebrush, of mountains shadowed in yellow pine and spruce and fir. They found elk and mountain sheep on the high elevations, and lower down there were deer, cougar, antelope, fox, coyote, wolf, rabbit, and wild turkey.

Most of these things they had come to know well in their wanderings, but in what is now New Mexico they found something they had never known. Having always lived at best a step ahead of hunger and often with it, the life of the Pueblo Indians represented a security and plenty inconceivable to them. With abundant game and cultivated fields they would never again fear want. In amazement they gazed on patches of corn, pumpkins, beans, gourds, and a wonderful fiber—cotton. They saw fine pottery decorated in geometric designs of numerous colors. They saw coiled woven baskets, rectangular and round, large and small. They saw stone hoes and axes and broad flint knives and many other ingenious tools, such as rubbers, polishers, and scrapers. They saw feather-cloth robes, and ponchos, blankets, and clothing woven of cotton. They saw mosaics, ornaments, and beads of turquoise and other beautiful stones. And they saw astonishing articles made of shells. The shells came from the far-off seas, from the Pacific, the Gulf of California, and the Gulf of Mexico.

Centuries before any European set foot in the Southwest there were transcontinental trade trails linking every part of North America. When the first French *voyageurs* reached the upper Missouri River country, the Sioux possessed shells from the Pacific and wampum from the Atlantic. When white men first encountered them, the plains tribes had bone harpoons of Eskimo origin, colored stones and moss agates from the Yellowstone, utensils made of eastern woods, and ornaments bearing designs used by natives of the lower Mississippi Valley. Tribes in the middle and southern plains had pottery dishes made by Pueblos and turquoise from New Mexico, cotton garments from the Hopis, shells from the Pacific and the Gulf of Mexico. It is known that Indians in southern Ohio sent expeditions to the Rocky Mountains prior to A.D. 1300—and they went on foot—to obtain grizzly-bear claws and obsidian.

This knowledge reflects on passages in the Navajo origin myths that relate that one of the four sacred mountains was adorned with abalone shells and another with turquoise. It is possible, of course, that migrating Navajos had seen these treasures among peoples living along the eastern slopes of the

Rocky Mountains or on the plains. But it seems unlikely that they would have seen them in quantities sufficient to inspire the inclusion of them in their legends and religion. A more plausible explanation would seem to be that they came to understand their value and to take delight in them after reaching the Southwest. If that is the case, then a time sequence may be given, at least in this small respect, to parts of the Navajo religious chants.

At the end of the long Navajo migration a new culture was born. Elements of the far northern woodlands, of the plains, and of the mountains would be preserved in it, but now, settled in their new home, the Navajos would exhibit qualities that not only distinguished them but graded them above many other peoples of their race: superior intellect, extraordinary perspicacity, and consuming ambition. And woven into the new culture—vital strands in its texture—would be many of the customs and beliefs of the Pueblo town dwellers whose wealth, sophistication, and beautiful, exciting religious ceremonies inspired the wanderers from the north.

Irrigated agriculture modeled after the Pueblo system was the initial significant transition in the primitive Navajo way of life. With it the Navajos also adopted Pueblo agricultural ritual, "although with some loss of form and much loss of meaning," for the Navajos were neither peaceful nor sedentary. They were wild, unpredictable, and cruel. They wanted both the freedom of the wind and the rewards of the patient laborer, wanted both to revere their own gods and pay obeisance to the gods of others, if by so doing they might gain benefits for themselves.

The Navajos were quick to understand the valuable discovery they had made. With irrigated farming—and that meant the establishment of permanent settlements—they could not only enjoy a stable food supply and an easier life but could develop other resources available to them. They saw only one way to acquire the Pueblos' security and luxuries (and the possessions of the Pueblos were nothing less than luxuries in the eyes of the impoverished Navajos), and that was to take them. Steal material things, and capture male craftsmen, killing them when they were no longer needed. Capture young female potters, weavers, cultivators, not only to serve as workers but to bear children to whom they could pass on their skills.

But the most significant developments in the new Navajo culture would not result from their contacts with the Pueblos. They would not occur until the Spanish had reached New Mexico.

# 2

STRANGE NEWS HAD COME UP the Rio Grande to northern New Mexico in the spring of 1536, perhaps brought by Indian traders, perhaps by hunters on their way to the plains east of the mountains. It came from the Jumanos, who dwelt in pueblos on the river below El Paso del Norte. Several moons earlier, it was reported, three men with beards whose skin was white and one big beardless man whose skin was black had come among them from the east, stayed twenty days, and then had gone on west to find the sea.

The Jumanos did not identify them, but the travelers left their own accounts. They were Alvar Nuñez Cabeza de Vaca, Andres Dorantes, Alonso del Castillo, and Estevanico the Black, the last survivors of the Narvaez expedition, which had been destroyed on the Texas coast, and the first Europeans to cross the continent north of Mexico, a feat that has few equals in the history of American exploration.

Some three years later, in 1539, more strange news filtered

17

into the country of the upper Rio Grande. This time it came from the Zuñis, who lived several hundred miles to the west. Estevanico the Black had reappeared there, wearing jingling bells and feathers, and with strings of turquoise covering his great black chest. With him was a large band of Opatas from Mexico, as well as a harem of Indian maidens. Estevanico told the Zuñis that following him were white men in gowns "sent by a great lord, who knew about the things in the sky," and that these men were coming to instruct the Zuñis "in divine matters." His words made the Zuñis "think that he must be a spy or a guide from some nation who wished to come and conquer them, because it seemed to them unreasonable to say that the people were white in the country from which he came and that he was sent by them, he being black . . . so they decided to kill him."

Just to prove that he was not a god who could survive death, the Zuñis cut Estevanico up and distributed pieces of his body among themselves and other tribes, and they sent messages down the trail to tribes in Arizona and Mexico to kill all black or white men who boasted of knowing about things in the sky.

Estevanico the Black, sent north by the viceroy with Fray Marcos of Nice (whom he had left far behind him) to find the fabled Seven Cities of Cibola, had opened the gate to the Southwest to white men. And like an awesome storm, the clouds of dust raised by Coronado's columns in the summer of 1540 marred the blue infinity of the New Mexico sky. There was the incredible sight of men wearing heavy beards and girded in armor that threw back the sun's light. There were the roar and fire of miraculous weapons that spat deadly missiles with unbelievable force and spoiled the air with an acrid odor. There were the clanging of metal on metal, the clinking of spur rowels, and the rattling of sabers and chains. And on the trails along the Rio Puerco, Rio

Grande, and Rio Pecos the Indians heard a strange thunder, a ragged beating on the earth that was unlike any cadence of the dance drums. In the camps of the *soldados* firelight caught on the sleek sides of great beasts, and there were peculiar sounds in the shadows, horses munching fodder and stamping, and the strange smells of their sweat and manure.

Into New Mexico poured a cascade of men, horses, and guns that were not only unknown to the Navajos, the Hopis, the Pueblos and the Apaches, but beyond the realm of their imagination. And the red peoples, wondering and terrorized, many of them bleeding and dying on the floors of their ancient houses, would make supreme efforts to stop the invaders, but they would not succeed.

None of the preserved documents of the Coronado expedition mention the Navajos, although detachments of the expedition passed through parts of their region. But if Coronado neither saw nor heard of Navajos, on the plains east of the Rio Pecos he met their relatives the Apache Athapascans, "who lived like Arabs"; he called them Querechos. Castaneda, one of the chief chroniclers of the expedition, told how Querechos "follow the cows [bison], hunting them and tanning their skins to take to the settlement in Cicuye." Cicuye was on the Rio Pecos in New Mexico.

The first documented encounter between Spaniards and Navajos occurred some forty years after the ill and dispirited Coronado had vanished in the west. In 1583 a small company led by Antonio de Espejo and Fray Bernardino Beltran, journeying north from El Paso, reached the Rio Grande pueblos. Moving westward from Zia, they met "peaceful Indian mountaineers who brought us tortillas even though we did not need them."

The "mountaineers" were Navajos. The "tortillas" were

probably some kind of corn cake they had learned to make from the Pueblos. Curiosity and perhaps apprehension undoubtedly caused them to approach the Spaniards bearing gifts. Such a gesture, unless employed to throw intended victims off guard, would seldom be known in years to come. Indeed, a few days after that first historic meeting Espejo would know more of the true character of the Navajos. At Acoma, he recorded, the surrounding area "gave promise of mines and other riches, but we did not go to see them as the people from there are many and warlike. The mountain people come to the aid of those settlements." Noteworthy as well is his statement that the Navajos "carry on trade with those of the settlements [Pueblos], taking to them salt, game, such as deer, rabbits, and hares, tanned deerskins, and other things, to trade for cotton mantas and other things."

A contingent of the Coronado expedition led by Pedro de Tovar had destroyed a Hopi pueblo, and as Espejo advanced toward their country Hopi emissaries appeared with warnings to him to turn back. The Hopis also appealed to the Navajos to aid them in repelling the Spaniards, and Espejo learned of "a great gathering of wild and warlike people to fight us." Espejo prepared to meet the threat by recruiting some 150 Zuñi warriors, enemies of the Hopis, and with this force and only nine Spanish soldiers he moved toward the Hopi villages. When he reached the pueblo that had been destroyed by Tovar, the Hopis, not willing to chance losing another one, sent the Navajos away and asked for peace.

Diego Perez de Luxan, one of Espejo's companions, wrote: "The Lord willed this that the whole land should tremble for ten lone Spaniards, for there were over twelve thousand Indians in this province with bows and arrows." The statement is a typical illustration of the inflated ego of the Spanish explorers and their blind confidence in their own powers.

If there had been 12,000 Indians in the area of the Hopi towns, ten Spaniards, even with the help of their guns and 150 Zuñis, would not have lived to write accounts of their adventures.

The Navajos were watching. They trailed Espejo for a time, and one night "some of them came to our horses and fled when they heard them, as they found the sound unfamiliar." If the Navajos had in mind stealing the Spanish horses, perhaps fear that they could not handle the unfamiliar beasts kept them from making the attempt. That fear would be soon overcome.

Like Coronado, Espejo had dreamed of finding mines in the north and of winning fame as the conqueror of a great new empire. Like Coronado, he returned to Mexico a disillusioned man.

But if Coronado and Espejo won no great riches for themselves, they opened a new and vital chapter in southwestern history. Their journeys impressed upon the Navajos and all other Indians of New Mexico the value of the horse as a means of transport and the supremacy of the gun as a weapon. The horse was far less incomprehensible to the Indians than the gun. The horse was flesh and blood. Like deer, antelope, buffalo, mountain sheep, and elk, it lived on grass, it left droppings. Its uses were also familiar: its meat was edible, its hide was useful, it propagated its kind, and it took care of itself. But the most desirable thing about the horse was that, unlike wild animals, it could be tamed and taught to serve a master.

Use of guns developed at a slow pace, for even after the Indians had learned how to use them, powder and lead were difficult to obtain in quantity. For two centuries after the Spanish had colonized the Southwest—and even after the Americans had taken over the country—Indians continued to fight with lances, bows and arrows, knives, hatchets, and

clubs, not only in intertribal conflicts but against white adversaries.

Persistent and successful raiders, the Navajos acquired horses and guns sooner than any of the sedentary Indians of New Mexico. Having subdued the Pueblos and made them a captive people, the Spanish were fairly successful in preventing them from obtaining guns and horses, but they were eminently unsuccessful in preventing the Navajos from stealing both. Yet, although they were the first "horse Indians" in the region, the Navajos never possessed sufficient firearms and ammunition to give them equality in this respect with the white military forces that waged offensives against them.

The horse gave the Navajos mobility that enabled them to extend their raiding over vast distances, but it was sheep more than anything else that would give stability to their economy.

The Coronado expedition had traveled with a large band of sheep, but many of the animals were lost through injuries or consumed en route. The small number that survived the hardships of mountain and desert travel were the first domestic sheep to reach New Mexico, but they too were soon killed and eaten.

It is Don Juan de Oñate who can be credited with introducing stock raising in the Southwest. Reputedly one of the richest men in Mexico, owner of mines and large ranchos, he arrived in New Mexico in 1598 as governor of the province. His purpose was to establish a colony on the Rio Grande, and he brought with him soldiers, priests, retainers, and settlers, numbering several hundred in all, a long train of heavily laden oxcarts, and thousands of horses, cattle, mules, goats, and sheep.

Spanish officialdom, from the highest to the lowest offices and not excluding viceroys, had steadfastly refused to be-

lieve that the gold for which Coronado and other explorers had searched did not exist in the north. Oñate was of a similar mind. He wandered over the Southwest from Kansas to Arizona in futile hunts for treasure, much to the detriment of the colonizing plan with which he had been charged. Desertions almost destroyed the colony he founded, but it was saved by the timely arrival of a few more settlers. In the years during and immediately following Oñate's tenure countless thousands of sheep, and cattle and horses in smaller numbers, were driven up the long trail along the Rio Grande from Mexico.

The Navajos were interested spectators. Moving cautiously out of their hidden canyon homes to the west, they gazed on the growing herds grazing in guarded pastures, and they saw the bands of sheep flowing like black and white waves over the hills. Whenever an opportunity arose, they made off with a few animals and a few prisoners, and they killed both Pueblo and Spanish herders. In the earliest years of Spanish settlement their raids were not highly profitable, but their proficiency as bandits rapidly improved. Each prisoner they took enhanced their knowledge and skill. Each horse they stole increased their mobility and striking power, gave them the means of swift attack and swift escape, and the element of surprise. They soon became masters of plunder.

Although they denied the Pueblos the privilege of owning horses, the Spanish permitted them to acquire small bands of sheep. The sheep were the *churro*, the scrawny, long-legged common sheep of Spain. (Only royalty could own merinos.) They were prolific, needed little care, adapted themselves readily to a new environment, and produced long, straight wool containing so little grease that it could be woven without being thoroughly washed. The Pueblos soon learned to shear the wool, dye it with indigo brought

from Mexico, and spin and weave it. Woolen breechcloths and wraparound blanket dresses began to supplement clothing made of native cotton.

The Navajos watched, raided, and learned.

If the Navajos might be termed nomads during the centuries of their migration from the far north, the description is not apt after they reached the Southwest and came in contact with the Pueblos. Groups of families built hogans in places where water and fuel were sufficient to fill their needs. These small population centers became permanent settlements. The people went out to hunt, to gather piñons, to raid, but always they returned to the settlements. Navajo clan names are chiefly place names. When agriculture became a subsistence economy, the Navajos concentrated in areas where enough water could be found to cultivate their fields. When they acquired sheep, they adopted the Spanish custom of moving the herds with the seasons from winter to summer grazing ranges. Some Navajos went with the sheep, but others remained at home to cultivate and harvest crops.

In arid New Mexico, of course, there were not many places where grass, wood, water, and security from attack could be obtained in desirable combination, and the size of a Navajo village was controlled by the extent of these necessary resources. Some of them remained small and isolated, perhaps containing no more than three to six hogans. However, as early as the middle of the seventeenth century, fifty years after the arrival of Oñate, there were Navajo settlements containing upward of fifty hogans. Most of the communities, whether large or small, were built on mesas that could be defended, with cornfields spread along the valley below. There was always a need for new sites, as the Navajo population increased steadily through births and the addition of captives, and they continually pressed westward. But the

popular belief that they were nomads in historical times is completely erroneous.

By no means all of the Pueblos living among the Navajos were captives. From the time of Oñate many of them fled their homes to escape Spanish oppression. Some went north and east, but large numbers of them found a haven among the Navajos, who always welcomed refugees. Ruins of homes constructed of rock and adobe in traditional Pueblo style have been found adjacent to the hogans of Navajo settlements.

The early Spanish officials of the province of New Mexico, with no exceptions of record, were arrogant, bigoted, greedy, intolerant, cruel, and stupid. They enslaved the Pueblos in violation of royal edicts prohibiting slavery of "Christianized Indians." Looking upon the Pueblos as heathens, they not only held them in bondage but accorded them less consideration than they gave to beasts of burden. Sheep and cattle were assigned a much greater value—at least they could be eaten.

The power of the Catholic Church to influence political and economic affairs in the colonization of New Mexico is indicated by Oñate's decree dividing the region into seven mission districts, each in the charge of Franciscan friars. In one of these districts lived the Navajos. It was "somewhere to the west," but the Spanish knew no more of its geographical boundaries than they knew of the people it contained. They were certain of only one thing, knowledge gained from the Pueblos and from their own experiences: the Navajos were to be feared.

The padre sent by Oñate to "Jémez and all Apaches in its sierra and neighborhood" was Alonso de Lugo. Jémez (both a pueblo and a mountain range) was on the eastern border of the Navajo country. This was the first appointment of a priest to serve Navajos, not only an unenviable assignment but, as it was soon discovered, a futile one. The Navajos were out there, but if they were to be seen at all it was only when they struck to plunder and then vanished like shadows in the night. Within a short time after Fray de Lugo had taken his station, Navajo raids in the Jémez area became so costly that soldiers were sent into the mountains for the purpose of "putting down the Apaches who were killing people and stealing horses." It was not a successful operation.

Oñate not only demanded tribute from each pueblo but forcibly expropriated food and clothing in such quantities that some of the peoples were made destitute and suffered from cold and hunger. In October 1598, Oñate, on one of his treasure hunts, passed Acoma, a Keres pueblo, with a large company. He wrote that the residents of the old town on the high mesa "furnished us liberally with maize, water, and fowls" and solemnly agreed to become Spanish subjects. A few weeks later Oñate's nephew Juan de Zaldivar reached Acoma with a contingent of soldiers. The Keres considered Zaldivar's demands excessive and rejected them. In the fight that ensued, Zaldivar and fourteen soldiers were killed.

At the time the Keres and the Navajos were friends and traded with each other. If Navajos were not actually in the pueblo when the fight occurred, they were not far away, for they were eyewitnesses to the terrible events that took place in January 1599, which ensured their undying hostility toward the Spanish.

Oñate sent another nephew, Juan de Zaldivar's brother Vincente, and seventy soldiers to punish the Keres "as a warning to everyone in this kingdom." Vincente de Zaldivar was to destroy the pueblo, and all those executed "you will expose to public view." If Vincente wished to show any leniency, "you should seek all possible means to make the Indians believe that you are doing so at the request of the friar. . . . In this manner they will recognize the friars as their benefactors and protectors and come to love and esteem them, and to fear us."

Vincente gave no thought to leniency. In a few days he and his soldiers, none of whom was killed in the battle, murdered at least eight hundred men, women, and children. When the Keres begged for mercy and offered payments of food and blankets, Vincente had prisoners brought out, cut to pieces, and their remains thrown off a cliff. Some five hundred women and children and eighty men were taken as captives to San Juan, and there Oñate pronounced the punishment they were to receive. Males over twenty-five years of age were to have a foot cut off and labor in "personal servitude" for twenty years. Younger males and all women were sentenced to slavery. Girls under the age of twelve were given to Fray Alonso Martinez, who was to distribute them as he wished to Spanish families "in this kingdom or elsewhere," and young boys were made the property of Vincente.

The Navajos soon launched a series of fierce raids on the Spanish towns and pueblos in which the captured Keres were held. In less than two years they helped most of those sentenced to slavery to escape. Bravely the Keres commenced the restoration of Acoma.

In August 1607 Oñate resigned, but his departure in no wise influenced the Navajos to decrease their raids. The viceroy wrote the king that their depredations—burning settlements, killing people, and stealing herds—were causing havoc in New Mexico and driving the colonists to despair. Moreover, New Mexico was contributing nothing to the Spanish treasury. Pueblos fled to the high country whenever tribute collectors appeared. The colonists had insufficient horses, and even the military was in need of mounts, because of Navajo raids. Slaves regularly vanished, presumably to live among the wild people to the west.

Orders came to the provincial government to have the Franciscans make greater attempts to pacify the Navajos. The friars were not enthusiastic about the idea, claiming that the actrocities of Oñate had inflamed all Indians to such an extent they were unwilling even to listen to their pleas. The soldiers complained that the friars were not interested in learning Indian languages, so the Indians could not understand them even if they were willing to listen. The settlers were ready to go home, saying that thefts were ruining them, and, besides, the few soldiers present were no match for their enemies—Comanches and Utes to the northeast, Apaches on the east and south, Navajos on the west, and rebellious Pueblos in the middle. Spanish patrols accomplished nothing.

Pedro de Peralta faced a distressing situation when he became governor of New Mexico in 1609. He had been given his orders: assemble the Pueblos in settlements where they could be held captive and prevented from trading with the unregenerate Navajos, and increase the activities of the Franciscans. Peralta, who transferred the provincial capital from San Gabriel to Santa Fe, attempted to perform the duties given him, but he was only nominally successful. Navajos, joined by Jémez Indians, raided pueblos and sent their occupants fleeing for their lives. One Jémez leader was captured and hanged, but the execution had no deterrent effect on either his own people or their Navajo allies. Internal conflicts kept the colony in turmoil. The Franciscans and secular officials engaged in a bitter contest for the control of Indian labor. Prominent colonists had been awarded *encomiendas*, that is, the right to employ a certain number of Indians and reap the rewards of their labors. The word "employ" was a euphemism. In reality it meant enslave. As *encomenderos* had done ever since the arrival of the Spanish in the Americas, those in New Mexico violated the statute requiring them to pay fair wages to their workers and arbitrarily took over Indian lands, depriving their owners of income and in many cases sufficient sustenance. Priests as well as settlers practiced this form of peonage.

The remoteness of the upper Rio Grande region from the seats of government and the church in Mexico City was a factor enabling the priests to acquire extraordinary secular powers. Caravans supplying the New Mexico missions moved on highly irregular schedules. Often two or even three years passed in which none arrived in Santa Fe. The priests—reportedly numbering about fifty in the 1620's—were in almost every respect their own masters. But isolation and lack of guidance cannot be blamed entirely for the steady deterioration of their relations with the Indians. They were neither good politicians nor competent administrators. Many were uncompromising religious fanatics. They were stern disciplinarians demanding of the government not only the authority to force religious doctrine down the throats of Indians but the right to control every phase of the social and economic life of the Spanish towns. Supported by the few civil and military authorities of the province, they were its real rulers. They commanded soldiers to enforce compliance by the Indians with all demands made of them. They ordered cruel punishment inflicted upon recalcitrant villagers. They demanded that runaways be pursued by armed contingents and brought back to suffer lashings and imprisonment. They condemned slavery, yet tolerated it, thinking themselves absolved by the act of baptizing the men, women, and children being given to Spanish families as servants or sent to labor in mines.

The Franciscans had been engaged in their missionary labors in northern New Mexico less than three decades when they reported that more than thirty thousand Indians regularly attended Mass. Soon thereafter they boasted that more than sixty thousand "red heathens" had been converted. Both claims were ridiculous, but the Franciscans were the chamber of commerce of the day and place. Certainly no Navajos had been brought into the fold, unless as prisoners destined to be slaves. And subsequent happenings demonstrated that if the vaccine of Christianity had been injected into large numbers of Pueblos, it was accomplished by physical force rather than persuasion and that the treatment failed to have any lasting effect on them.

Neither the priests, the civil administrators, nor the military appeared able to understand that they were dealing with people of old and advanced culture, people fully capable of progressing under intelligent and humane guidance. The Pueblos, and especially the Navajos, could not be easily driven into abject submission or forced to abandon without a desperate struggle the religious beliefs instilled in them through cherished caremonials deeply rooted in their past.

# 3

THE CAMPAIGN OF DEATH and destruction launched by Oñate would be continued by the Spanish for more than two centuries. As witnesses if not victims at its outset, the Navajos conceived an enmity for the invaders that would not diminish. When they themselves became targets of Spanish suppression their fury rose to new intensity. If they entered into an agreement to maintain peace—and they did on numerous occasions—it was done only for the purpose of gaining time in which to prepare for new assaults. Only their complete annihilation could have brought an end to the vicious offensives they waged against the two majesties, the king and the God of the Spanish. And in New Mexico and Arizona, the Spanish, with all their trained soldiers and all their power of arms, would not come close to achieving a decisive victory in combat against them.

In 1628, Fray Bartelomé Romero and Fray Francisco

Muñoz went among groups of Navajos whose leaders they identified as "Quinia" and "Manases," and who "lived fifty leagues from the Pueblo of Santa Clara, and west of the Rio Grande." The priests built a small church at the *rancheria* of Quinia, "who is well known for being so belligerent." These Navajos, one account relates, "rebelled after the captain [Quinia] and his wife and his children had been baptized; and they wished to kill the Father who was catechizing them. And having their arrows already pointed at him, they did not dare to do it, and fled from the *rancheria* and left the Father there."

Romero and Munoz hurried back to safety among the Pueblos. This is the first known attempt to convert Navajos in their own country, but it would not be the last time the gospel bearers failed to win them to Christianity. Missionaries of many denominations are still meeting with defeat on the Navajo reservation today.

In 1629, less than a year after Fray Romero and Fray Munoz abandoned the first church to be erected in the Navajo country, Navajos, perhaps the same bands led by Quinia and Manases, were reported to be living only "one day's travel from Santa Clara," and it was in this little pueblo that the celebrated Fray Alonso de Benavides took his place in Navajo history.

In 1629 Fray Benavides had been a religious in the New World for more than three decades. From 1621 he had held the office of Father Custodian of the province of New Mexico. Now he was preparing to return to Mexico City, where he had been ordained and had long served, "to finish my days there if He will allow me to do so."

During his tenure in New Mexico he had traveled extensively through the immense region, the boundaries of which, especially on the north, were vague at best. He had performed his duties in many pueblos scattered over hundreds of miles, and he had shown zeal and courage by assigning to himself the perilous task of attempting to propagate the gospel among the savage Apaches of the upper Gila River. A keen observer, he had acquired a vast knowledge of the Indians inhabiting his enormous jurisdiction, and he prepared a comprehensive report—he called it a memorial—to be submitted to the king of Spain.

In the Benavides *Memorial* the name "Navajo" appeared for the first time on a printed page.*

Benavides was campaigning to have more priests sent to New Mexico, and he consistently overstated the number of Indians to be converted, the number of towns in need of resident priests, and the opportunities for the saving of heathen souls. If a historian can find no justification for his rash claims, it is possible to understand his reasons for making them.

Obviously, if no one could delineate the boundaries of New Mexico with any degree of accuracy, no one could state with certainty how many Indians inhabited it. Strained as Benavides' estimates were, he could offer an example to support them. To the west of the pueblos in north-central New Mexico, he told the king, was the "province of the Apaches of Navajo." No one could be sure how far it extended, except that it was known to be enormous, and no one could say how many people lived in it, except that it was known to contain an inconceivably large number.

His designation "Apaches of Navajo" revealed significant intelligence gained from the Pueblos. The early Spaniards

* In 1626 Fray Zarate Salmero, in his Relaciones de Nuevo Mexico, wrote of the "Apaches de Nabaju," as far as is known the first written use of the word. However the Relaciones was not finished for some years thereafter. Unfortunately for historians, the Spanish used the names "Apache" and "Navajo" interchangeably in their writings for two centuries.

had heard the word *Apachu* used by Indians. It came from
the Zuñi language and meant enemy. In Spanish it became
*Apache,* and it was applied to all the Dineh. Oñate had
been the first to call them Apaches in official communications.

Within a few years after the establishment of Santa
Fe as the provincial capital (1609–10), civil, military, and
church authorities had reason to give a separate designation
to the Apaches of northwestern New Mexico. Unlike the
Apaches to the south, they did not eat all the sheep and
cattle taken in their raids, but grazed them in their remote
country and built up the herds. Nor did they consume all the
corn and seeds they stole, but put some aside for planting,
and they cultivated fields with flood waters and stored
harvests. While carrying on their plundering they were
building an agricultural economy.

Once more an Indian language supplied the needed
word. It was *Navahu,* the name of a Tewa pueblo that
stood near an extensive area of excellent farming land. In
the Tanoan language, which the Tewas spoke, *Navahu*
signified a place of cultivated fields. So the northern New
Mexico Dineh became Apaches of Navajo in Benavides'
*Memorial,* and he enlightened the king with the explanation: "These of Navajo are very great farmers . . . that Navajo
signifies—great planted fields."

The *Memorial* was published in several European coun-
tries, and in it Benavides expressed the opinion that the
Navajo province was "the most bellicose of all the Apache
nation." It contained many deposits of "rock alum," valuable
in dyeing, and as all the Pueblo Indians were

inclined to dyeing, to have wherewith to dye their
clothing, they need alum, which exists only in those
[Navajo] ranges. And to go after it two or three thou-

sand [Pueblo] Indians unite; and to meet these in war
the said Navajo Apaches sally in defense of their territory; and over the affair there are very very many
deaths. Unless it chances that they [the Pueblos]
arrive in a time when the Navajos have withdrawn to
other ranges to hunt. . . . When the Navajos know
that the Pueblos have come to take away their alum
from them, they unite very purposefully and come to
make war on the Pueblos in revenge for their having
entered upon their lands. And the Navajo people is
so numerous that in two days there come together more
than thirty thousand.

Benavides must have known the figure was absurd. The
Pueblos could have told him that the Navajo population
probably did not exceed four thousand men, women, and
children. However, as far as the Spanish settlers and the
Pueblos who had been victims of Navajo forays were concerned, even that was too many. That the Navajos were
incomparable raiders Benavides well understood, and he
knew as well how often the Spanish had failed to combat
them, for he remarked that although "sundry times the
Spaniards have gone there to chastise them for the many
Christian Indians they kill, although they assaulted them
at daybreak and caught them off their guard, they always
found the fields curdled with Navajos beyond number."

After describing the Navajo hogan—information never
before published—Benavides thought that "perhaps it will
be to Your Majesty's taste" to hear how he had tried to
make peace with the Navajos and imbue them with the
principles of Christianity. In September 1629, he wrote, he
was ministering temporarily at the church at Santa Clara,
where resided the Tewas, "who were dwellers on the frontier and received many damages from the Navajos. Thither

more than usual these Navajo Apaches repaired to do havoc."

Benavides had hoped to capture a Navajo warrior,

but having seen that I could not catch a one—to regale him and send him again to his land to tell his captains that I wished to treat for peace—I adventured and determined to send to them twelve Indians of my Christians. . . . I called the captains and the old men of the [Santa Clara] pueblo, and communicated to them the desire I had that this peace could be made; as well as to stop so many deaths, as they might treat and have reciprocity in their agriculture, and that we might by this road attain their conversion, which was my principal end.

It was a dramatic and historically valuable, if somewhat unbelievable, episode that Benavides recounted for the Spanish sovereign. His emissaries to the Navajos "went forth with very great courage and spirit. . . . God knoweth the constriction in which my heart was, seeing the manifest risk in which I was putting those Indians."

The Tewa delegation moved cautiously into the country of "that untamed and ferocious nation," and when in view of the hogans of a *rancheria* they made signs that they came in peace. The Navajos replied that they might proceed in safety, "whereupon they went drawing nearer, although slowly and with mistrust."

A representative of the Navajos came forward to meet them. They delivered Benavides' message and gave him a packet of tobacco and a rosary. Having never seen a rosary, the Navajo "asked what it signified that the thread had so many beads." It signified, said the Tewas, that Fray Benavides was sending to every Navajo "word that he would be his friend."

Putting the rosary about his neck, the Navajo declared that he welcomed peace, but it was apparent to the Tewas that "he was suspicious that they might have some double dealing." To be certain that no deceit or trickery was involved, the Navajo announced that "he would come and see us in our pueblo."

Here is an illustration of the haughtiness of the Navajos and the disdain with which they regarded both the Pueblos and the Spaniards. A Navajo leader—Benavides did not supply his name—was unafraid to go with only three companions to counsel in the midst of people who had suffered grievous losses of life and property at the hands of Navajo raiders. Benavides was overjoyed. He assembled a throng of Indians from several pueblos to welcome the important guests to Santa Clara, and "next to the altar I ordered a chair set upon a rug" in which to sit when he received them.

Solemn and impressive ceremonies followed during the next three days. A Pueblo "offered his own bow and arrows to the Navajo captain," declaring that "before God, who was on that altar . . . he gave those weapons in earnest of his word that he would never break the peace." Not to be outdone, the Navajo proffered one of his own arrows with the pledge, "And so to that God, whoever he may be, I likewise give my word and faith, in the name of all my people . . . and that for my part and that of my people the peace and friendship shall never fail." Bells were rung and trumpets sounded and hymns were sung, "all of which pleased the Navajos much to hear, since it was the first time."

Upon departing, the Navajo leader declared that he would return in a few weeks and would bring with him a great number of his people, as well as gifts "to make a big fair . . . and from that moment he assured the Pueblos they might enter his territory to hunt . . . and that they should be treated as friends. And so it was."

So it was not.

Benavides' *Memorial* delighted everyone who read it, including the king, but they could hardly have been expected to know—and Benavides did not trouble to tell them—that no Navajo, no matter what his rank or position, could speak for all Navajos. No Navajo possessed the authority to negotiate singlehandedly a treaty of peace. Like many western Indian tribes, the Navajos maintained an almost pure democracy. Decisions reached in councils ruled them, not chiefs. Leadership was not hereditary. Leaders were appointed, but they were subject to replacement at any time, and any prerogatives granted them could be quickly rescinded.

The Navajo who went boldly to Santa Clara knew that every pledge he made was open to rejection by his people. Even more important, he understood that the Navajos were not interested in securing peace with the Spanish, that only through a continuation of their raiding could they maintain their economy. Very simply, the Navajo had gone to Santa Clara to spy, to determine what treasures the agent of the white man's God possessed, and the feasibility of plundering them. But he had been no more deceitful than Benavides.

Benavides was aware of the futility of the show he had staged. He knew that it was a meaningless display, but it bolstered his ego, was guaranteed to please his superiors and the Spanish court, and provided him with a thrilling story to recount. He gave his king false information mixed with a few grains of truth, at the same time revealing that he fully understood that the abyss between the Navajo and Spanish worlds could not be bridged by a single act of his own.

"And this Navajo province," Benavides wrote in conclusion, "is the one which has given most pain and anxiety to New Mexico . . . because there are in it more than two hundred thousand souls, judging by the times when the Spaniards have seen them going to fight."

There were not 200,000 Indians in all of New Mexico in 1629, and Benavides knew it better than anyone else. He knew, too, that his negotiations would bring no lasting peace. And there was no peace.

Priests continued to arrive and take up stations among the Pueblos, but they did not journey unescorted through the country. That would have been a sure method of achieving martyrdom, and not all of them would have welcomed that. They were more interested in acquiring farms and herds and *encomiendas*. Wherever they went they were accompanied by soldiers. The banner of Christ waved not only over his emissaries but over firearms and artillery.

In 1629, when priests were assigned to Acoma, Zuñi, and the Hopi towns, Governor Silva Nieto himself accompanied them with thirty soldiers. Acoma had been restored, and housed more than two thousand Indians. They made no protest against Spanish demands, and no trouble occurred. Fray Juan Ramirez was welcome to stay with them, if that was his wish. They would not bother him. Things were not as easy for Fray Roque de Figueredo at Zuñi. He obtained a house to serve as living quarters and church, but the Zuñis showed their displeasure at his presence, and he endured what Benavides termed "many difficulties and travails, because of the great resistance the sorcerers [medicine men] make."

Governor Nieto was too timid to travel beyond Zuñi, and with eighteen soldiers to protect him he turned back to Santa Fe. However, he ordered two lay brothers and twelve soldiers to deliver Fray Francisco de Porras to Awatobi. The Hopis gave them a cold welcome, and sent off messengers with news of their arrival to the Navajos, with whom, at the moment, they were on good terms.

Fray Porras wasted no time in condemning Hopi idols, and "at this the sorcerers were irritated; and seeing that they were being deprived of the jurisdiction which as infernal ministers they had over those souls, they persuaded all the people that the padre and all those who accompanied him were so many liars." Whereupon Fray Porras, after a prayer, is supposed to have spat on his hands, made a mud ball, and daubed it on the eyes of a blind boy, whose sight was immediately restored. If the incident occurred, Fray Porras made a serious mistake. It did nothing to endear him to the medicine men. Shortly afterward he was stricken vio- lently ill and died. Who had put poison in his food was never learned.

In the next few years six priests were murdered by Taos, Zuñi, Hopi, and Jémez Indians, all of whom were at peace with the Navajos. These acts of violence brought swift reprisals, adding to the terrible ordeals being suffered by all Pueblos. Meanwhile, the Navajos repeatedly raided both Spanish ranchos and the Indian towns that had not negotiated peace pacts with them.

The total Spanish population of Santa Fe in 1630 was less than 250, yet they owned more than 700 Indian slaves. How many children of mixed blood existed in the capital is not a matter of record, but reports indicate the number was considerable.

The Pueblos, captives in their towns, were the main support of the Spaniards. Without their forced labor and the expropriation of their farm products and the goods they made, there would have been no colony, for the settlers could not have produced sufficient food and articles to sustain themselves and at the same time bear the cost of Navajo raids. Benavides was pleased to inform the king that the presidio was not supported by "pay from your Royal coffers, but by making the soldiers *encomenderos* of those pueblos."

The Spaniards might have continued to live in moderate comfort had they not brought down their own economic roof by fighting among themselves. The conflict was caused by the greed of both the Franciscans and civil officials, and each faction's consuming jealousy of the authority of the other.

Through the regimes of a series of governors—most of them of short duration—the controversy increased in bitterness, until at last it degenerated into actual violence. In defiance of a government edict, the Franciscans established factories in which Indians were forced to work, and they insisted on the right to distribute Indian slaves to settlers. These were prerogatives each governor claimed. Accusing the Franciscans of attempting to gain a monopoly of wealth in New Mexico, Governor Luis de Rosas threw a priest into jail.

The Franciscans charged that Rosas was encouraging Navajos to steal horses owned by the missions. The Navajos needed little encouragement to steal horses from whoever possessed them—horses were horses. Nevertheless, while Rosas was in office they made so many raids, killed so many mission Indians, and stole so much stock that the Franciscans declared that the Spanish military, even with the aid of civilians, was unable to defend the colony. Rosas sent no troops against the Navajos, although he made slave raids and caught a few of them in his net.

Rosas' next move was to appear at several pueblos and order the inhabitants not to obey the Franciscans. The Pueblos of Taos and Jémez promptly revolted and murdered priests stationed with them, and several other Spaniards. Other Pueblos assisted Navajos in making off with mission cattle and horses. Rosas made no effort to punish the rebels. Instead, he sent soldiers to confiscate their possessions and take a large number of Pueblo children to be sold into slavery. Under his orders, soldiers drove the priests from Nambe, San Ildefonso, Santa Clara, and other towns.

Since their position in the pueblos was swiftly becoming untenable, the Franciscans abandoned them and moved to Santo Domingo, where they fortified themselves. In league with a number of soldiers and settlers who had joined them, the priests adopted Navajo tactics and launched raids against the herds of the governor and the settlers loyal to him. The Navajos, taking advantage of the situation, stole stock from both factions as well as from the helpless Pueblos. For two years this three-sided war of attrition continued.

In 1641, Juan Flores de Sierra y Valdéz arrived in Santa Fe to replace Rosas, but died a short time later. Rosas had not yet departed, and the Franciscans stormed into the capital, took control of the provincial government, clapped Rosas into prison, and plotted his death. Arrangements were made with a Señora Ortiz to be found by her spouse committing adultery with Rosas in his cell. Although Rosas was purportedly under guard, the allegedly outraged husband was permitted to enter the cell in the night and murder him.

The Franciscans next sought retaliation against the Navajos, and throughout 1642 waged a relentless war against them in their own country. The priests proved to be competent military strategists. They took numerous prisoners, killed a large number of warriors, destroyed Navajo communications, and burned crops and stores of food. As they customarily did under the pressures of a costly offensive, the Navajos sent a delegation of old men to ask for peace. The Franciscans agreed, and withdrew, believing that the

Navajos were decisively beaten. They had not yet reached Santa Fe before Navajo raiders were again on the rampage throughout the land.

When Governor Alonso Pacheco de Heredia took office late in 1642, he sought to remedy matters with forceful measures. He executed eight Spaniards who had aided the Franciscans. The Franciscan faction injected a racial issue into the controversy with the charge that Pacheco's support came from "a Portuguese and mestizos and sambahigos, sons of Indian men and Negroes and mulattos." Pacheco issued an order forbidding Pueblos to travel from one town to another without a license, and he doubled the taxes and tribute all Pueblos were required to pay. Pueblos continued to travel, but not from one town to another. They fled the country, many of them to plains tribes and some to the Navajos. Out of the 150 pueblos occupied when the Spanish colonized New Mexico and Arizona, only forty-three contained inhabitants when Pacheco left office in 1644.

In the ensuing decade the population, prosperity, and power of the Navajos continued to increase. Despite military offensives against them, they kept the Jémez frontier in such turmoil that in some places the Franciscans were unable to maintain missions. In 1650 the Spanish discovered that the Tewas, Keres, and Jémez were conspiring to revolt and were in league with the Navajos. These Pueblos, said a Spanish report, "under the pretext that the Navajos were doing it, turned over to them in the pastures the droves of mares and horses belonging to the Spaniards, which are the principal nerve of warfare. They had already agreed with the said apostates to attack in all districts on the night of Holy Thursday, because the Spaniards would then be assembled."

Quick action by Governor Hernando de Ugarte y la

Concho prevented the first organized Pueblo revolt from succeeding. Nine of the leaders, from Isleta, Alameda, San Felipe, Cochiti, and Jémez, were captured and hanged, and many of the people were sentenced to serve as slaves for ten years. Although he punished the Pueblo plotters, Governor Ugarte placed the blame for the aborted uprising on Navajo medicine men. He sent soldiers into the Navajo country, but they accomplished nothing. Navajos had to be found before they could be killed.

The bitter feud between the Franciscans and the civil officials had abated somewhat by the time Governor Bernardo Lopez de Mendizabal arrived in 1659, but he had been in office only a short time before passions flared once again. Lopez quickly made a reputation as a slaver, dispatching "squadrons of men to capture the heathen Indians and send them to *reals* and mines . . . to sell." This trade in human captives involved mainly the Apaches and other tribes in eastern New Mexico, but Lopez had his eyes on the Navajos. It was his contention that because the Navajos had made no overtures of peace, they must be punished. He sent a force against them, but only two Navajos were captured. Lopez announced that it was learned from the captives that another revolt was being planned. The Franciscans accused him of endangering the entire colony by sending troops on a wild goose chase.

Lopez was openly anticlerical. The Franciscans sought to prohibit all native religious ceremonials. Lopez told the Pueblos to hold their own dances when they desired. When the Franciscans attempted to rebuild the church that had been destroyed by rebellious people in Taos, Lopez named as native governor of the pueblo a Taos Indian who had murdered a priest. Fray Luis Martinez was sent to serve in Taos, but Lopez told the Taos not to obey him, and charged that after raping an Indian woman Fray Martinez had cut her throat and buried her under his house.

Unable to capture Navajos in their own country, Lopez watched for opportunities to seize them in other places. When he was informed that a large band was en route to trade with the Jémez, he waylaid them, killed the men, and sold the women and children into slavery.

Retaliation for this unconscionable act came within a few weeks. Out of the west rode Navajo raiders, striking simultaneously in several areas, killing converted Indians and Spaniards wherever they were encountered, burning buildings, and driving off herds of livestock. The cost to the colony for Lopez's barbarity was many times the profit he had made from the enslaved Navajos.

Governor Diego de Peñalosa came upon the stage to make his contribution to the swiftly deteriorating conditions. Besides continuing the slave trade and exacting tribute from Indians already impoverished—many were dying of malnutrition and disease—Peñalosa ordered that all "enemy Indians," even though they were at peace, were to be prevented from engaging in trade with the Pueblos. It was his theory that if Navajos and Pueblos could be kept apart they could not conspire to rebel. Moreover, the Pueblos would then be obliged to do all their trading with the Spaniards, and could be swindled with ease. It was all very simple to Peñalosa, but not quite as simple as he was himself. Before he left office, Navajos had increased their attacks in virtually every section of northern New Mexico to such an extent that travel on any road, except by a large military force, was completely unsafe.

Governor Fernando de Villanueva inherited from Peñalosa a land not only aflame with warfare but stricken by famine. The normal exchange of food and commodities, upon which both Pueblos and Navajos greatly depended, had been disrupted. Crops had failed in many sections. The Navajos could move to mountains where game could be found, but the Pueblos were prisoners in their own towns, and hundreds of them were dying of starvation. At the same time, a mysterious disease swept through New Mexico with devastating effect, killing both people and livestock.

Despite the disasters coming one upon the other, the Navajos and Pueblos continued to make plans for a united revolt. Death and devastation appeared to act as fertilizer for the seeds of rebellion.

The fuse was burning, and Villanueva was unable to put it out. He did his best, executing Indians suspected of plotting against the king and the Catholic faith and selling scores into slavery, but it was no use. The Navajos could not be stopped, and now they made it clear that their raids were not carried out solely for the purpose of increasing their herds and taking captive women. Their goal was to keep the Spanish from entering their country at all, for any reason whatsoever.

In 1671, Governor Juan de Miranda was on his way to take office in Santa Fe. The train with which he was traveling was attacked by Navajos, four men were killed, and the wagon mules were stolen. Upon reaching the capital, Miranda sent soldiers to chastise the Navajos. A few were killed, but the Navajos continued to burn churches, kill Spaniards, steal livestock, and murder priests.

Miranda gave way to Governor Juan Francisco Trevino. He was greeted with an unprecedented situation. The Pueblos were not only plotting rebellion, but openly calling for it. Making the situation worse, the Indians were brazenly resuming their religious ceremonials. Trevino received reports that priests were being "bewitched"—perhaps a way of saying they were being scared out of their wits—"with the result that half a dozen had dropped dead." Trevino did what any Spanish governor of the time would be expected to do. He hanged three Tewas suspected of defying the faith, and lashed forty-three other "convicted and confessed idolators" and sold them into slavery.

In 1679, Governor Antonio de Otermin faced a discouraging prospect. Some seventeen thousand Pueblo Indians were still alive in New Mexico. How many Navajos there were was not known, for there was no way of counting them. All that could be said was that, whatever their number, there were too many. Dutifully, Otermin determined to combat them, for not only were they continuing their raids of death and destruction against the Spanish and the few Pueblos who had been subjugated by the Franciscans, but it was plain that they were encouraging the Pueblos to rebel.

Otermin's strategy called for a two-pronged campaign, using reinforcements who were expected from Nueva Vizcaya. One column would move westward from Taos and the other would start at Zia.

It was too late. August 10, 1680, the fuse reached the bomb.

Navajos and Pueblos, under the generalship of Popé, a medicine man of San Juan, swept through northern New Mexico in waves too powerful to be resisted. It was a well-planned and well-executed uprising. Quickly more than four hundred colonists and twenty-one priests were slain. A few of the most attractive women were taken alive and turned over to the Indian leaders for their pleasure. The Spaniards, converted Indians, and servants who escaped the initial onslaughts fled to Santa Fe and barricaded themselves with Governor Otermin and other residents of the capital in government buildings. There for ten days they successfully withstood assaults by several thousand warriors.

The bravery of the Spaniards was extraordinary. On August 20 a hundred soldiers and daring civilians broke out in a surprise counterattack. Under the fusillades from their guns, the besiegers, armed only with bows and arrows, lances and knives, were routed. Three hundred Indians were slain, and forty-seven taken alive were hanged in the plaza of Santa Fe.

The Spaniards understood that any hope of containing the revolt was futile. To remain meant starvation and death. In the dawn of August 21 they began a retreat that would not halt until they had reached El Paso.

The province of New Mexico was abandoned to the Indians. And they, determined to destroy every trace of the invaders, continued to rampage through the land, burning the Spanish churches and missions, their factories, farms, and homes. And every person who had been forcibly baptized by the Franciscans was scrubbed with yucca suds.

# 4

THE CHANGES THAT TOOK PLACE in the Navajo way of life between the time of the colonization of New Mexico by the Spanish and their departure in the great revolt of 1680 provide a record of acculturation that has no equal in American Indian history. Almost every Navajo custom, religious ceremonial, social system, and economic practice had been affected, being either discarded or blended with the Pueblo culture, in some cases to the extent that original forms were largely obscured.

Prior to the Spanish period Navajo acculturation had been confined within relatively narrow limits. Chiefly involved were agriculture and agricultural ritual obtained from the Pueblos. True, captives contributed artistic and domestic skills, but change was gradual in these cultural areas. Navajo contacts with Pueblos were intermittent, and generally under hostile conditions. From the beginning of the Spanish occupation Pueblos sought a haven among Navajos, but there were not enough refugees to cause rapid changes in Navajo culture. Those that did occur were not of transcending significance.

Following the revolt, however, the conditions of contact between the two peoples were suddenly and drastically altered. No Spaniards stood between them. It was not from simple choice that hundreds of Pueblos deserted their towns after the uprising and flooded into Navajo country. It was fear, the abiding fear that the Spaniards would soon return in great force and exact terrible vengeance upon them.

The Spaniards did not return for twelve years, but in that brief period was created the foundation for a pattern of organization that would endure in some pronounced aspects to the present day. The Navajos would adopt modified Pueblo styles of architecture, manufacturing techniques, and religious ceremonials. They would develop the Pueblo clan system. They would supplant patrilineal descent with matrilineal descent. Origin myths would be given conformity and would find general acceptance.

The Pueblos came from numerous towns, but if there was a babble of tongues in the beginning, there were interpreters. The two peoples were brought together by common needs and desires. Children with the blood of both in their veins would augment the strength of the union; they, and even more so the second generation, would be Navajos, speaking the Navajo language, knowing only the ways of life created by the assimilation, and taking pride in their heritage.

The number of clans increased to sixty or more. To a Navajo, "relatives" meant the members of his or her clan whether consanguineous or not, and they were of equal importance to both men and women. A Navajo could deliver no greater insult than to say of another: "He acts as if he didn't have any relatives." Descent was through the mother. Although most clans had descriptive names—such as Standing Horse, Parallel Stream, Bitter Water, Trail-to-the Garden, Red House, Salt—they may have had their origin in a group of several women from a single pueblo, or even from a single woman. One clan reputedly originated with a lone Spanish woman brought home as a captive by a Navajo raider. But although every Navajo belonged to the clan of his mother, he honored the clan of his father. To identify himself a young man might say: "I am Standing Horse, born of Bitter Water." Marriage between members of the same clan was prohibited. Navajos considered such a union a repulsive crime, and believed that perpetrators of it (it seldom occurred) would become insane.

Women were accorded high standing in other ways. In the Blessing Way Chant, woman is depicted as supreme in the hogan. She could enjoy individual ownership of livestock and jewelry and other possessions, and her husband could never take them from her, even if their marriage was dissolved. Some of the most powerful and important deities were female: Changing Woman, Spider Woman, Salt Woman. The poles of the four directions were Earth Woman on the east, Mountain Woman on the south, Water Woman on the west, and Corn Woman on the north.

Many things, however, and especially natural resources, belonged to all the people. Water, timber, salt brush, and grazing lands were communal property, but their use was subject to proprieties. A man did not, for example, cut wood close to the home of another or use another's water unless he was on a journey or his own supply failed. A Navajo family established a home and grazed their sheep on the adjacent range, but their only right to the land was through "inherited use-ownership," and it could not be given away by any member of the family. To a certain degree, the "inherited use-ownership" concept also applied to livestock owned by a family. Every family member, including young children, would be assigned animals, but that did not mean they could dispose of them at will. The welfare of the family had to be given first consideration. Each "owner" had to contribute meat in his turn, and provide animals to be slaughtered for a ceremonial or to feed guests. But he could look upon sheep bearing his private earmark or brand and feel a sense of security that otherwise would not have been enjoyed.

New land was a constant requirement as the population increased, and year by year the Navajos pushed westward into less occupied country. Thus, members of clans might live out their lives without seeing one another or meeting only on rare occasions, but no one forgot who his relatives were, even if he didn't know them. A Navajo was always linked to his clan, and his life was guided by its ritual and regulations.

In Navajo myth, the Dineh learned to weave from the greatest weaver of all, Spider Woman. But, of course, they learned the art from the Pueblos, and, as they did in almost every other occupation, they came to excel in it. They were never good potters. After the Pueblo influx they attempted to make painted pottery, but the results were poor imitations of Pueblo types. Their seeming lack of talent for this work may have been simply lack of interest. They were material-ists, and pottery was of small value to them as an article of trade. They could obtain all they needed from the Pueblos, and nothing was to be gained by creating a surplus. If they had been able to manufacture a superior pottery for which there would have been a wide demand, their economy would have benefited. As this obviously could not be ac-complished, pottery making died out.

Although the Navajos adopted Pueblo agriculture, manu-facturing techniques, and ceremonials, they did not become Pueblos. The reason is that they absorbed those customs

they believed would benefit them, and those that most delighted and appealed to them, but rejected all other Pueblo
ways of life. They became competent farmers, but they did
not give up raiding. They accepted the Pueblo "religious
riches," but not without adapting them to their own thinking. They used the Pueblo "framework of theology and
ceremony, but into it they poured their own feeling for
movement and some of the lore of every region they had
traversed." Pueblo ceremonials were communal activities.
The Navajo transformed them so that they might be held
for an individual, who would pay the singers and the think-
ers and the sand painters. Yet even though the medicine
men might be performing to aid an individual, all who
cared to attend the ceremonies were welcome. So the great
Navajo chants, songs, and dances originated, and in this
sense they were community affairs. Navajos might travel
for days to participate in a squaw dance or Yeibechai. To
the Pueblo ceremonials the Navajos gave incomparable
primitive drama and grandeur.

The Navajos began to grow rich from what they learned
and obtained from the Pueblos, and by the time the
Spaniards returned, although widely scattered and elusive,
they were a well-organized, united, and powerful tribe.

New Mexico was reconquered in 1692 by Captain General
Don Diego de Vargas Zapata Lujan Ponce de León. With
two hundred heavily armed soldiers, two cannon, three
priests, and a long supply train, Governor de Vargas rode
up to the pueblo walls of Santa Fe and called upon the
Indians within them to surrender. After hours of haranguing
and negotiating, the Indians capitulated.

For the next two months de Vargas moved through the
country, going as far west as the Hopi towns, and negotiated
numerous peace pacts. Many of the pueblos were deserted,
however, and de Vargas was informed that the peoples who

had occupied them would not submit to him. He made no effort to pursue them, knowing the hardship and the cost that would result. One might as well try to reduce the Jews without the Inquisition, he wrote, as runaway apostate Indians without strong military forces.

Although de Vargas was restrained, maintaining a policy of peaceful approach and striving to avoid violence, he left no doubts in the minds of the Indians with whom he talked that he expected them to submit to Spanish civil laws, abandon their ceremonials, and adopt Catholicism. No exceptions would be permitted when he returned in the coming year with settlers to re-establish the colony of New Mexico. He avoided the Navajo country as much as possible in his journey, convinced that his presence there would make war inescapable. Navajo scouts watched him as he moved westward, and at Zuñi made their first strike, slipping into the Spaniards' camp and stealing sixteen horses.

Navajos told the Hopis that de Vargas was on the way to attack them, and when he reached Awatobi he found a thousand warriors arrayed against him. At least three hundred of them were mounted, and many were armed with Spanish swords and guns. De Vargas succeeded in convincing them that he came in peace, and only wished to notify them that the Spanish province of New Mexico would be resettled. At the Hopi town of Walpi, de Vargas saw "a great number of warriors," and was told that many of them were Utes, Navajos, "and their allies." He made inquiries about minerals in the vicinity, and was told the location of a vermilion mine. He obtained samples—he thought the vermilion might contain quicksilver—but decided against visiting the deposit, as he had received a report of a new gathering of Navajos in the area. His horses were in poor condition, and he could not chance having more stolen, leaving him stranded amid formidable enemies. He went back to Zuñi, and then set out directly for El Paso and Mexico.

In mid-December 1693, de Vargas was again at the gates of Santa Fe. With him this time were a hundred soldiers, eighty families of settlers, eighteen priests, a large group of halfbreed Indians, and an odd assortment of mercenaries, ex-convicts, men and women of good birth, lawyers, and hopeful shopkeepers.

The pueblo of Santa Fe had been fortified, and as de Vargas and a group of priests entered the plaza singing hymns, the Indians stood at their battle stations, silent, their weapons poised. The defenders showed no sign of willingness to negotiate. There was no response at all. Still hoping that he could make a peaceful entry, de Vargas sent word that he would allow the Indians time to evacuate the city, and he ordered a camp established on the outskirts. It was bitter cold, and snow covered the ground.

For two weeks de Vargas waited. The suffering of the colonists was severe, and twenty-one soldiers died of exposure. De Vargas was unnecessarily patient, but that was not a sign of weakness. As the year of 1693 neared an end, he attacked. After two days of fighting, the Indians fled. Seventy captives were hanged.

The story was the same in other pueblos as de Vargas led his soldiers in a winter campaign up and down the Rio Grande. Only four pueblos capitulated without a battle. Hundreds of Indians were killed as they fought to defend their homes.

The priests followed the soldiers into the fallen towns and began to rebuild the churches that had been destroyed thirteen years earlier in the revolt. But peace was still far from restored. Navajo raiders swept boldly into Santa Fe, killed a boy, and made off with a number of horses before the soldiers could intercept them. Reports reached de Vargas that the Taos, Picuris, Jémez, Cochiti, and Navajos had united to attack the colony.

"With full sails we forge ahead," de Vargas declared with a confidence he did not feel. While he girded for the assault, he moved some sixty newly arrived families to a new settlement at Santa Cruz. As more colonists came up the long trail, Bernalillo was established. Drought added its burden to the smoldering spasmodic warfare. Crops failed, and the specter of starvation stalked the country.

Revolt was in the air during the winter of 1695–96. Some priests fled their stations and returned to Santa Fe. In June the united Pueblo and Navajo warriors made a furious strike. Five priests and twenty-one soldiers were killed. Again the pueblo churches were destroyed.

De Vargas moved fast and without mercy against the rebellious towns. He had some help now from Pueblos who realized the futility of defying the Spanish. Before the year ended, the rebellion had been put down. Pueblos began to return to their homes, but not all of them. Once more a large number fled into the Navajo country. It was a repetition on a smaller scale of the influx of 1680, but it was an important event in the record of Navajo acculturation. The Pueblos who would not surrender to the Spanish under any circumstances were largely from San Felipe, San Cristóbal, Santa Clara, Jémez, and Cochiti. Navajo legend recounts that the Jémez sent them all their unmarried young women with the request: "Find husbands for our girls so that if our pueblo is destroyed the Jémez blood will be preserved." The Jémez blood was preserved in a new Navajo clan, the Coyote Pass. Another new clan was the Black Sheep, the founders of which were women from San Felipe.

The final organized revolt of the Pueblos failed. They were a beaten people.

But out of the war had risen a new, strong, and uncon-quered people. The Navajos had become the lords of New Mexico. They would never capitulate as the Pueblos had done, never submit to Spanish domination.

As the eighteenth century opened, they continued their vicious incursions against the white invaders, but they also turned their eyes toward new and more distant fields. The Navajos, according to reports reaching Santa Fe, were raid-ing French and Pawnees on the Great Plains! Three hundred, four hundred miles from their home country!

It was unbelievable, but seemed to be proved by the Navajos who were boldly appearing at fairs, such as those held annually in Taos, with guns, powder flasks, clothing, and other merchandise of French origin. These could have been obtained in trade with plains tribes, but there was other evidence that left no doubt of Navajo raids to the northeast. On one occasion they brought into Taos a num-ber of Pawnee children whom they hoped to sell to the Spanish. At the moment, official Spanish policy was against trading with the most formidable enemy of the provincial government. When no buyer was forthcoming, the Navajos beheaded the Pawnee youngsters. They wanted no Pawnee blood in their tribe.

These were murders as fiendish as any committed by Oñate and other Spaniards. The Pawnees avenged them by ambushing and wiping out, with the help of French *voya-geurs*, a large band of Navajo raiders.

Fear that a French invasion of their northern colonies was in the making caused the Spanish to adopt a strategy that involved inducing Indians to fight one another. Tribes were encouraged to take captives, especially young ones, among plains peoples who traded with the French and deliver them to Spanish slavers. The Spanish also made slave raids into the Great Plains, under the pretext that they were military moves to stop the French advance.

In the case of the Navajos, the Spanish could offer two acceptable reasons for conducting slave raids against them: they were bandits, and they were enemies of the church.

The result of these forays was a sharp increase in the human chattel that could be purchased on the New Mexico market for delivery to Mexico. Taos was one of the main centers of the diabolical commerce. There Spanish traders

> gathered to trade and barter with Indians for deer and buffalo hides, and what is saddest, for Indian slaves, men and women, small and large, a great multitude of both sexes . . . the richest treasure for the governors, who gorge themselves first with the largest mouthfuls. . . .
>
> When these barbarians bring a certain number of Indian women to sell, among them many young maidens and girls, before delivering them to the Christians who buy them, they deflower and corrupt them in the sight of innumerable assemblies of barbarians and Catholics, without considering anything but their unbridled lust and brutal shamelessness, and saying to those who buy them, with heathen impudence: "Now you can take her—now she is good."

The philosophy of the Navajos was defined in their maxim: "Poor is the man who can see farther than his horses graze." Their consuming greed extended to all domestic animals, but horses were prized above all. Nothing delighted a Navajo more than the sight of horse herds cropping the sparse grass of the high ranges. Horses were riches, and in the reasoning of the Navajos there could be no such thing as a surplus.

A calendar of events for the entire eighteenth century

would present a monotonously repetitive record of Navajo plundering, Spanish reprisals, Spanish-Navajo peace agreements, and Navajo plundering. The pattern was generally the same. A band of Navajos, its size governed by the amount of resistance expected—it was not unusual for as many as five hundred warriors to unite in a raid—with terrifying howls would sweep upon a Spanish community, murder defenders, carry away women captives, and drive off as many head of livestock as possible under the need for quick flight.

Soldiers, usually supported by Indian and Spanish civilian volunteers, would set out in pursuit of the raiders but seldom overtook them. In most cases a punitive expedition would gain revenge by shooting on sight any Navajos they encountered and destroying any Navajo livestock, hogans, and crops they chanced to find. Frequently these drastic measures would bring a peace offer from some Navajo leader. The Spaniards had no alternative but to agree to it, for even a short respite from Navajo assaults was better than none at all. The Navajos would keep a promise only as long as it served to their advantage. Normally this involved just enough time to re-establish the destroyed settlements— sometimes in new locations—strengthen their defenses, and make plans to renew their plundering. There were occasions, however, when they suffered such severe punishment from both Indian and Spanish forces that their recovery was slow and difficult.

In the execution of hit-and-run tactics the Navajos were masters, but they appeared unable to achieve the organization and discipline that are essential in sustained warfare. In 1702 Governor Pedro Cubero, with 250 men, set out to attack them, but when the Navajos learned of the size of this well-armed force they quickly sent a chief to Taos to make amends. Cubero accepted the plea and called off the campaign. Comparative quiet prevailed on the Navajo frontier for almost three years, but in 1705 they went on the rampage again, and Captain Roque de Madrid led a strong contingent against them.

Madrid left the Rio Grande near Taos and moved northwestward, defeating the Navajos in several engagements. This offensive might have been continued had not a large number of Navajos who had taken refuge on a high mesa witnessed what they considered a remarkable feat of magic. The horses of the Spaniards were suffering from thirst. A priest knelt in the sand of a dry wash and lifted his arms toward the heavens. Almost at once dark clouds appeared. A heavy rain fell, and flood waters swept down the wash. The Navajos were so terrified by the seeming miracle that they threw down their arms and pleaded for amnesty.

But the fears engendered in them by what they took to be the padre's spiritual powers and the deadliness of Madrid's guns were soon overcome by their ungovernable lust for wealth. In 1706 they raided the pueblos of San Ildefonso, Santa Clara, and San Juan, and between 1708 and 1710 attacked numerous Spanish settlements. Only by sending punitive forces into Navajo country to ravage their villages were the Spanish able to enforce submission. In the year 1709 alone five campaigns were conducted against them. Numerous offensives were carried on in the ensuing years until 1720, but the results were always the same: after short periods of inactivity the Navajos began a new series of strikes.

However, an unprecedented peace between the Spanish and the Navajos prevailed for more than three decades after 1720. The tranquillity was heartily appreciated by the provincial government, which had all it could do at the time to combat assaults on the colony by Apaches and other plains tribes.

The prolonged interval during which the Navajos halted

their raids was not the result of a change of heart, a desire for friendship with the Spanish, or a decrease in their craving for plunder. They were forced to give full attention to combating the onslaughts of two formidable foes: enemy Indians and drought.

Intertribal conflicts occurred with seasonal regularity. The Utes attacked from the north, seeking booty and captives. This pressure steadily increased, forcing the Navajos to maintain strong defense forces along the northern perimeter of their country. Indian raiders also struck spasmodically from the west and south, and the frequency of these incursions necessitated constant vigilance by the Navajos.

Insufficient summer rain caused crop failures in several years between 1720 and 1750, but an extremely severe drought occurred in the latter part of this period. It and vicious assaults by the Utes forced the Navajos to abandon numerous villages and move southward in New Mexico and westward into Arizona.

Of the two foes, Utes and drought, the Navajos considered the Utes the more menacing. Droughts came and went—they had survived many—but the Utes gave every indication of growing more powerful and more destructive.

Navajo leaders put their heads together and contrived a crafty plan. They appealed to the Spanish governor, Joaquin Codallos y Rabal, for protection against the Utes. In return for this aid they would reconsider their antipathy to the Catholic Church, and would be agreeable to engaging in discussion about the matter should the governor care to send religious emissaries to them.

They knew what they were doing. Nothing could have delighted the provincial government and the priests more than the prospect of unfurling the banners of Christianity throughout the Navajo country and securing the submission of Indians who had for so long rigorously opposed every effort to convert them. Attempts would be made to induce the Utes to halt their attacks.

With soaring hopes and prayers for success on their lips, Padres Delgado and Irigoyan set out with Pueblo interpreters to confer with the Navajos. Traveling westward from Jémez, they were courteously received wherever they went. Large groups respectfully listened to their pleas and their sermons. On their return they joyously reported that they had "interviewed" more than four thousand Indians, and that Navajo leaders had promised to send a large delegation to meet the governor at the next full moon. An urgent dispatch was sent to the viceroy to inform him of the triumph. By the time the news reached Spain the four thousand Navajos "interviewed" had become more than five thousand "converted," and the king ordered the viceroy to "sustain the friars and help along the good work."

The Navajos kept their word, and a group appeared in Santa Fe. They were received by the governor, who presented them with handsome gifts and assured them he would do all in his power to protect them. All he asked was that they become Catholics, and thereby assure themselves of salvation. They readily pledged fealty to the church. The governor's proposal that four missions be established in the Navajo country, with some thirty soldiers assigned to protect them, was approved in Mexico City in 1746. Padre Menchero, the *visitador*, personally directed the project. He persuaded six hundred Navajos to settle at Cebolleta, where a mission was to be established. Another mission would be located at Encinal, and Navajos began to move to that area. Shortly after the missions were completed in 1749, serious trouble occurred between the "converts" and the priests.

A new governor, Tomás Velez Cachupin, had taken office. Because of Apache raids he had been unable to send

soldiers to guard the missions, but in the spring of 1750 he
sent investigators to determine the cause of the dissension.
They quickly found it. Padre Menchero had been too liberal
and had promised more gifts than he was able to deliver.
The Navajos angrily complained that they had not received
half the rewards promised them, and that the priests stationed at the missions were too poor to make any gifts at
all, having hardly enough clothes to cover themselves and
nothing of any value.

The Navajos maintained that they had been deceived by
the church. Nothing had been done to stop the Utes, and
they were continuing their onslaught. Therefore, they had
gained nothing by establishing themselves at Cebolleta and
Encinal and had decided to abandon the communities.

The Navajos returned to their free life, scattering to un-
known locations in the west. The priests went back to Santa
Fe. In the summer of 1750 the missions at Cebolleta and
Encinal were deserted.

As long as they ruled in New Mexico—for almost another
three-quarters of a century—the Spanish government would
make no further efforts to convert the Navajos. They would
be considered as hopelessly addicted to idolatry and abandoned to their heathenish life.

The awarding of immense land grants created a new and
serious controversy between the Spanish and the Navajos.
Some of the grants, notably those between the Rio Puerco
and Mount Taylor, included lands claimed by the Navajos.
They had resumed their raiding to recoup losses suffered at
the hands of the Utes, and now they included in their targets the new settlements growing on Spanish grants encroaching on their country. The pueblos of Laguna and Zia
were raided in 1774, and the grants of Rio Puerco and Cebolleta were attacked so ferociously and with such success
that they were abandoned. The Spanish retaliated by send-

ing two punitive expeditions out from Albuquerque that destroyed large amounts of Navajo property.

For five years, between 1775 and 1780, the Navajos were strangely quiescent and gave the Spanish little trouble, but during the interval a plot was formulated that would spread the flames of a vicious war throughout the Southwest. In 1777 the Gila Apaches, or Gilenos, and the Navajos concluded an alliance. The pact opened to both tribes vast areas for plunder, and formidable forces of the united warriors conducted raids into southern Arizona and even into Mexico.

The famed explorer, army officer, and colonizer Colonel Juan Bautista de Anza took the oath of office as governor of New Mexico in August 1777, but did not reach Santa Fe until the late fall of 1778. The Navajo-Gila alliance presented a perilous situation, and he had orders to spare no effort or cost in suppressing it.

Initial Spanish strategy involved winning the friendship of the Moquis (Hopis) and establishing both a mission and a garrison in their towns. At the time the Moqui region was suffering from a devastating drought, and recent Navajo raids had taken a heavy toll of lives and property.

Anza notified the Moquis that he would bring them gifts and food, and that any who wished to migrate to the Rio Grande area could do so with the assurance that they would receive care and protection. Some 150 accepted the offer, and he found homes for them in various pueblos. More would have come, he was informed, had they not been fearful of being waylaid by Navajos. With more than a hundred soldiers and Indian allies and a packtrain of foodstuffs, Anza left Santa Fe for the Moqui towns early in September 1780.

On the Rio Puerco, Anza encountered Navajos. They fled at sight of him, but he sent signals that he was not marching against them and some of them returned. He gave them tobacco and warned them against disrupting the peaceful relationship between the Spanish and the Moquis. Anza understood that more Moquis were waiting for him to escort them to the Rio Grande region, but he was not aware of the atrocities already committed by Navajos against the Moqui migrants. Not until he had traveled several days west of Zuñi did he learn that forty Moqui families—perhaps 160 to 180 people—had set out for Santa Fe after receiving assurances from the Navajos of a safe passage. As the large group of hungry and impoverished Moquis trudged eastward, hoping to meet Anza, they were captured by Navajo warriors. The men were murdered in cold blood, and the women and children carried away to be absorbed into the Navajo tribe.

Never in their history was the utter faithlessness of the Navajos demonstrated with greater brutality than in this case. Anza found the Moquis on the verge of extermination. In 1775 Fray Silvestre Velez Escalante had visited the Moquis and reported that they numbered nearly eight thousand persons living in seven pueblos, possessed many cattle, horses, and sheep, and cultivated extensive croplands. Drought, pestilence, and Navajo and Ute raiders had combined to destroy them. Anza was appalled to discover that two pueblos were without any residents and that less than eight hundred people inhabited the other five towns. In five years nearly seven thousand Moquis had either perished, fled their homeland, or had been taken captive. The Moquis possessed no cattle at all, only five horses and no more than three hundred sheep.

Logistical difficulties of supplying troops on offensives, the problems of exchanging communications over vast distances, and incredible red tape caused Spanish military campaigns to proceed with agonizing slowness. Anza drove

southward to Sonora and established a military line between
the territories of the Gila Apaches and the Navajos at the
Rio de la Laguna (the present Rio San José). The Gilas
suffered serious defeats from Spanish forces moving north
from Sonora and Nueva Vizcaya between 1782 and 1784,
and it remained for Anza to strike the blows in the north
that would destroy the Navajo-Gila alliance.

Anza and his superiors thoroughly understood not only
the perfidious nature of the Navajos, but their economic
condition, the political structure of the tribe, and the precarious situation in which they existed as a result of enemy
pressures from three directions. Anza added a fourth pressure by stationing a force on the Rio de la Laguna and no-
tifying the Navajos that any of them found in Gila territory
south of the stream would be "treated as declared enemies,
seized and taken to the Villa of Santa Fe to receive the punishment which may appropriately be imposed." He also forbade all trade and communication between Navajos, Pueblos, and Spanish, warning all colonists and peaceful Indians
that violations of the order would bring severe penalties.

Trade was vitally important to the economy of the Navajos, and the tactics had the result of dividing them. A strong
group led by a man the Spaniards called El Pinto wanted
to maintain the alliance with the Gilas, and an equally
powerful group favored its dissolution. The theory of the
Spanish was well recounted by the commander general in
a letter to the viceroy. Cut off from trade with the Pueblos
and Spanish and with their bitter enemies, the Utes and the
Comanches, a constant threat, "It is not presumable in such
a situation the Navajos would take lightly the propositions
which I have ordered made to them when, because of the
opportune application of the means and principles inspired
in the governor [Anza], they see themselves obliged to take
a side." By "fostering the germs of the Navajo discord," it

was believed that the "desired rupture between the Gilas and Navajos could be achieved in terms rendering impossible their reconciliation in the future."

The strategy was effective. Some forty Navajo headmen, bearing the authority to speak for their respective followings, gave Anza their word that they would join the Spanish and would attack the Gilas. Shrewdly Anza "stirred up as a rival" to El Pinto a strong Navajo leader whom he called Coton Negro. El Pinto capitulated. He appeared before Anza, "confessing his infidelity and past alliance [with the Gilas], asked pardon and promised him that as much as he had been opposed to the Spanish before, he would be devoted and faithful in the future."

Displaying extraordinary skill as a negotiator and politician, Anza succeeded in uniting the great majority of the Navajos. In a council held at Santa Fe early in 1796 most of the Navajo settlements were represented by ranking delegates. They asked that Anza appoint a single chieftain to lead them in forays against the Gilas, and they submitted the names of two of their leaders, both of whom were present, whom they "judged most fit and worthy" to hold the distinction of being their general. Both the candidates "were sons of the two old men most friendly to the Spaniards."

Anza selected both, expressing the view "that because of the scattered condition in which their nation existed, it was necessary that a lieutenant be named for the general, with whom he might share the affairs of government." He requested the Navajos to make the choices themselves by voting. When that had been done, Anza, ignoring Navajo names—probably because he was unable to pronounce them —called the general Don Carlos, and the lieutenant Don Joseph Antonio. In the name of the Spanish king he presented them with medals signifying their respective ranks. Then, "to avoid conspiracies among the discontented,"

Anza suggested that the Navajo leave all "present captains of rancherias in possession and exercise of their offices." It was a shrewd move, for it had the effect of precluding internal squabbling on lower levels. The council accepted the suggestion without dissent, obviously very much pleased.

On several occasions during the summer of 1786 the Navajos demonstrated their intention to abide by their pact with Anza by attacking the Gilas and driving them southward. The general and the lieutenant made several trips to Santa Fe, ostensibly to confer with Anza and to receive orders. However, they disclosed the major concern of the Navajos with a plea that Anza rescind his order forbidding them to engage in trade with the Spanish and the Pueblos. Anza not only withdrew the order, but opened wide the trade gates, allowing Pueblos and Spaniards to enter Navajo country to barter and granting Navajos permission to attend trade fairs.

Ugarte had become commander general of Spain's interior provinces in October 1785. A year later he wrote Anza that he had "observed with satisfaction that you have already triumphed, not only completing the rupture of the old link which bound the Navajo Indians to the Gilas . . . but also succeeding in moving the former to make war on them. . . . Thus your lordship justly deserves my approval of all your dispositions. Of these I shall inform his Majesty."

In addition to opening trade doors, Anza opened the doors of the churches to Navajos. Not many passed through them for the purpose of accepting Christianity or marrying into so-called Christianized tribes. Anza also failed in his attempt to establish a mission in the Navajo country. The Navajos coldly opposed the idea, and Anza abandoned it, fearing that if he persisted the peace he had achieved might be jeopardized. The gulf between Navajo paganism and Christianity would not be bridged.

Anza left office in November 1787. Shortly after, Navajos raided Abiquiu and Rio Abajo. A year later Anza died in Arizpe. As he was laid to rest, the system of alliances he had so skillfully constructed had begun to disintegrate.

Anza's successor as governor of New Mexico, Fernando de la Concha, was soon faced with Navajo uprisings. By 1792 the old order of things once more prevailed. Many Utes and Navajos, instead of attacking each other, united to raid Comanche camps on the plains. Navajos and Gilas still fought below and above the Anza line, but warfare between these two peoples, which Anza had brought about, lasted only until 1796, when the Gila-Navajo alliance was restored.

All along the northern New Mexico frontier Navajos were once more on the rampage, and once more the Spanish were forced to drive against them. Military columns moved deep into their country, ravaging the land and killing them wherever they could be overtaken.

Spanish intelligence estimated the Navajo population at approximately four thousand, of whom one thousand were warriors. The estimates were probably conservative. The Navajos were spread over an immense area, and it was unlikely that all of them were observed. Penetration by Spanish forces would send them retreating into remote regions. Not always were the soldiers able to engage them in battle, for the Navajos fully understood that the superiority of Spanish arms gave them little chance of victory in a direct confrontation. Most of the engagements that occurred were running fights. Raiding was a different matter, for the Navajos enjoyed the advantage of surprise. The number of Navajos known to have participated in single raids—often several hundred—indicates that they could have mustered more than a thousand fighting men.

In the first years of the nineteenth century Spanish troops were constantly in the Navajo country. Navajos plundered several pueblos and Spanish towns despite desperate efforts of the military to stop them. The increasing boldness of the Navajos prompted Governor Chacon to order a winter campaign against them. In January 1805, Lieutenant Antonio Narbona led a strong force into the Canyon de Chelly, after learning from Pueblo scouts that a large number had retreated into that area.

The Navajos were forewarned of Narbona's approach. Women, children, and old men were taken to a large cave high on a great wall of a branch canyon—later to be known as Canyon del Muerto—which was believed to be an impregnable position. The only access to the cave was a precipitous and narrow trail from the top of the wall. The Navajo men then scattered and concealed themselves in the towering rocky precipices of the adjacent area.

As Narbona led his men through the magnificent Canyon de Chelly and into Canyon del Muerto he saw no sign of human life. Hogans were deserted. Some sheep had been seen grazing on the mesa lands outside the canyons, but no animals were found on the snow-covered floors. The immense chasms were silent, cold, and deserted.

Narbona might have turned back, had not the scream of a woman suddenly pierced the stillness. An old Navajo squaw had been unable to control herself and rose in the cave shrieking raucous curses at the Spaniards.

Narbona and his men observed that the cave had a sharply sloping roof. They opened fire, and bullets striking the roof ricocheted in a deadly rain on the Navajos. Some troopers had found a way to the top of the wall and discovered the trail. Slithering down it, they entered the cave and waded among the trapped men, women, and children, clubbing and bayoneting them to death.

Navajo warriors engaged Narbona in a running battle, but suffered heavy losses. In the report he submitted when he reached Zuñi he claimed that he had "killed ninety bucks, with 25 women and children, besides capturing 36 (men), with 30 women and children; also 30 horses and 350 sheep." One Pueblo scout was killed, and sixty-four Spaniards sustained wounds.

It was a major defeat for the Navajos, and in the early spring they sent emissaries to Santa Fe to ask for peace. Governor Chacon drew up a treaty that imposed severe penalties, but the Navajos readily agreed to it and made their marks on the document. It was the same old story. Within a year they were raiding again, and Chacon's successor, Joaquin del Reál Alencaster, was forced to launch offensives against them.

Alencaster's greatest problems, however, had nothing to do with Navajos. In 1803 the enormous Louisiana Territory had been sold by France to the United States. The first American traders, defying Spanish regulations, had reached Santa Fe. Rumors that American military forces were pushing into the Great Plains and attempting to enlist the Indians in attacks on Spanish settlements came with the regularity of the moons. In January 1807 the first American spies, Zebulon M. Pike and Dr. John H. Robinson, and a small group of American soldiers were taken prisoners on Spanish territory. Intelligence of Aaron Burr's conspiracy with General James Wilkinson, commander in chief of the American forces in Louisiana, to launch a filibustering expedition against New Mexico and Texas had alarmed Spanish authorities. Patrols stationed along the northern boundaries claimed by Spain to guard against the anticipated American assault, and other troops sent against the Navajos to prevent them from making northern New Mexico uninhabitable.

The condition would endure until Mexico won independence from Spain in 1821; the changes in the Navajos' relations with the incoming Mexican regime would be for the worse.

The last two years in which the Spanish flag flew over New Mexico were marked by bloody clashes. Troops dispatched by the last Spanish governor, Facundo Melgares, invaded the Navajo country in January 1819, killed a number of warriors, and again forced the Navajos to ask for peace. Melgares prepared a treaty, but before it could be negotiated the Navajos took to the plunder trail again. The Spanish sent two more expeditions against them in February and March. In these campaigns large numbers of Navajos were driven westward to the vicinity of the Moqui towns, and now the Moquis, who had suffered so greatly from Navajo raiders, appealed to the Spanish for protection. With a revolution raging in Mexico, the Spanish were in no position to send a permanent garrison to the Moqui country, but Governor Melgares was able to induce the Navajos to sign a peace treaty in August. It was effective only a few months before the Navajos broke it, but on this occasion they had good reason to return to the warpath. Forty Navajos who appeared at Jémez to trade were murdered by inhabitants led by the local mayor. Melgares arrested and imprisoned the killers, who were Mexicans, but they were released when Mexico came into power.

The treaty of 1819 was the last between the Spanish and the Navajos.

The Navajos made no distinction between Spaniards and Mexicans. The change of flags brought no changes in policies that were beneficial to the Navajos. They were taken prisoner and sold into slavery by the Mexicans just as they had been by the Spanish. In 1823 the first attempt by the Mexicans to sign a treaty with the Navajos was made—with an ultimatum that unless they agreed to terms, a campaign would be launched against them. Fearing they would sustain crippling losses, the Navajos signed.

The Mexicans were acting with diabolical intentions. At the time of the peace conference, the Mexican governor José Antonio Vizcarra, and his lieutenants "were debating how to divide the booty and captives which the campaign they were secretly planning would surely net." Without waiting to learn if the Navajos would abide by the treaty, they completed a plan of war.

Indeed, the major provision of the first Mexican-Navajo pact had to do with the subject of Indian captivity. Land issues and boundaries, even Navajo raiding, were of lesser importance to Vizcarra and his conspirators. The Navajos were to return all captives they held "without hiding any, and the same with the fugitives, if there are any." This could be construed as meaning all Indian slaves held by the Navajos, including the children born of Navajo men and captive or fugitive Indian women. It would have been a fruitful harvest for Mexican slavers.

The Mexicans sought to make the Navajos believe they would reciprocate in the exchange of captives, but the wording of the clause made plain the falseness of their promise: Navajos who had "fled to us"—there were very few, if any— would be returned "whenever they may wish to go back; but if they should wish to receive the saving waters of Baptism, it does not appear the desire of Catholics to deny them."

The treaty had no sooner been signed than Governor Vizcarra launched his slave raid on the Navajos. For four months his column—mostly armed civilians, for there were few soldiers in New Mexico at the time—swept through the Navajo country. The governor was disappointed by the results. The Navajos were elusive, and only fifty warriors were killed and thirty-six women and children captured to be sold into bondage.

Continued slave raids, many of them conducted clandestinely by civilians without government sanction, forced the Navajos to wage both a defensive and an offensive war against the Mexicans between the years 1822 and 1846. The Navajos retaliated against invasions of their country, not only for the purpose of plundering settlements but in the hope of recovering men, women, and children forcefully taken from them. They attacked the Mexican slave-trading centers of Abiquiu, Cebolleta, Jémez, and Cubero. Twice in October 1832 they struck at the military garrison at Soccoro with such success that the commander reported his troops were unable to give chase because they had no horses.

The Navajo children could be sold for 150 pesos. The priests "saved the souls" of these small boys and girls by baptizing them before they became the servants of Mexican families. According to one source, in a five-year period there were more than 250 recorded baptisms of Navajo captives. The actual number was undoubtedly higher, as many captives baptized were described simply as "Indians."

Because they had few soldiers at their command, the Mexican governors engaged Utes, Pueblos, and civilians to conduct slave raids for them. These mercenaries were paid in booty, which included Navajo prisoners as well as livestock.

The war raged through the years with bloody fury, both in and outside the Navajo country. Repeatedly both sides offered to make peace. On the part of the Mexicans, the proposals were totally worthless, for they had no intention of keeping them. Moreover, a treaty negotiated by a provincial governor had no legality until it had been ratified by the authorities in Mexico. None of the treaties made between Navajos and Mexican officials in Santa Fe—and there were eight or ten of them—was ratified as Mexican laws required. On the part of the Navajos, they were unable to abide by any treaty because Mexican slave hunters continued to attack them.

This was the case in 1837. Mexicans violated a peace agreement by laying waste Navajo settlements near Ojo del Gallo, Chuska, and Canyon de Chelly, killing twenty Navajo defenders, taking as many captives, and stealing some seven thousand sheep.

A year later Governor Manuel Armijo, having just assumed office and eager to line his own pockets, led a drive against the Navajos and delivered a demoralizing blow. Seventy-eight warriors were killed, and seventy-six young Navajos were captured. Armijo marched back to Santa Fe with his prisoners tied to saddle horns, his servants driving 2,500 sheep and mules loaded with more than 1,500 bushels of corn taken from Navajo storehouses, and many packs of woven Navajo cloth and silver ornaments—all of which was salable at a good profit to him.

Despite Mexican campaigns against them, despite their serious losses of life and property, both the culture and the economy of the Navajos continued to develop. Even under the burden of almost unceasing warfare they remained irrepressible, determined and clever learners. Navajo acculturation during both the Spanish and Mexican regimes was extensive. They adapted Spanish equipment and ornaments to their own needs. Navajos who escaped from Spanish captivity, many of them after years of servitude, brought back with them skills taught them by their captors. Raiders returned not only with livestock, but also bridles, saddles, and other articles adorned with silverwork. They learned silversmithing from captives they took, from their own men who had been prisoners of the Mexicans, and from Pueblos to whom the Mexicans had taught the art. Spanish and

Mexican influence became apparent in their clothing, although dress that was the most suitable to their own way of life predominated.

What is probably the first description of Navajos to appear in an American publication was supplied to the *Missouri Intelligenser* by Samuel Patton, who ventured into the Southwest during the Mexican period. The Navajos' "skill in manufacturing," Patton reported, "and their excellence in some useful and ornamental arts show a decided superiority of genius over all other tribes of the Western Continent. They have fine flocks of sheep, abundance of mules and herds of cattle of a superior kind. They have gardens and peach orchards. Several articles of their woolen manufacture equal the quality of ours." Navajos wore blankets draped over one shoulder, in the manner of Mexican gentlemen, and short trousers "which came halfway down the calf and were split at the knee." Some of the trousers were made of Spanish cloth, others of soft "excellently tanned" buckskin. Clothing of both men and women often was "decorated along the seams with silver buttons." A Navajo leader killed by Mexicans "wore shoes, fine woolen stockings, small clothes connected at the sides by silver buttons, a hunting shirt and a scarlet cloth cap, the folds of which were also secured with silver buttons."

Pueblo style prevailed among the Navajo women. Generally they wore a double-blanket dress of woolen material, fastened at the shoulders and hanging down front and back. It provided freedom of movement for working about a cooking fire, herding sheep, or riding. Their jewelry consisted of turquoise, coral, and silver pendants, bracelets, necklaces, and buttons.

No lasting peace was possible between the Mexicans and the Navajos. Only by killing or capturing the Navajos could the Mexicans hope to protect their property. And so long as their children were held as slaves, the Navajos would not cease their raids to recover them. It was a vicious circle that might have been followed for years had not an event occurred that changed the entire course of western history—war between the United States and Mexico.

A friendly Ute married to a Navajo woman—a union that was a rarity—brought word to his wife's clan that "a certain people are going to come to us. From below where the sun constantly rises, they are going to come to us. Their ears are wider than anything. They extend down to their ankles. And these people at night, covering themselves with those ears of theirs, lie down to sleep."

The same news, in somewhat different form, had reached Santa Fe, and Governor Armijo had no time to think about Navajos. The American army was moving toward New Mexico, and American civilian emissaries had arrived in Santa Fe to advise Armijo that it would be useless for him to attempt to defend the capital in the face of the overwhelming force that was marching south from Bent's Fort on the Arkansas River.

Armijo made a pretense of "saving his responsibility as a Mexican officer" by calling upon the people "to rise and repel the invader." The response was decidedly half-hearted, and those who proclaimed their patriotism and willingness to fight were poorly armed. Nevertheless, Armijo led his few soldiers and the auxiliaries, perhaps two thousand in all, out to Apache Canyon, a short distance east of Santa Fe, and announced his intention to make a stand. However, when scouts—some of whom had been captured and released by the Americans—informed him of the strength of the approaching force he changed his mind, sent his defenders home, and fled south to safety.

The Americans met no resistance as they occupied New Mexico.

# 5

IF THERE WAS ANY DIFFERENCE between Spaniards, Mexicans, and Americans, the Navajos were unaware of it. To their way of thinking white men were white men, and all of them were enemies. They had fought the Spaniards for two centuries. To a Navajo, a man calling himself a Mexican was still a Spaniard, imbued with Spanish ideas, adhering to Spanish customs, speaking the Spanish language. As for the priests, they had remained as uncompromising under the Mexicans as they had been from the beginning, unceasingly denouncing Navajo deities, unrelenting in their efforts to destroy Navajo beliefs and ceremonials.

The Navajos had seen few Americans—perhaps some beaver hunters in the mountains of the upper Rio Grande basin or Santa Fe Trail traders. Now the Americans claimed all the land under the sky, but that was no reason to believe conditions would change for the better. Only a few Mexicans had left the country because of the war between

Mexico and the United States. Most of them, as far as the Navajos could learn, were ready to welcome the conquerors. That could mean only one thing: Mexicans and Americans embraced the same policies, the same beliefs, and they would be united in their enmity toward the Navajos. The slave trade would not be stopped. The Navajos were fully prepared to fight Americans as they had fought the Spaniards and Mexicans.

Another factor influenced the Navajos. Banditry had been the original foundation of their economy. Some of them were rich, owning large herds and employing servants to manage them and to cultivate fields, manufacture jewelry and decorations, and weave cloth. These *ricos* opposed raiding and advocated war only when necessary to protect their property against invaders, but they were few in number. Most Navajos were relatively poor, and some had to struggle to obtain the barest necessities. Having seen the prosperity that raiding had brought to some Navajos, the have-nots demanded the right to achieve it for themselves. This was especially true of the young warriors. After all, raiding had been the way of life of their forefathers. It had made the Navajos strong. It could give an individual stature among his people, and it could give him ease and comfort. They would not give it up, and they would not be controlled by rich men who for their own reasons counseled restraint.

The Spanish had been united under the banner of one faith. It had been woven into their political structure, in many respects given the force of law, and it had wielded a powerful influence on their thinking and their actions. Among the conquering Americans, be they soldiers, civilian settlers, tradesmen, or government officials, were to be found adherents of at least three faiths, Protestant, Catholic, and Mormon. This disunity did not, however, indicate an absence of intolerance or bigotry. If these malevolent emotions were not as vociferously proclaimed as they had been by the Spaniards it did not mean that they were less deeply ingrained in Americans. It meant that under the American political system antagonistic sectarians might find themselves the victims of crippling adversities, for they would not receive, nor could they legally demand, legislative or political support.

If constitutional provisions—which theoretically governed the actions, if not necessarily the thinking, of the Americans —were beyond the comprehension of the Navajos in 1846, they would come to realize that the vaunted American freedom of worship, at least as it applied to them, was highly qualified.

Religion would have a forceful bearing upon the course of American-Navajo history. The faith of the Spanish was the warp and woof of their lives, and they were as unyielding in their demands that Indians accept it as they were in demanding that Indians obey their civil laws. That was something the Navajos could understand. Although the American territorial government itself made no religious demands on the Navajos, it permitted the Navajo country to be turned into a religious jungle, where all manner of sects, while seeking to devour each other, tried to force their doctrines down the throats of their captive audience. That was something the Navajos could not understand.

In most other respects there was little difference between the Spanish and American regimes of the nineteenth century. Both were poisoned in almost equal proportions by corruption, greed, and stupidity.

The Americans, with a few notable exceptions, not only did not understand Indians but, even more lamentable, made little effort to understand them. They laughed at them. They derided them. They aped them in fiendish and crude pantomime. They supported, even encouraged, the slave trade.

They raped Indian women. They scalped Indian men, took the bloody mementos back to their homes, and enjoyed the shudders of their relatives. They ruined fields by stabling their horses in them. With ghoulish delight they robbed Navajo graves and stripped the corpses of Navajos they killed.

In August 1846, as the Army of the West took possession of New Mexico, its commander, Brigadier General Stephen Watts Kearney, assured the populace that American military forces would put an end to Indian depredations. Speaking from a rooftop in Las Vegas, he said: "The Apaches and Navajos come down from the mountains and carry off your sheep and your women whenever they please. My government will correct all this. They will protect you in your persons and property."

In the proclamation he issued a few days later at Santa Fe, he declared: "The undersigned has instructions from his government to protect the religious institutions of New Mexico. . . . Also to protect the persons and property of all quiet and peaceful inhabitants within its boundaries, against the Utes, Navajos, and others."

Kearney appeared to have heard only one side of the problem—that of Navajo raids. These, of course, had to be stopped. Another serious problem remained to be resolved, but if Kearney was aware of it he chose to ignore it: he said nothing of the slave raids conducted against the Navajos by the New Mexicans. Early American policies included no provisions for disrupting the traffic in Indian slaves. Indeed, for a time certain regulations would encourage it.

The first major mistake made by American military leaders was their assumption that with proclamations, manifestos, and regulatory demands they could effect a tripartite peace between themselves, the New Mexicans, and the Navajos. With almost inconceivable naïveté they took it for granted that signatures on a piece of paper would bring an end to hatreds that had festered for centuries.

The conquered New Mexicans held the American soldiers in contempt and bitterly resented the treatment received from them. The ragtag and bobtail contingents that marched into the New Mexico towns were boisterous, ill-mannered, and lawless. Writing from personal observations, a British explorer, George F. Ruxton, described the volunteers from the Midwest as "the dirtiest, rowdiest crew I have ever seen collected together." The soldiery in New Mexico, said various newspaper dispatches, "have degenerated into a military mob, are the most open violators of law and order, and daily heap insult and injury on the people. . . . About one-fifth of the whole command have died from the effects of dissipation." Another report stated: "Nearly the whole territory has been the scene of violence, outrage, and oppression by the volunteer soldiery against all alike. . . . The civil authorities find themselves utterly powerless. . . . All is hubbub and confusion here; discharged volunteers leaving, drunk, and volunteers not discharged remaining, drunk." Critics were unanimously agreed, however, that the average American soldier was "brave under fire, a good shot and a good fighter."

As detachments of the American army were stationed along their frontier, the Navajos received false intelligence that the Americans planned to join with the New Mexicans and the Pueblos in a campaign to exterminate them. The rumors were circulated by New Mexican loyalists who hoped the Navajos would attack American garrisons, and by Utes who were seeking to induce the Navajos to join them in war upon the "new men," as the Americans were called. The propaganda proved disastrous to its disseminators. The Navajos increased their raids against both the Utes and the towns. During the first few months after Kearney's arrival,

New Mexicans reported that Navajos had "killed more than fifty citizens or carried them into captivity, and had stolen more than 60,000 head of horses, mules and sheep." The figures undoubtedly were exaggerations, but they were instrumental in spurring military action against the Navajos.

Original military plans called for Kearney to continue on to California and for Colonel Alexander W. Doniphan to take troops down the Rio Grande and engage the Mexicans in Chihuahua. The continuing Navajo depredations, however, caused Kearney to postpone the Chihuahua campaign. He ordered three companies of Doniphan's command, under Lieutenant Colonel Congreve Jackson, to Cebolleta, on the Navajo frontier sixty miles west of Albuquerque, and sent another contingent commanded by Major William Gilpin to Abiquiu. These two garrisons were established, but attempts to halt Navajo raiding failed.

Kearney set out on his famous march to California. En route he received dispatches advising him of the growing necessity to strike against the Navajos. He sent back orders to Doniphan to move into the Navajo country in force without delay. Thus the first American military campaign against the Navajos took place in October 1846, less than three months after New Mexico had been occupied.

It was a poor time of year to begin an offensive, for winter would soon grip the high red-rock country, but Doniphan did not hesitate. He ordered Jackson and Gilpin to move west from Cebolleta and Abiquiu by different routes, "chastise the Navajo wherever they appeared hostile," and unite at Bear Spring (southeast of Gallup, New Mexico). Doniphan planned to join them there for the purpose of negotiating a treaty with the Navajos.

Doniphan's instructions countermanded previous orders under which Jackson already had acted. Upon being sent to Ceboletta, Jackson had been told to summon Navajo headmen to Santa Fe to negotiate a treaty. Jackson had engaged Antonio Sandoval, leader of a small group of Navajos living among New Mexicans near Cebolleta, to carry the request to Navajo leaders. He could not have made a worse choice for an emissary.

Sandoval was the Benedict Arnold of the Navajos. He and his followers—probably fewer than two hundred men, women, and children—were known as *Dine ana'ih*, "Enemy Navajos." Not only had Sandoval, whose Indian name was Hastin Keshgoli ("Crooked Foot"), served as a spy and scout for New Mexican forces campaigning against Navajos, but he had led private slave raids against them and sold the captured Navajo children to New Mexican families. That he had not been killed was one of the unsolved mysteries of the time.

After an absence of two weeks, Sandoval returned to Cebolleta and informed Jackson that the Navajo headmen were fearful of going to Santa Fe before talking with Americans in their own country and being assured that American soldiers would protect them from the New Mexicans. A Captain Reid volunteered to take a small contingent to talk with the Navajos and convince them they would receive the protection they demanded, and Jackson consented to the plan.

It was a daring venture. Reid took with him only thirty volunteers and enough provisions for a reconnaissance of fifteen days. The little company, with the untrustworthy Sandoval serving as a guide, rode nearly a hundred miles westward. In that distance they encountered no Navajos, but that they had been carefully observed became apparent when, after an exhausting week of travel, they reached Bear Spring. There, prepared to talk with them, was one of the greatest of all Navajo leaders, Narbona, aged and crippled by arthritis. After being told the purpose of Reid's mission, Narbona sent Navajo riders out to summon other headmen to meet with the American officer.

Within three days several hundred Navajos had ridden into Bear Springs. A member of Reid's group recorded that the beautiful valley swarmed with "mounted warriors, with their feathers streaming in the wind, their arms raised as for conflict, a sight unequalled in display of horsemanship."

Narbona, a celebrated orator, was called by his people Hastin Naat'aani ("Man Speaking Peace"), and he merited the name. Many of the Navajo leaders present at the council were opposed to going to Santa Fe under any conditions, but Narbona persuaded them that it would be to their advantage to accept the proposal. After long and heated discussion the Navajos agreed to send a delegation to the New Mexico capital to confer with Doniphan and the first American civil governor, Charles Bent.

Reid hastened back to Cebolleta, only to learn that his hazardous mission had been a waste of time. Instead of waiting for the Navajos to meet him in Santa Fe, Doniphan had decided to negotiate with them at Bear Springs. By the first of December he was riding westward with Jackson's command, while Gilpin's troops were moving by another route into the heart of the Navajo country. The rendezvous at Bear Springs was set for December 20.

Gilpin sent out Pueblo scouts to inform the Navajos of the transfer of the council site from Santa Fe to Bear Springs. By December 18 he was caught in deep snow at the mouth of Canyon de Chelly. With a few troops and a number of Navajos, Gilpin left his column and set out on a fast ride to Bear Springs. His command, encumbered by its supply train, was instructed to follow as rapidly as conditions would permit. He reached Bear Springs on December 21, the day after Doniphan had convened the peace meeting.

A score of the most prominent Navajo headmen sat at the

council fire with Doniphan, Jackson, and Gilpin. Camped nearby were some five hundred Navajo warriors and more than three hundred American cavalrymen. The Navajo councilors were cool and reserved. They told the Americans that there were matters they could not comprehend, questions for which they wanted answers; that the American negotiators spoke with straightforwardness and conviction, but words and manners could be deceptive, and they knew nothing about these "new men" or about their true intentions.

The United States government in Washington, declared Doniphan, desired to live in peace with the Navajos, but at the same time it had an obligation to protect all citizens, including New Mexicans, and if the Navajos continued their depredations, the American army would have no alternative but to fight them. The warning brought Nataallith to his feet. Called Zarcillas Largo ("Long Earrings") by the New Mexicans, he was recognized as the most influential Navajo medicine man.

"You have a strange reason for threatening to make war on us," he told Doniphan. "We have fought the Mexicans for years and with good cause. Now you recently made war on them, too, and you have many guns and soldiers, and you have beaten them. That is what we have been trying to do for years. Now you threaten us for attempting to do what you have done yourself. We do not understand why you quarrel with us for fighting Mexicans on the west, while you do the same thing on the east."

Doniphan replied that it was the way of Americans to look upon enemies they had conquered as friends. It was an unsatisfactory explanation to the Navajos, and only increased their bewilderment. However, after giving the difficult matter more thought overnight, Doniphan struck upon an argument that tipped the scales in his favor:

"If you will allow us to settle in New Mexico peacefully," he told the Navajos, "profitable trade can be established between us. You can obtain all the goods you need from us at fair prices. Therefore, we would both benefit."

The Navajos' attitude changed. Americans were obviously rich in goods of all kinds. After a lengthy consultation with the council, Largo again addressed Doniphan:

"If it is the intention of the Americans to hold New Mexico and to stop the Mexicans from attacking us, we will stop our raids. Under these conditions there can be peace between us, and we will welcome trade with you."

The first treaty between Americans and Navajos was signed by Doniphan, Gilpin, Jackson, and fourteen Navajo headmen, whose Spanish names were Largo, Caballada Mucho, Alexandro, Sandoval, Cayatanita, José Largo, Narbona, Narbona Segundo, Pedro José, Manuelito, Tapio, Archuleta, Juanico, and Savoietta Garcia. Most of these Navajo leaders were *ricos*, owners of large herds, extensive fields, and fortunes in silver, turquoise, and coral adornments. Thus they had good reasons for hoping that Americans would bring peace to the land.

Although they were men of great influence, the political structure of the Navajos denied them absolute power to control the actions of their people. They could advise but not dictate, and the Navajos had no supreme chief whose commands were law. The New Mexicans explained these facts to American authorities, and predicted that the Bear Springs treaty would prove to be of no more value than scores of previous pacts, that is, a mere scrap of paper.

If Doniphan harbored any skepticism, he did not reveal it. A former Missouri lawyer and legislator, he looked upon a treaty as a contract, legally binding on all parties and not to be changed without their mutual consent. In the view of the Navajos, a treaty meant nothing unless it was implemented by force. This was something that Doniphan, and probably most American officers and civil officials, did not realize.

Doniphan went on to Chihuahua, eager to participate in the Mexican War and believing that he had brought peace to New Mexico. The treaty he had drafted was, indeed, a sound document. Its five main provisions covered the crucial points of contention:

(1) A firm and lasting peace would henceforth exist between Navajos and Americans;

(2) Residents of New Mexico, including Indians, were to be considered Americans;

(3) Mutual free trade would be carried on without molestation and with full protection for all parties;

(4) Women and children taken as captive slaves, both Indian and Mexican, were to be restored to their people;

(5) All property illegally obtained by either Mexicans or Indians since New Mexico became an American territory was to be returned to its owners.

The Bear Springs treaty was never ratified by the American Congress, but even if it had been, it would have been worthless under conditions prevailing in New Mexico. The New Mexicans ignored it and continued their incursions into Navajo country to recover stolen animals and capture women and children to be sold on the slave market. The Navajos retaliated with raids. Moreover, a revolt by New Mexicans and some Pueblo Indians against the Americans was in the making.

Colonel Sterling Price, who replaced Kearney as military commander in New Mexico, had some two thousand soldiers with which to keep the territory under subjection, but many of them were incapacitated with venereal diseases and other afflictions. The garrisons were so widely separated that patrols were unable to prevent violence in their respective areas. Fights and raids by both New Mexicans and Navajos—as well as by Utes, Comanches, and Apaches—were carried on almost with impunity.

The inability of the Americans to control the vast territory they had conquered was thoughtfully noted by both the Navajos and New Mexicans. Neither, of course, had any real understanding of American military might, and judged the situation by events occurring before their eyes. Although American civil authorities and military officers strove to protect the residents' legal rights, the volunteer soldiers "were overbearing, abusive, and quarrelsome, taking no pains to conceal how much they despised all that was Mexican; and instances of individual insult and outrage were frequent. The Natives were naturally revengeful, many of them vicious, ignorant, and ready to listen to the exaggerated charges and promises of the few reckless characters . . . bent on stirring up a revolt."

Both Navajos and New Mexicans observed "the inroads of sickness among the invaders, their difficulty in obtaining supplies, their comparatively small number, and their distance from reinforcements," all of which gave the impression that Americans were not so formidable as they had been purported to be. To the Navajos it had an additional meaning: the Americans were not able to enforce the Bear Springs treaty.

The leaders of the uprising were Tomás Ortiz and Diego Archuleta, who, if it was successful, would become governor and commander general, respectively. They had strong support from several priests, notably Juan Felipe and José Manuel Gallegos. The plan called for a concerted attack by several hundred rebels on Santa Fe on Christmas night, when Americans would be engaged in holiday festivities and off their guard. The plot was revealed to the American military by the wife of one of the conspirators a few days before

Christmas, giving Price enough time to make numerous arrests. Ortiz and Archuleta fled to the south, and it was believed that the revolt had been successfully thwarted.

American authorities had not given enough thought to the machinations of the Pueblo Indians who had intended to participate in the uprising. In mid-January 1847, Governor Bent and his Mexican wife, feeling assured that all danger from rebels had ended, went to Taos, where they maintained their permanent residence. They were joined by Sheriff Stephen Lee, attorney James W. Leal, Prefect Cornelio Vigil, Narcisso Beaubien, son of Superior Court Judge Charles Beaubien, and Bent's brother-in-law, Pablo Jaramillo.

On January 19 a group of Taos Indians demanded of Sheriff Lee that he release two prisoners who had been arrested for conspiring with the rebels. When he refused, they killed him and the prefect, Vigil. Shortly afterward they forced their way into the Bent home and murdered the governor, Leal, young Beaubien, and Jaramillo.

The insurrection was far from over. Many New Mexicans joined the rebellious Pueblos, and for the next eight months guerrilla warfare raged through central and eastern New Mexico. Several hundred Indians and New Mexicans were killed, and a score of rebel leaders were taken prisoner and executed. American battlefield deaths were considerably fewer in number, probably less than sixty officers and men, but many soldiers succumbed to wounds sustained in the engagements.

With Americans occupied by the revolt, Indians took advantage of the opportunity to go on the warpath. Comanches, Pawnees, and Arapahoes attacked packtrains on the Santa Fe Trail, killing traders and making off with livestock and goods. Out of the west, during the spring and summer of 1847, swept Navajo raiders. Thousands of sheep, horses, cattle, and mules were stolen from pueblos and New Mexican communities, and many women and craftsmen were carried into captivity.

The Bear Springs treaty had long since been forgotten by both Americans and Navajos. With the arrival of reinforcements, as well as government funds, from the east, and the rebellion all but ended, American military commanders could give their attention once again to the problem of halting the vicious and costly plundering of the Navajos.

The best fighting men had been sent to Mexico, and the newly arrived reinforcements were green recruits, callow youths poorly trained and without battle experience. But action against the Navajos could not be postponed. In September, Major W. H. T. Walker was sent west with a battalion, supported by a contingent of New Mexicans and Pueblo guides, and a battery of field guns. The force was well equipped and carried supplies for a campaign of two months.

Walker started from Santa Fe on September 10, 1847. A local newspaper reported that "nearly every man left drunk." On October 13 he brought his troops, sober and hardened by the strenuous ride, back to the capital. They had ridden to Bear Springs, through the Red Lake district, and had penetrated the Canyon de Chelly labyrinth for several miles. They had encountered few Navajos; meanwhile the Navajos had continued their raids on New Mexican settlements. It was believed that the expedition had accomplished nothing. This was not the case, however. Walker had made a show of force that greatly impressed the Navajos, who had carefully observed the column during its trip, and, shortly after Walker returned, a delegation of Navajos appeared in Santa Fe and asked for peace. In a council they agreed to abide by the provisions of the Bear Springs treaty.

If American authorities had studied the record of negotiations of the Spanish and Mexicans with the Navajos they would have realized that the Navajo offer was a ruse, that it was designed to relieve the Navajos of being driven from their homes and suffering extreme hardships in deep snows and subzero temperatures. But even a tentative peace was advantageous to the American military, for the troops were not equipped for a campaign under the severe weather conditions of winter in the high Navajo country.

Between November and March the Navajos remained quiet. In the spring of 1848 they once again were on the plunder trails. The desperate situation of the American military was disclosed in orders issued by Colonel E. W. R. Newby, then commanding in Santa Fe:

> The Colonel Commanding is deeply pained at the intelligence which he daily receives of the frequent outrages, committed on the persons and property of peaceful inhabitants by the Navajos.
>
> This painful feeling, not a little enhanced by the fact, that three-fourths of the force remaining in this Department are infantry, and are powerless against the rapid movements of mounted men, who are familiar with every inch of the country, and that, in consequence, his garrisons are compelled to sit still while murder and robbery is committed under their very eyes.
>
> In consideration of the circumstances, that as the only means of protection remaining, it is ordered that the Mexican inhabitants of this Department, be authorized to arm and equip themselves—organize in parties or bands and hold themselves in readiness to repel all incursions and to recover the property that may have been taken from them by the Indians.

If the order had the effect of strengthening defense against the Navajo onslaughts, it also gave legal sanction to raids against them by New Mexicans whose object was to enrich themselves with Navajo booty and livestock and take captives to be sold into slavery.

Newby did not delegate the entire task of fighting Navajos to New Mexican irregulars. In May he moved west with cavalry and infantry, and killed a number of warriors in skirmishes. The rapidity with which the Navajos fled before him convinced Newby that he had taught them a lesson and that they would behave. In response to his ultimatum a number of Navajo headmen signed another treaty of peace. Newby was satisfied.

Once again the American territorial authorities demonstrated their inability, or their unwillingness, to understand that a few Navajo leaders could not speak for all their people. The Americans insisted upon considering the Navajos as a tribal entity, and they stubbornly refused to recognized the Navajo clan system or the fact that a band of plunderers was subject only to the command of its leader and to no other person. Thus it followed that Navajos living closest to the settlements often suffered punishment for depredations in which they had not taken part but which had been perpetrated by Navajos living far to the west.

For two decades after the Mexican War there would be no genuine peace between the Americans and the Navajos. The blame for the almost continuous hostilities could not be placed on the Navajos alone. Armed bands of New Mexicans attacked Navajo settlements under the excuse that the American territorial government had accorded them the right to recapture livestock stolen from them, but not infrequently these incursions were slave raids. While the New Mexicans were appealing to the American military to halt the Navajo plundering, they were doing the same thing against the Navajos.

Also, the American occupation had opened the gates of the Southwest to a new faction of troublemakers, unscrupulous white traders. No regulations had been enacted to govern their activities, and they traded guns, knives, ammunition, foodstuffs, and raw whisky for pelts, livestock, blankets, silverwork, jewelry, and other Indian goods at exorbitant profits. Conflict stimulated business, and they supplied the Navajos with weapons to be used against the American soldiers and the New Mexicans.

The first Indian agent assigned to New Mexico was James S. Calhoun, a native of Georgia. A veteran of the Mexican War, in which he won promotion from captain to lieutenant colonel, a close friend of President Zachary Taylor, and a self-pronounced rabid Whig, Calhoun was a man of integrity. He reached Santa Fe in July 1849. His salary was $1,500 a year, and he was allowed $2,300 annually for expenses and contingencies. Although he had no previous experience in handling Indian affairs, he quickly demonstrated his capacity for recognizing the underlying causes of the oppressive situation facing him. His reports to Washington were blunt, objective, critical, devoid of political mumbo-jumbo, and constructive. In 1851 he would be appointed governor, but would also continue to serve as Superintendent of Indian Affairs for New Mexico.

Calhoun agreed with Colonel John M. Washington, the new commander at Santa Fe, "that any attempt to conciliate the tribes who have caused the recent and present troubles in this territory, would have a very serious tendency." They must be "properly chastised" before peace could be established. Yet, while advocating a policy of meeting force with force, it was his hope that a strong invasion of the Navajo country would have the result of "awing them into submission" and that extreme violence might be averted. With

Colonel Washington he formulated plans for an extensive campaign, which was started less than a month after he had taken his Santa Fe post.

Two companies of artillery, four companies of infantry, one company of mounted dragoons, and one company of mounted New Mexican volunteers left Santa Fe on August 16, 1849, for the pueblo at Jémez, where they would be joined by the garrison stationed there under the command of Captain Henry Linn Dodge. It was a formidable force of more than three hundred heavily armed fighters, accompanied by a long supply train and a contingent of Pueblo and Mexican guides. Engaged to serve as an interpreter was the traitorous Sandoval, who appeared to possess some mysterious power to convince American commanders that he was indispensable to them. The chronicler of the expedition was Lieutenant James H. Simpson, an engineer, a competent artist, an amateur archaeologist, and a lover of grand views and Arizona sunsets. He would submit a journal valuable for its geological, archaeological, geographical, and ethnological content, the first scientific report on the Navajos and their homeland.

Flags and guidons waving in the breeze, swords and guns catching the brilliant sunlight, the long column snaked through Chaco Canyon in the last days of August. In the valley of the Rio Tunicha, reached on August 30, a large number of Navajos were encountered. Their hogans were spread among cornfields along the river. Simpson recorded that the women "wore blankets, leggins, and moccasins—the blankets being confined about the waist by a girdle. They bestrode their horses *à la mode des hommes.* One of them, on horseback, had a child at her breast confined on its back to a board, the upper portion canopied by a frame of willow-work." Several of the Navajo men "wore helmet-shaped caps which were in some instances heightened in picturesque

effect by being set off with a bunch of eagles' feathers . . .
One had hair approaching red . . . Some of them were almost naked—one of them entirely so, excepting his breech
cloth, his whole person at the same time looking ghastly on
account of a kind of whitewash with which it was covered." The water in the little stream was "amply sufficient . . . The pasture is but scant, and therefore the cornfields of the Navajos in the vicinity have to be drawn upon.
It having been represented that the Navajos would resist
the troops in cutting the corn, Captain Dodge, with a command, was sent to enforce the order."

Although several hundred Navajos watched with pained
eyes as troopers took the corn they had stored for winter,
and cavalry horses ruined the stalks still unharvested in the
fields, they offered no resistance. With a strong escort of
warriors three chiefs rode into the camp and requested to
talk with Washington and Calhoun. They were the crippled,
aged Narbona, José Largo, estimated to be seventy years
of age, and Archuleta, a somewhat younger man, all of
whom had signed previous treaties with the American military.

Washington excoriated them for the failure of the Navajos to keep their promises, and instructed the interpreter
to announce that he had come to give them another chance
to keep the peace. "Tell them," he said, "that I wish them
to go to Chelly, so that a treaty may be made with the whole
nation."

Any hope Calhoun may have held that a durable peace
could be achieved without resort to force was forever destroyed by the tragedy that occurred as the council ended.
A New Mexican officer attached to Washington's staff reported that a horse being ridden by a Navajo had been
stolen from him. Washington ordered a Lieutenant Torez,
officer of the guard, "to seize the horse and rider and bring

them before him," Calhoun wrote. "The moment the guard was ordered forward, every Navajo Indian in the crowd, supposed to number from three to four hundred, all mounted and armed, and their arms in their hands, wheeled, and put the spur to their horses; upon which Washington ordered the guard to fire."

The celebrated old leader Narbona was killed instantly, and six warriors were mortally wounded.

As the crowd of Navajos moved off, Simpson wrote in his journal, "Major Peck also threw among them, very handsomely—much to their terror—a couple of round of [artillery] shot." Narbona was scalped by one of the half-breed New Mexicans. Two civilian brothers, Edward M. and Richard H. Kern, cartographers assisting Simpson, were "furious with themselves because, in the excitement, they had failed to secure Narbona's head for their scientist friend and associate at the Philadelphia Academy of Natural Sciences, Samuel George Morton."

Washington appeared unconcerned by the killings and marched on to Canyon de Chelly, camping near the mouth of the great gorge on September 7, not far from a large number of hogans. Presumably for the purpose of terrorizing their occupants, he ordered them destroyed. Simpson thought it "somewhat exciting to observe the huts of the enemy, one after another, springing up into smoke and flame, and their owners scampering off in flight."

Navajo headmen readily responded to Washington's order to meet him on September 9. "The parties there entered into a treaty," wrote Simpson, "by which the government of the United States assumed the paternal control it has been in the habit of exercising over the tribes of Indians. . . . All that could be accomplished by the expedition, then, may be considered as having been accomplished. . . . The Navajos have put themselves under the jurisdiction and control of the United States."

Before the Washington troops had returned to Santa Fe, Navajo raiders made furious strikes on the pueblos of San Ildefonso, Santo Domingo, and Santa Ana, and the New Mexican communities of Cebolleta, Abiquiu, Cubero, La Purgarita, and Corrales. Large numbers of livestock and several young New Mexican shepherds, both boys and girls, were taken, and a score of New Mexicans were murdered, in some places almost within sight of Washington's soldiers.

Washington had accomplished nothing. Indeed, the needless killings of six warriors and Narbona, a man revered by all Navajos, in a dispute over a stolen pony, and the senseless burning of hogans had inflamed the Navajos to vicious retaliation. They continued their devastating raids throughout the remainder of the year. Calhoun wrote to Indian Commissioner William Medill: "Not a day passes without hearing of some fresh outrage, and the utmost vigilance of the military force in this country is not sufficient to prevent murders and depredations and there are but few so bold as to travel alone ten miles from Santa Fe."

# 6

In 1851 the War Department received a report from Inspector General George A. McCall on the dire situation in New Mexico. He estimated the Navajo population at nearly eleven thousand men, women, and children, and voiced his conviction that "the future prosperity of New Mexico will depend in great measure on the impression now to be made on these Indians."

McCall advised a program under which the Navajos, "the richest of all and most civilized, except the Moquis"—a poor comparison, for the Moquis numbered only 2,400—might be contained. He recommended stationing a strong military force, no less than five hundred men, in the Navajo country, "to show them that a treaty is something more than idle talk." Under such circumstances they might "be induced to settle permanently like the Pueblos, and thus in time be controlled, in which case they would be invaluable allies."

The same flaw was to be found in McCall's proposals that

was contained in other military reports: they said nothing of halting the lawless activities of the New Mexicans and the white traders.

While Calhoun agreed that permanent garrisons should be established among the Navajos, he also thought that a reservation should be set aside for them, "their limits circumscribed, and distinctly marked out, and their departure from said limits be under certain prescribed rules." He estimated that between 1846 and 1850 New Mexican ranchers in two counties had suffered losses of 151,000 sheep, 800 mules, and 1,300 cows. Other reports gave much larger figures. He pleaded to no avail to the War Department and Bureau of Indian Affairs to "spend your million now, if necessary, that you may avoid the expenditure of millions hereafter."

Calhoun had been informed by Pueblo allies that after Colonel Washington had left Canyon de Chelly, white traders operating in the Zuñi country told the Navajos—obviously for the purpose of increasing trade with them—that the Americans, New Mexicans, and Pueblos were organizing an immense force, and that it would soon march to kill every living Navajo without mercy.

Calhoun, aware that the traders were not above such tactics, took what measures he could to drive unscrupulous members of the fraternity out of business. Washington had been replaced as commander by Colonel John Munroe, and Calhoun obtained Munroe's approval of a regulation requiring all traders to obtain federal licenses. Its provisions were stringent: "Applicants must be citizens of the United States, produce satisfactory testimonials of good character, and give bond in the penal sum of five thousand dollars . . . that he will not trade in fire-arms, powder, lead, or other munitions of war. . . . No license will be granted authorizing trade with Apaches, Navajos, or Utahs."

Reputable traders applied for licenses, but the regulation had little effect in the Navajo country. Without Indian agents or soldiers to enforce it, illegal trade was carried on among the Navajos almost without interruption.

Calhoun advocated the organization of a strong militia that could be called upon to support the small regular garrisons, but neither funds, arms nor supplies in sufficient quantities were available for such a purpose. Moreover, a policy of permitting civilians to arm themselves and attack the Navajos at will was favored in Washington.

Calhoun had been governor and Superintendent of Indian Affairs a few months when Colonel Edwin Vose Sumner, a veteran of several Indian campaigns and the Mexican War, took command in Santa Fe of the newly created Ninth Military District. Sumner did not agree with the "volunteer campaigns" plan, which permitted New Mexican civilians to invade the Navajo country. He set about reorganizing the military structure of the territory to make it more effective in combating Indian raids. He and Calhoun were soon embroiled in violent disagreements.

Calhoun bitterly complained to Washington: "Without a dollar in our territorial treasury, without munitions of war, without authority to call out our militia, without the co-operation of the military authorities of this territory, and with numberless complaints and calls for protection, do you not perceive I must be sadly embarrassed and disquieted?" Despite the lack of finances and equipment he authorized New Mexicans to organize "volunteer companies" to combat the Navajos. Yet it was made obvious by his own correspondence that the Navajos could hardly have been expected to remain peaceful so long as the New Mexicans were free to conduct raids against them.

Calhoun had no money with which to pay the New Mexican "volunteer raiders," but he devised a means by which they could recompense themselves. He issued a proclamation directing that "property which may be captured from any hostile tribe of Indians, by any [civilian New Mexican] company . . . shall be disposed of in accordance with the laws and customs heretofore existing in this territory—until legislative action shall be had upon the subject, either by the Congress of the United States or the Legislative Assembly of the Territory."

That order had the effect of encouraging slavers. As Calhoun well understood, "an average Navajo boy or girl (age five to fifteen) brought as high as $200 on the auction block." More than ten years would pass before congressional action halted the slave trade in New Mexico.

Calhoun was a desperate governor, beset with more burdens than he should have been asked to bear. His policies conflicted with one another in numerous respects. While he was allowing New Mexicans to raid the Navajos and sell captives, he was recommending that the Navajos be given the protection of American laws "regulating trade and intercourse." He was appealing to the federal government to establish among the Navajos "trading houses, liberally; give to them agricultural implements . . . allow them blacksmiths, and carpenters, and locate among them such agents as will Americanize their labor." In this proposal Calhoun was many years ahead of his time, and the Indian Bureau looked upon it as radical, if not idiotic.

Colonel Sumner saw the Calhoun slave proclamation for what it was, an implement inciting the Navajos to greater depredations. Being powerless to rescind it, he took the only alternative open to him: the use of military force to halt the hostilities. The breach between him and Calhoun had steadily widened, to the extent that he rejected almost every recommendation Calhoun submitted. Calhoun wanted to make a trip through the vast country under his jurisdiction, and requested a military escort. Sumner replied that no troops could be spared for such a purpose. He refused to escort Indian subagents to their posts. He refused Calhoun's request to accompany him on the expedition he was planning to the Navajo country, yet his orders from Secretary of War Charles M. Conrad had specifically stated: "In all negotiations and pacific arrangements with the Indians, you will act in concert with the Superintendent of Indian Affairs in New Mexico, whom you will allow to accompany you in the expeditions into the Indian Territory."

Conrad had ordered Sumner to "make an Expedition against the Navajos, as early as practicable, and inflict upon them a severe chastisement." By the end of August 1851 Sumner was at Bonito Canyon, six miles north of Window Rock (Arizona), with a strong force of cavalry, infantry, and artillery. The site, which the Navajos called Tsehotsohih ("Meadows-Between-Rocks"), had long been a Navajo holy place. Shrines stood about the springs, and into the bubbling waters Navajos dropped shells and bits of turquoise with pleas to their deities for good health and other blessings.

Sumner selected the place for the first military establishment to be built in the Navajo country, giving it the name of Fort Defiance. Traveling on, he led his troops to Canyon de Chelly. En route they were troubled by Navajo snipers, but suffered only minor casualties. No Navajos were found in Canyon de Chelly, but many were seen on the rim, and at night their myriad campfires glowed like red jewels among the stars. Headmen made no effort to confer with Sumner, and after destroying a few cornfields and orchards —the troops ate the fine ripe peaches in Canyon de Chelly— he went back to the Fort Defiance site. He ordered the construction of a large facility, appointed Major Electus Backus commander of a garrison to consist of two companies of cavalry, two of infantry, and one of artillery, and returned to Santa Fe. There he learned that during this campaign the Navajos had raided settlements along the upper Rio Grande. A few days later they struck within eighteen miles of the capital.

The territorial legislature passed a resolution calling for the organizing of a militia, and Calhoun sent it on to Washington.

Under the interpretation then prevailing, Indian tribes were considered "foreign nations," and therefore the State Department was involved in relations between them and the federal government. The basis for this conception, which was later rejected, was in the provision of the Constitution delegating to the legislative branch of the government the power "to regulate commerce with foreign nations and among the several states, and with the Indian tribes." Because the terms "foreign nations" and "Indian tribes" were contained in the same sentence, Congress, for nearly a hundred years, would hold to the view that the framers of the Constitution intended that both were to be considered in the same category.

Calhoun wrote Secretary of State Daniel Webster late in 1851: "Col. Sumner's expedition to the Navajo Country has been productive of no good, as yet, and if an effort I am now making fails, the people of the Territory, to some extent, will be forced to take care of themselves, or consent to lie down quietly, and be plundered and butchered." At the same time he informed Indian Commissioner Luke Lea: "The Military officers and the executive cannot harmonize, and I am not certain that the public interests would not be promoted by relieving us all from duty."

Calhoun finally succeeded in obtaining authority from Washington to muster a company of mounted militia and supply it with arms and other equipment from the quartermaster depot at Fort Union, in northeastern New Mexico. Colonel Sumner was obliged to obey the order, and he instructed the commander at Fort Union to make available seventy-five flintlock muskets, ammunition, and other equipment to the volunteers, who would be led by a civilian, Preston Beck of Santa Fe. Sumner, however, imposed strict conditions under which the arms might be used. The militia company was not to conduct forays against the Navajos unless acting in support of regular army troops. The equipment was to be returned to Fort Union upon his demand. The restrictions made it impossible for Beck and his volunteers to operate as an independent company, and the plan failed.

Justifying his actions in a report to Washington, Sumner stated that the war between Navajos and New Mexicans had been carried on for two hundred years, "quite time enough to prove that unless some change is made it will be interminable."

> They steal women and children, and cattle, from each other, and in fact carry on the war, in all respects, like two Indian nations.
>
> This system of warfare will interfere very much with my measures, and indeed do away with all the advantages that I confidently expect to reap from the establishment of Fort Defiance. This large post in the very midst of the Indian country cannot fail to cramp them in all their movements . . . provided, they find that the post can protect, as well as punish.

Calhoun threatened to send out militia without consulting Sumner. Sumner replied that he would halt "any such marauding party" with regular troops. A parley with Navajo headmen was scheduled to be held at Jémez on Christmas day, 1851, and this time Sumner agreed to let Calhoun go along. At the council Sumner bluntly warned the Navajos that unless they remained peaceful, "troops from Fort Defiance would prevent them from raising a single field of grain." Sumner was opposed to giving any equipment or supplies to the Navajos until they had demonstrated for at least six months their intention to halt their raiding, but Calhoun defied him and presented them with several thousand dollars worth of agricultural implements, cloth, wire, and other articles.

It appeared that Sumner's program was having the desired effect, for throughout the winter of 1851–52 the Navajos made no trouble. The garrison at Fort Defiance was strengthened, troops patrolled the country, and Navajos began to appear in the towns on trading missions. Sumner's warning that he would turn back with force all "independent incursions" into the Navajo country kept the New Mexicans in check. Many Navajos visited Fort Defiance, and Major Backus supplied them with cast-off clothing and surplus foodstuffs, and instructed them in the use of agricultural implements.

As January 1852 neared an end, several score Navajo headmen and warriors arrived in Santa Fe. Calhoun was seriously ill, but they were received by acting agent John Greiner. As a gesture of good will, they delivered to him three New Mexican captives and promised to abide by the demand that they restore all stolen property.

"We like the Belaganas [Americans]," a chief named Armijo told Greiner. "We have eaten their bread and meat. Smoked their tobacco. The clothing they have given us has kept us warm. With the hoes they have given us, we will cultivate our lands. We have gratitude."

That was all very well, Greiner replied, but reminded them that many New Mexican women and children taken by them remained to be returned. The American chief would not be satisfied until all captives held by the Navajos had been restored to ther homes. Mention of the old issue immediately clouded the atmosphere of the meeting.

Armijo struggled to restrain his anger as he demanded:

> Why can't the Americans understand there are two sides to this question? My people are all crying in the same way. Three of our chiefs now sitting before you mourn for their children, who have been taken from their homes by the Mexicans. More than two hundred of our children have been carried off. [Presumably he meant since the American occupation of New Mexico, for many times that number of Navajos had been sold into slavery during the Mexican regime.] The Mexicans have lost few children in comparison with what they have taken from us. Since the time of Colonel Newby we have been trying to get our children back. Is it American justice that we must give up everything and receive nothing?

The delegation departed much less happy than they had been upon arriving. But hostilities did not occur, and Calhoun succeeded in having S. M. Baird appointed as special agent to the Navajos, with headquarters at Jémez. By this time Calhoun's health was so bad that he was confined to his bed. In April 1852 he wrote Sumner: "You are perhaps advised of my weak, feeble, and almost helpless condition—and I feel that I am speaking almost as a dying man. . . . For the last four weeks I have been unable to stand alone."

Calhoun wanted to be buried in Washington, but not until late in May could he muster enough strength to attempt the long journey across the plains. On May 31 Greiner wrote the Indian Bureau: "On Wednesday last Governor Calhoun left Fort Union for the States with very little probability of ever reaching there alive—he takes his Coffin along with him."

He was accompanied by W. E. Love, his son-in-law, his secretary, D. V. Whiting, and a small group of Pueblo chiefs journeying eastward to confer with the Indian commissioner. He died on the Great Plains in June.

New Mexico knew a strange peace during the year 1852. Small incidents occurred that sent cavalry riding, but they led to no serious hostilities. William Carr Lane, former army officer and a Missouri politician, succeeded Calhoun as governor and ex-officio Superintendent of Indian Affairs. Lane believed that the Navajo problem could be solved by "feeding them, not fighting them," and he attempted to put his policy into operation. It had merit, but being ignorant of all factors involved, Lane soon learned that he had not struck upon a panacea.

The turncoat Sandoval gave Lane his first taste of serious trouble. It was Sandoval's contention that Pueblos were stealing water that he and his band needed to irrigate their fields near Cebolleta. When Sandoval's complaints to the Indian office in Santa Fe went unheeded, he spread a report among the Navajos that Lane and Sumner were planning a campaign to exterminate them. From Fort Defiance and other stations came word that Sandoval's propaganda had made the Navajos uneasy and that young men were talking of taking to the warpath. Lane ordered agent Baird to assure the Navajos that Sandoval's claims were without substantiation and to distribute gifts and foodstuffs among them.

Baird had not been a success as an agent at Jémez. He was more interested in furthering his own career than in serving the Navajos. The building of Fort Defiance and the granting of trading privileges to the Navajos had brought numerous traders into the Navajo country. The business was lucrative, and for a time Baird had considered leaving the Indian Bureau and opening a trading post. Lane soon came to the conclusion that Baird was not suited by nature or inclination to be an agent, and complained to Washington that Baird "gave little attention to his official duties, and gave most of his time to private business."

Except for a few thefts of livestock in the Las Lunas and Pena Blanca areas—nothing to get excited about—the Navajos were peaceful in the spring of 1853, but in May a tragic incident occurred near Chamas that convinced Lane that a general Navajo uprising had begun. Four Navajos killed a New Mexican sheep owner, Ramón Martin, and took away as prisoners his eight-year-old son, Librado, his young nephew, José, and three shepherds. The raid obviously was in retaliation for thefts made by New Mexicans, for the three shepherds were released and sent home with word that when livestock recently stolen from Navajos was returned, the two boys would be set free.

Lane's investigators learned from Pueblo Indians at Jémez that the murderers were well-known Navajo raiders led by a renegade named Jasin, and that they resided near Tunicha. Donaciaro Vigil, territorial secretary, who spoke the Navajo language and was a friend of numerous headmen, with an escort of nine Jémez Indians, went to the Tunicha Valley in search of the two youths. There he conferred with two prominent chiefs, Armijo and Aquila Negra, warning them that Lane considered the crimes "a justifiable cause for war."

Armijo and Negra knew Vigil to be a truthful man, and they arranged to have the captives delivered to him. Vigil demanded that the murderers also be surrendered, but Armijo and Negra pleaded that Jasin and his companions belonged to a clan over which they had no authority and therefore they were powerless to act in the matter. Knowing the futility of further argument, Vigil instructed the chiefs to appear in Santa Fe and explain the situation to Lane, and departed with the two young captives.

Early in June, Negra and a group of headmen appeared

in the capital for a conference with the governor. Lane was now running for Congress, and he believed that by being unrelenting in his demands on the Navajos he would win votes among the New Mexicans. He wrathfully rejected the explanation that if Negra and Armijo attempted to deliver the murderers, the clan to which they belonged would take to the warpath.

Lane, believing that he was in a position to gain a political advantage, requested Sumner to send troops against the Navajos. Sumner refused, giving several reasons for his stand:

(1) It was unfair to hold an immense tribe of ten to twelve thousand Indians responsible for the wanton acts of four or five uncontrollable outlaws;

(2) A general campaign against the Navajos would not only be extremely expensive, but would be futile, for it was virtually impossible to draw them into a confrontation;

(3) All that would be accomplished would be the destruction of Navajo crops, homes, and herds belonging to Indians who in no way could be held responsible for the murder of Martin, and who in all probability did not know it had occurred.

Under continued pressure from Lane, however, Sumner at last agreed to send a contingent of troops from Fort Defiance on a swing through the Navajo country to make a show of force. The mission was assigned to Captain Henry L. Kendrick. He was fortunate in having with him Henry Linn Dodge, a former army officer whom Lane had chosen to succeed the incompetent Baird as agent to the Navajos.

On their tour Kendrick and Dodge conferred with hundreds of Navajos. Kendrick sought to impress upon them that if Lane succeeded in persuading the army to make war upon them, "it would be the last war necessary," for not only the soldiers but the New Mexicans and the Pueblos "would be let loose upon them, their flocks seized, their men killed; their women and children taken prisoners," and that they would lose a great part of their homeland, for they would be confined west of the Chuska Mountains.

Lane was not pleased with the report submitted by Kendrick and Dodge. It stated their unqualified conviction that Navajo depredations were the work of "a few bad and irresponsible men" and that most Navajos were sincerely anxious to keep the peace.

Lane suddenly lost desire to punish the Navajos. Indeed, when he was defeated in his race for Congress, he lost interest completely in the affairs of New Mexico, resigned the governorship, and went back East. His secretary, William Messervy, served as acting governor until President Franklin Pierce appointed David Meriwether to the office.

Meriwether was a veteran frontiersman. He had been a trapper for John Jacob Astor's American Fur Company in the mountains of the Far West. In 1819 the company sent him with a band of Pawnees to attempt to open trade with New Mexico. Captured by the Spanish, he was taken to Santa Fe and accused of being an American spy. Lacking evidence to substantiate the charge, the Spanish released him after holding him prisoner for a month.

Meriwether advocated a policy of "containment" in dealing with the Navajos. He proposed that a buffer zone be created between the Navajo country and the western New Mexican settlements, with the federal government holding title to the land. This, he believed, could be achieved through a treaty with the Navajos under which they would give up lands they claimed east of the Chuska Mountains in return for substantial annuities.

Disregarding Meriwether's advice, Washington continued the practice of granting annuities to the Navajos and reiterated the warning that depredations would bring troops against them. The program concurred with the thinking of the military, and especially with that of Kendrick at Fort Defiance, who expressed to his superiors the belief that "the most efficient rod in terrorem [sic] to be held over these people is the fear of a permission being given to the Mexicans to make captives of Navajos and to retain them, a permission at once wise and philanthropic and one which would at an early date settle the question."

That, except for a few minor incidents, peace prevailed for almost three years after Meriwether took office was not due to the effective execution of any policy whatsoever, but to the work of one of the most daring and competent men to enter upon the stage during the period of the Indian wars. He was Henry Linn Dodge, appointed by Governor Lane as special agent to the Navajos.

Dodge, a former army captain, was the son of Senator Henry Dodge of Wisconsin and a brother of Senator Augustus Caesar Dodge of Iowa. He had served with Rocky Mountain exploring expeditions and with troops escorting caravans on the Santa Fe Trail, and had accompanied Colonel Washington through the Navajo country in 1849.

After leaving the army Dodge, an irrepressible adventurer, had wandered over much of New Mexico and Arizona. In 1851 he made a small gold strike in the wilderness of the upper Gila River. At the time of his appointment as agent he was thirty-six years old and was engaged in furnishing supplies to frontier military posts and operating a trading post near Cebolleta. He spoke Navajo and Spanish with sufficient fluency to make himself understood without an interpreter.

Dodge established his agency headquarters at Fort Defiance and then set off with only a few Indian companions on a long tour of the country. Never before had the Navajos known an American who traveled among them without a military escort. He had no fear, Dodge told them, because he was their friend and his intentions were honorable.

"If I give you bad advice," he declared, "you can kill me. I intend to live among you, not in the safety of Santa Fe or Jémez. I am here to work with you and to keep peace in this country, and I propose to do both to the best of my ability."

Dodge believed he could wield greater influence if he were not under the watchful eye of the military, and he moved his agency from Fort Defiance to the vicinity of Sheep Springs. There he "acquired a Navajo belle for a wife. Her near relationship to the chief, Zarcillas Largo, without any doubt played an important part in his congenial relationship with the tribe."

During his first year as an agent, Dodge, whom the Navajos called Red Shirt, rode with groups of warriors and headmen throughout most of his immense jurisdiction to familiarize himself with the country and gain knowledge of local problems. His long absences caused concern in Santa Fe and Fort Defiance, and officials complained that he was derelict in keeping in touch with them and failed to file the customary weekly reports of his activities. His only reply to his critics was to the effect that if he had anything to report that required the attention of Washington he would report it. Meanwhile, he was "pleased to state" that most of the Navajos were prosperous, crops were good, herds were large, and the headmen had a profound wish to keep the peace. As for his absences, it was his opinion that an agent could not hope to exercise the necessary influence unless he lived among the Indians, understood them, and was constantly in touch with their leaders.

On one occasion Dodge rode into Santa Fe at the head of a colorful column of a hundred Navajos, among them Largo and other chiefs, which gave the residents a few moments

of concern. Every member of the band was armed, either
with lances and bows and arrows or with rifles, and all were
garbed in their finest buckskin raiment and blankets and
adorned with silver, turquoise, and coral jewelry. Dodge set
up a camp not far from the Palace of the Governors. To the
great relief of both townspeople and officials, during the
three days the visitors remained not one of them became
drunk or was even seen to take a drink.

He had not, Dodge told Governor Meriwether, brought
the delegation either to celebrate or to sign another worthless treaty. They had come to pay their respects to the governor and to discuss matters of importance. Meriwether, although not without suspicion and apprehension, agreed to
hold a council. He was firmly resolved, he told the delegation crowded into the palace, to keep the peace between
them and the New Mexicans, and he would always "hear
the complaints of the white man with one ear and the red
man with the other." After carefully weighing the evidence,
he would make his decisions "with impartiality and they
would be irrevocable and must be obeyed by both factions."

This was straight talk, and the Navajos nodded their heads
in approval. Meriwether then presented Largo with a large
medal and appointed him "head chief of the Navajo nation."
Dodge privately advised Meriwether that under their political system Navajos were not obligated to recognize a
supreme chief, but the governor did not feel that he could
rescind the appointment. To Dodge's surprise, the Navajos
registered no objections, and some of them took the attitude
that Meriwether's act might well be wise. After all, Americans had a Great White Father, and perhaps the Navajos
would benefit if they adopted more American customs. At
any rate, Largo was henceforth recognized as "leading chief,"
even if his authority remained limited and many Navajo
headmen refused to take his advice or obey his commands.

Largo, however, was a shrewd man, and he did not attempt to impose his power on those who refused to accede to it.

After a feast that Meriwether provided, the Navajos staged a night dance in the plaza, the townspeople crowding about the fires and thoroughly enjoying the spectacle. In the morning they and Dodge vanished into the west.

Meriwether hastened to report to Washington, telling Commissioner Manypenny: "I am inclined to doubt the policy of bringing these Indians into our settlements for many reasons. In the first place it is expensive, and then it brings them acquainted with our country. . . . And last though not the least objection which I will mention is that I think it best for both races that they should have as little promiscuous intercourse as possible with each other"

Meriwether held strong racial prejudices, and he was irked with Dodge for having married a Navajo. What he failed to take into consideration was the fact that since Dodge had been agent, Navajo depredations had all but halted.

Dodge was a determined exponent of settling disputes by peaceful means, but he did not hesitate to use force if he believed a situation demanded it. When a Navajo killed a soldier in an argument near Fort Defiance, although the soldier had provoked the fight, Dodge set out in pursuit of the murderer, taking with him a lieutenant and a squad of soldiers. The fugitive was tracked to the domain of the chief Armijo, and Dodge demanded that he be surrendered to the military for trial. Armijo, in accord with the Navajo custom, offered a liberal payment of horses and sheep in compensation for the slaying. Dodge refused, insisting American law required that a criminal be tried and, if found guilty, punished. The penalty for murder was death.

Armijo, realizing Dodge's determination, at last agreed to surrender the wanted man. That was easier promised than accomplished. In the attempt by Navajos to capture him, the fugitive put up a fierce fight, and was taken only after being severely wounded. Dodge nevertheless took him back to Fort Defiance, where he was identified by several soldiers as the slayer and, as Dodge reported, "hung until he was dead, dead, dead."

As the year 1855 began, the Navajos remained at peace. Dodge begged the Indian Bureau to appropriate money with which he could purchase farm tools for them. This was an innovation the officials were not prepared to endorse, but he persisted in his requests, and at last he wrote that he had "the pleasure of receiving one hundred and fifty hoes and twelve axes. . . . The spring has been unusually wet and bids fair to be a good cropping year." Dodge was able to obtain additional implements at Fort Defiance and Santa Fe. He secured the authority to employ a blacksmith and a silversmith, and he established them at his agency to instruct Navajos in these crafts. He borrowed a thousand dollars from his father and spent it on equipment, which he distributed to worthy Navajos.

That spring Dodge and Meriwether had reason to report "there was every prospect of the peace continuing," but suddenly clouds arose to darken the bright outlook. Word came from Kit Carson that the Capote Utes, for whom he was agent, had taken to the warpath. Reports were received that both Utes and Jicarilla Apaches had raided communities in northern New Mexico, killed about twenty people, carried off some women and children, and had stolen hundreds of sheep and horses.

Navajos reported to Dodge that the Utes were urging them to join in the war, but they had refused. Dodge wrote Meriwether that the Utes claimed to have killed eight hundred whites, and boasted to the Navajos that "we are an easy prey for them." While admitting that a few Navajos were always eager for war, he was convinced that the great majority wanted to continue the peace and would join him in putting forth every effort "to prevent the viciously disposed part of the tribe from joining the enemy." But there could be no doubt that "pressure upon them by warring tribes threatened constantly to destroy every gain made."

The situation was made more precarious by action of the New Mexico legislature. New Mexican and American stockmen, covetous of Navajo grazing grounds, had long pressured the legislature to pass a bill permitting them to move their herds into the Navajo country. Failing to obtain the measure, they appealed to the Federal District Court and obtained a ruling that declared that "under the laws of Congress there is no Indian country in New Mexico." The decision was all the stock raisers needed. It opened the Navajo country to invasion, not only by them but by all manner of traders. Soon afterward Major Kendrick reported from Fort Defiance that herds owned by New Mexicans were as far west as Zuñi, and "now that our peaceful relations with the Navajos have a fair prospect of being consolidated, it is to be regretted that owners of flocks . . . are placing an almost irresistible temptation to robbery before a people under whose exactions New Mexico has groaned for a third of a century."

Navajos complained bitterly to Dodge of the encroachments. The territory they claimed as their homeland was enormous, but its grazing grounds were limited, for most of it was arid. The Navajos owned at least 250,000 head of sheep, and Dodge understood that if this number were greatly increased the land would soon be dangerously overgrazed and suffer damage from which it would not recover.

Troops could stop the Utes, but the invading stockmen were operating within the law. Dodge believed that the only way of halting their intrusions upon Navajo grazing lands was to establish a permanent Navajo reservation. This was not a new idea, and he and others had long advocated that it be adopted. By the time Dodge renewed his plea to Washington to set aside Navajo tribal lands, Congress had already authorized the enactment of a treaty under which Navajos would be guaranteed "the right of occupancy" of their homeland. Communications between Santa Fe and Washington were extremely poor, and were subject to the hazards of weather and marauding Indians. It took no less than three months, and often four, for dispatches to be transported over the great distance. Indeed, eight months elapsed after Congress had passed the Indian Appropriations Act of 1854 before Meriwether received word that he had been "designated by the President to enact articles of convention with the Navajos."

The governor and Dodge consulted together on the matter. Meriwether's orders said:

> You will make such arrangements as will provide for the Indians, within the country in which they may respectively reside and the possession of which they claim, a suitable tract or tracts, limited in extent, for their future permanent home; and will guarantee to them the possession and enjoyment of the reserve assigned them, with provisions that hereafter the President may cause the land reserved to be surveyed, and to assign to each single person over twenty-one years of age, or head of a family, a farm containing from, say, twenty to sixty acres, according to the number of persons in each family.

Meriwether was not opposed to the treaty, but he was not enthusiastic about going out to the Navajo country. The trip would consume weeks, and he had many other matters weighing upon him. Perhaps the treaty could be prepared, and the reservation boundaries delineated and agreed to by the Navajo chiefs, in Santa Fe. Dodge responded with a blunt *no*. To begin with, no chief, or even two or three of them, had the power to sign the treaty by themselves. A general council with all Navajo headmen was necessary. Also, he felt strongly that if the proposed treaty was to be taken seriously by the Navajos, the governor himself should discuss it with them and explain the terms, provision by provision. Issues of transcending importance were involved. All previous treaties could be forgotten, for now for the first time boundaries of the Navajo country would be established. The effect of this would not only be to keep white stockmen from invading Navajo grazing grounds, but would also set limits that marauding Utes and Apaches would be forbidden to cross. It would give protection the Navajos badly needed, and provide them with a homeland they would have every right to defend.

Meriwether agreed to make the journey. He notified the new commander, General John Garland, of his plans and ordered papers and maps prepared. Dodge could enthusiastically report:

A treaty will be made in the early part of next month [July 1855] with the Navajos by Governor D. Meriwether at which Genl. Garland has assured me he will be present. . . .

*A liberal and enlightened policy towards this tribe for a few years will fix their destiny as an agricultural, manufacturing, and stock raising community. That these results can be speedily attained by them no person will doubt who is acquainted with their habits of industry, temperance, and ingenuity.**

Dodge recommended as a council site Laguna Negra,

* *I have italicized these words not only because they were prophetic, but because they demonstrate how far ahead of Indian Office officials who followed him Dodge was in his understanding of the Navajos and their problems.*

fourteen miles north of Fort Defiance, and it was approved. He hurried there to make preparations for the meeting. On the shore of the lake he established a camp and built a large *ramada* of poles and cedar boughs. Couriers were sent out to summon the headmen, and when Meriwether and Garland, with their military escort, interpreters, and servants, arrived on July 16 more than two thousand Navajos, among them almost every headman of the tribe, were assembled to receive them.

It is improbable that any other man could have inspired in the Navajos the confidence and trust they held in Henry Linn Dodge. It is even more improbable that they could have been induced by anyone else to sign a treaty that was decidedly unfavorable to them in several respects.

The meeting was not completely peaceful. A notorious renegade, Cach'osh nez ("Tall Syphilis"), and several warriors forcefully invaded the *ramada*, shouted curses at the negotiators, and threatened Meriwether's life. A young chief, Hastin Chilhajin ("Man of Blackweed"), grappled with Cach'osh nez, while others surrounded and held his followers. The disrupters were removed before anyone was injured.

Zarcillas Largo caused a sensation by returning the medal he had received from Meriwether in Santa Fe and resigning his commission as "head chief." "I am too old," he said. Meriwether requested the headmen to name another man to fill the office. Negotiations had to be suspended while the Navajos discussed the matter among themselves for some two hours. At last they announced that their choice was Man of Blackweed.

Meriwether attempted to place the medal about his neck, but Man of Blackweed pushed it away, explaining that if he wore it "on the same string used by Largo, his authority would not be respected." He accepted it only after it had been restrung. At the time Man of Blackweed was thirty-seven years old, a man of extraordinary intelligence, and a brilliant orator. Dodge reported that although he was highly respected, and was a strong advocate of peace, he also possessed an unshakable determination to defend the rights and claims of his people and would unhesitantly defy the Americans if he believed they were attempting to impose unjust conditions on the Navajos. This analysis would prove to be completely accurate. Man of Blackweed, who would come to be better known as Manuelito, would be one of the outstanding leaders in all Navajo history, and Americans would be forced to reckon with his power and shrewdness. He would in time, however, be ruined by *todithit*—white man's whisky.

When Meriwether announced the boundary lines of the proposed Navajo homeland, Manuelito registered vehement objections. The Navajos, he declared, claimed a much larger area. Moreover, the lines as they were drawn deprived the Navajos of many of their holy places. Only one of their four sacred mountains would be included. Meriwether thought that "one sacred mountain would be sufficient." Manuelito also pointed out that the Navajos would be excluded from the *salinas* south of Zuñi, where as long as anyone could remember they had gone for salt. Meriwether promised that he would issue a special order permitting the Navajos to visit the *salinas*.

The treaty stipulated that the Navajos must surrender title to all lands they claimed east of Chaco Canyon. Manuelito protested that many Navajos had lived in this region for centuries, and that it included Dinetah—"Old Navajo Land," the home of their ancestors. Meriwether replied that the Navajos would not be giving up the region (it was the area of the proposed buffer zone) for nothing. They would be recompensed with annual payments of $10,000.

Dodge gave his full support to the treaty, and it was approved. He believed it would be beneficial to the Navajos, for under its terms they would receive much-needed annuities, implements, and teachers to instruct them in means to improve their agriculture and animal husbandry.

All men have blind spots. In the case of the dedicated Dodge it was his faith in the federal government. He firmly believed that the United States would fulfill the commitments he and Meriwether had made to the Navajos. But the promised funds, supplies, farming implements, and instructors failed to materialize: the treaty was not ratified by Congress. Dodge was a disappointed and distraught man. He was fully aware that if the government failed to keep its word, the Navajos could not be expected to adhere to their agreements. He renewed his appeal to Manypenny for funds, tools, and instructors. He was the first agent to request that the government establish a school for the Navajos.

Although he endorsed Dodge's requests, Meriwether advised Manypenny that

> the necessities of the Navajos does not require the payment of a large sum annually to enable them to live in comfort and improve their condition. Indeed, these Indians may now be considered in a prosperous condition; they have a large number of horses and sheep, together with their domestic animals; have planted some four thousand acres of grain this season, and by another year will be able to raise a sufficient amount to feed the whole tribe plentifully, after which time I hope that they will have a surplus sufficient to supply the wants of Fort Defiance, which now has to be hauled over one hundred miles at great cost to the government.

By the spring of 1856 Dodge understood that events were leading to a tragic situation. The winter had been one of the severest and longest ever known in the Southwest, and the Navajos had suffered heavy losses of stock. Utes were attacking their settlements south of the San Juan, and many Navajos were fleeing to Fort Defiance for protection. Not only Meriwether complained that the fort was extremely expensive to maintain. The War Department took a similar view, and issued an order reducing the garrison to some 160 officers and men. Dodge somewhat wrathfully told Meriwether: "The Navajos are no fools and see at a glance that the troops are too few to prevent them killing and stealing."

Manuelito boldly grazed his stock on lands set aside under the treaty for military herds. Ordered by Major Kendrick to remove them, Manuelito defiantly replied: "Drive me off if you think your force is sufficient. If you try, I will call around me in one day a thousand warriors." Meriwether ordered Dodge to investigate. Dodge did, and advised that no action be taken, for "the soldiers are barely able to protect themselves and the government herds without attempting an offensive movement against the Navajos."

New Mexican stock raisers continued to trespass upon Navajo grazing lands, ignoring the Meriwether treaty. Members of the territorial legislature, under pressure from their constituents, made new attempts to have the Navajos restricted to smaller areas. As both Dodge and Kendrick had predicted, Navajos raided New Mexican herds that had been eating Navajo grass for more than a year. Late in March 1856 several thousand New Mexican sheep were stolen, and three shepherds who attempted to protect their flocks were slain.

Sent to investigate the thefts and demand that the animals be restored to their owners and the slayers delivered to the military for trial, Dodge learned that the raiders had not been "wild, uncontrollable young outlaws," as had been reported to him, but were the sons of three chiefs. He got some of the stolen sheep back, but advised Meriwether that all "the chiefs and head men with whom I have conferred say that it is impossible to give up the murderers, that it would produce a civil war among themselves in which the Utahs would take part on the side of the offenders." Dodge's own opinion was that "it would be madness in the extreme to effect any thing with the small force at Fort Defiance at the moment, as any small party going out to capture the murderers could be surrounded by a thousand warriors before going twenty-five miles."

Dodge was disillusioned and sick at heart. "That the dreadful scourge of war should not be visited upon the Navajos I have labored and suffered many privations, but I fear to little purpose," he told Meriwether. Some of his Navajo friends were showing coolness to him, and one, the son of a *rico,* Jon Largo, was threatening "to steal and kill all persons—Americans, Mexicans and Utes—that may be so unfortunate as to fall into their hands."

For the first time, Dodge disclosed his conviction that many Navajo leaders would not submit to the restraints placed upon them by the Meriwether treaty, adding that, in view of the circumstances and the failure of the government to abide by its commitments, he could not blame them. "I give it as my opinion," he wrote Meriwether, "founded upon many years of experience with these people, that if a strong force is concentrated at different points in their country, and that they have to pay the expenses of the war if the offenders are not delivered, they will give any assistance that may be required of them."

For once, the War Department took heed of Dodge's advice, and sent new troops to serve in the Navajo country. The reinforced garrison at Fort Defiance convinced Manuelito that it would be prudent to remove his herds from military grazing grounds, but New Mexican stockmen continued to encroach on Navajo ranges, and neither Meriwether nor the military did anything to stop them.

In the fall of 1856 a new threat to peace arose, this time coming from the south. Coyotero and Mogollon Apaches carried out a series of raids on both Navajo and Zuñi herds. Dodge joined a small contingent of troops, commanded by Major Kendrick, that was dispatched to track them down and punish them.

In mid-November the cavalrymen were in the vicinity of Zuñi. On the morning of November 19 Dodge, who knew the country well, set off alone with the hope of killing a deer. He was ambushed and shot to death by the Apache renegades.

# 7

THE TERRIBLE WARFARE that raged throughout the Southwest between 1858 and 1864 was in no sense the result of a
single irreconcilable controversy between Indian peoples
and the United States. Quite to the contrary, the roots of its
causes were deeply embedded in conflicting economic, political, philosophical, religious, and judicial concepts. From
these diverse wellsprings came the tensions that aroused
the bitterness and determination of the numerous factions
involved.

There was no common front, but an almost uncountable
number of salients scattered from Mexico to Colorado, from
western Texas to the Grand Canyon. The operations of
American military commanders were frequently disrupted or
defeated by minor conflicts waged by adversaries they were
unable to control. Chaotic situations often arose, and in the
face of them the military could do little more than hope the
participants in the unauthorized clashes would exhaust their

resources—or better, kill each other off, so the troops could proceed with effective offensives.

The murder of Dodge had brought an intensive campaign against the Apaches. The objective was not only to subdue them but to drive them onto a reservation to be established on the Rio Pecos in eastern New Mexico.

The plains tribes were on the warpath, killing settlers and attacking wagon trains and military contingents.

The Capote Utes were raiding settlements in Colorado and northern New Mexico. They, the Paiutes, and other Indians were being furnished guns and ammunition by the Utah Mormons, who were hopeful of inducing all tribes to unite and drive the "gentiles" out of the Southwest.

The western Pueblos were fighting Apaches and raiding Navajo herds.

The New Mexicans were conducting independent forays against both Utes and Navajos, chiefly for the purpose of taking slaves. Their pretext was that they were attempting to recover stock stolen from them.

With the beginning of the Civil War, many officers whose sympathies were with the South resigned their commissions and departed to fight for the Confederacy.

Forever ended was the long era in which the Navajos raided only for the purpose of enriching themselves. With enemies on every side of them—Americans, Utes, Pueblos, New Mexicans, Apaches—they were encompassed by a circle of death that each year tightened about them. They struck back , often in force, but not with the objective of acquiring new plunder. They were attempting to cripple their antagonists, and at the same time recover livestock and women and children taken from them.

Under these conditions, peace was impossible. The American military demanded from the Navajos strict compliance with the Meriwether treaty, and was itself guilty of violating the treaty's most significant provisions. No effort was made to adhere to the promise to protect the Navajos from forays conducted against them. Indeed, both New Mexicans and Utes were encouraged to attack them. If the Navajos retaliated, they were charged with breaking the treaty. Navajos were shot on sight, and without provocation, by New Mexican slave hunters. They were killed on roads, while laboring in their fields, while herding their sheep. Few attempts were made by either the civil government or the military to apprehend the murderers or to restore the Navajo captives carried off by New Mexicans.

An entirely different attitude was displayed by the American authorities with the slaying of a Negro slave owned by Major Thomas H. Brooks, then commanding at Fort Defiance. The innocent victim, identified only as Jim, was shot in the back with an arrow by a crazed Navajo who appeared at the post ostensibly to sell blankets. The killer dashed away on his horse, and escaped from soldiers who attempted to apprehend him. It was learned that a few days before he committed the heinous crime he had lost an argument with his squaw and had determined to kill someone "to appease his wrath."

Brooks immediately summoned the aged headman Zarcillas Largo and demanded that the murderer be surrendered. In coldly refusing, Largo reminded Brooks that, a few weeks before, soldiers had wantonly shot to death sixty head of Navajo cattle because the stock was found grazing on land reserved for military horses. The owners had not been reimbursed. Moreover, said Largo, the Americans were making no attempt to prevent New Mexicans and Utes from killing Navajos. Navajo headmen, among them the powerful Manuelito, could only assume that the Americans had no intention

of keeping the pledges made by Meriwether, and therefore
the Navajos must take what measures they could to protect
themselves.

Brooks wasted no more time in argument. Advising the
military department commander, General John Garland, of
the situation, he recommended that a large force be sent to
capture the Negro's slayer and punish the Navajos. He advocated, as well, that sanction be given the Utes to strike
against the Navajos simultaneously, and that New Mexicans
be engaged to aid and guide the American troops. Garland
concurred in the proposal and sent Lieutenant Colonel Dixon
S. Miles with a company of infantry and a company of
cavalry to Fort Defiance.

Here the devious Sandoval re-entered the picture. Miles
engaged him as an emissary to inform the Navajos that they
had a week in which to deliver the killer or face a concentrated campaign against them. Sandoval disappeared. In a
few days he was back with word that the wanted warrior
had been slain in a fight with Navajos who attempted to
comply with Miles's ultimatum. Sandoval asked for an army
wagon with which to bring in the body, but Miles refused to
provide the vehicle and gave him a blanket.

On the morning of September 8, 1858, five hundred
mounted Navajos were gathered at Fort Defiance. Presently
Sandoval rode into the post with a body wrapped in the
blanket and placed it before Miles. It was, declared Sandoval, the body of the murderer—or so he had been informed by the Navajos who had given it to him. Medical
examination by the post surgeon revealed that the Navajos
had attempted to deceive Miles by delivering the corpse of a
young New Mexican.

Miles refused to negotiate with the Navajos, although a
number of headmen were present, and sent Major Brooks
and a newly appointed Indian agent, Samuel M. Yost, to

announce that a state of war would exist as of eight o'clock the next morning. The Navajos vanished into the surrounding canyons.

Miles marched on schedule. Between September 9 and 14, when he brought his troops back to Fort Defiance, no major engagements took place. In skirmishes with small groups of Navajos two soldiers were killed and several were wounded. The Navajos were elusive, and avoided a direct confrontation. Only six warriors were known to have been slain. Miles burned a number of hogans and cornfields, confiscated some six thousand sheep, and brought back seven prisoners: one man, three women, and three children.

Garland was transferred to an eastern post. His successor was Colonel Benjamin Louis Eulalie de Bonneville, a veteran officer who had been previously engaged in directing a campaign against the Apaches. Bonneville, who had graduated from West Point in 1819, was nearing the end of a long career marked by unsavory episodes for which he had been publicly criticized by both military colleagues and prominent civilians. In 1831 he had obtained a two-year leave from the army under the pretense that he would, without cost to the government, explore the unknown West.

Bonneville's true purpose was to engage in the fur trade, and he was financed in the enterprise by some New York investors, among them a former associate of John Jacob Astor. From a business standpoint, the venture was a failure, although Bonneville was made famous by Washington Irving's fictional account of his adventures during the four years he spent roaming the West with an expedition of trappers.

Because Bonneville had overstayed his leave by two years, without even troubling to request an extension, he was dropped from army rolls. When he applied for reinstatement, the War Department refused his request, but was overruled by President Andrew Jackson. Bonneville had shown Mr. Jackson some maps of the West, and the President praised them as significant contributions to the geographical knowledge of the country. Bonneville had copied the maps in large part from ones prepared by several outstanding authorities, among them former Secretary of the Treasury Albert Gallatin, General William H. Ashley, and the great explorer Jedidiah Smith. On them, Bonneville gave his name to the Great Salt Lake, "an arrogant presumption when we consider the utter lack of any connection which his work had with that body of water."

Historian H. H. Bancroft would write of Bonneville that "being in his coarse way a *bon vivant* and voluptuary, he preferred lording it in the forest with a troop of red and white savages at his heels, and every fortnight a new unmarried wife flaunting her brave finery. . . . To shoot buffalo were rare fun; but men were the nobler game, whom to search out in their retreat and slaughter and scalp were glorious." This may have been unwarranted calumny, but there was no doubt that Bonneville was thoroughly disliked by many officers, and that he was pigheaded, egotistic, and totally without compassion in his treatment of an adversary.

Assuming the unenviable task of commanding at Santa Fe, Bonneville openly praised his predecessor, but it soon became apparent that he felt Garland had not been sufficiently forceful in dealing with the Indians. He immediately sent reinforcements to Fort Defiance and ordered another strike against the Navajos.

The campaign was carried out by Miles in late September and early October, but with no more effectiveness than the previous effort. With some three hundred infantry and cavalry and a company known as Blas Lucero's Mexican Spies—who, Major Brooks had advised headquarters, "could be employed at a very low price, if a portion of the booty taken was offered as payment for their services"—Miles moved this time through the Chuska Valley and penetrated numerous adjacent canyons, an area containing a large Navajo population. On two occasions detachments pursuing fleeing Indians narrowly escaped an ambush and were forced to retreat. Casualties were light: four troopers and ten Navajos were killed, and a score of soldiers and New Mexicans sustained wounds. The number of Navajos wounded was not known.

The booty comprised five thousand sheep, seventy-nine horses, and various articles taken from Navajo hogans, a large number of which were destroyed. To the great disappointment of Lucero's Spies, no women and children were captured.

Avoiding American patrols, Navajos attacked and looted New Mexican settlements, killed several herders, and drove off thousands of head of livestock. Under heavy pressure by both the citizenry and the territorial government to stop the raids, Bonneville determined to undertake a campaign "to destroy and drive from that part of the country every vestige of this troublesome tribe." He ignored complaints from Navajos and reports from his own officers that New Mexicans and Utes were attacking them.

Six companies of infantry and cavalry had arrived from Fort Leavenworth, and Bonneville ordered them to Jémez. Two powerful columns would be sent through the Navajo country in a pincers movement. One force, commanded by Major Electus Backus, would move through the Tunicha Valley, Blanco Canyon, and Washington Pass. Another force, commanded by Miles, would come up from Fort Defiance. The two columns would meet at the northern end of the Tunicha Mountains.

The plan was carried out, but the most that was achieved was the engagement of a few Navajos in running fights. Although large groups were sighted, they vanished before soldiers could overtake them. The united columns moved on to Chinle, at the mouth of Canyon de Chelly. There scouts reported that Navajos were to be found in large numbers near the Hopi villages. Advancing rapidly, the troops passed Black Mesa and penetrated the Hopi country, but few Navajos were encountered.

On the circular campaign the forces of Backus and Miles had traveled some 350 miles. Only four Indians had been killed, and only four were known to have been wounded. Scores of hogans and fields had been destroyed, but less than four hundred head of livestock had been slaughtered or confiscated.

However, the Navajos had been thoroughly frightened by the sight of such a formidable force of soldiers, Utes, and New Mexicans in their country, and a delegation of headmen appeared at Fort Defiance to ask for peace. Neither agent Yost nor the field commanders were empowered to negotiate a formal treaty, but to give themselves time to consult with Bonneville and Indian Superintendent James L. Collins, who were in Santa Fe, they agreed to an armistice of thirty days. At the expiration of the armistice the chiefs would appear in Fort Defiance for a council. Meanwhile, under the terms of the temporary pact, the Navajos would return all livestock stolen from the military, would nominate a principal chief who would thereafter be spokesman for the entire tribe, and would deliver to Fort Defiance the murderer of Major Brooks's Negro slave, Jim—should they catch him.

It was the conviction of Miles and Yost that with winter swiftly approaching, a tentative peace was better than none at all, and they shared the hope that the period of amnesty would lead to the enactment of a new treaty "on a sure basis; which would be binding on the United States as well as the Navajos."

Bonneville and Collins vehemently rejected the armistice and severely reprimanded Miles and Yost for acting without the sanction of their superiors. Their chief objection was that the armistice terms included no provision for protecting the New Mexicans from Navajo raids and did not obligate the Navajos "to indemnify the citizens of New Mexico for all losses resulting from their raids." In their protest they said nothing about New Mexicans returning either livestock or slaves taken from the Navajos. Bonneville angrily demanded that if the Navajos wished to have peace, their headmen must appear in Albuquerque and sign a treaty, the terms of which would be written by himself and which would not be open to amendment.

Bonneville and Collins established a new eastern boundary for the Navajo country, arbitrarily moving the lines delineated by the Meriwether treaty considerably to the west and depriving the Navajos of some of their finest agricultural and pasture lands. The new boundary transected the Albuquerque road near Window Rock and Fort Defiance. The circle was drawing tighter.

Both Miles and Yost were strongly opposed to the restriction. Miles did not choose to argue with his commander, but he wrote Yost that although many of the best Navajo farming and grazing areas remained west of the Bonneville-Collins line, "the largest and best lands under cultivation by the Navajos and also grazed on by them . . . lie east of a longitudinal line passing through Fort Defiance."

Yost, who by reason of his main vocation—he was publisher of the Santa Fe *Gazette*—was inclined to give editorial support to the views of his American and New Mexican advertisers, nevertheless did not hesitate to condemn the

Bonneville treaty as impracticable. Its terms, he wrote Collins, "are of such a character that they cannot be endorsed by any enlightened mind." If enacted, the treaty would drive the Navajos from the peaceful pursuits of agriculture and industry to robbery and plunder "by depriving the best of the Indians of the grounds they cultivate and graze— whereon they raise corn and wheat enough to support the whole nation—12,000 souls, and sustain 250,000 sheep and 60,000 horses, thus forcing them to either violate the agreement forced upon them, or compel them to abandon cultivating the soil and stock raising or become pensioners of the government or plunderers."

The Navajos refused to go to Albuquerque for a council, and Bonneville and Collins were forced to travel to Fort Defiance to meet the headmen. It was a trip that demonstrated the physical fitness of Bonneville, who was sixty-four years old, for it was made in December through bitter cold and deep snow, and the entire party suffered extreme hardships.

Bonneville bluntly rejected proposals made by the Navajos—and which were endorsed by Yost—that provisions be written into the treaty that would obligate the military to take action against Ute and New Mexican raiders. He was adamant in his demand that the document be accepted as it stood. Sign or face punitive measures, the Navajos were told. On Christmas day they signed. Collins requested, and received, Yost's resignation.

Beginning with the melting of the snow and sprouting of new grass on the ranges in the spring of 1859, Navajo raiders struck with fury on the settlements and ranchos. The Utes were again on forays, and war parties were formed with the full knowledge of the Ute agent stationed at Abiquiu. The New Mexicans and bands of unscrupulous traders were invading the Navajo country for booty and captives. Collins, if not the stubborn Bonneville, had some new thoughts. Navajo leaders, Collins informed the Indian Bureau, seemed unable to control the malcontents of the tribe, and he concluded that the chiefs themselves "were conniving in the raids."

Collins may or may not have known at the time how right he was, but it would soon be made forcefully apparent to him that the Navajo chiefs, almost to a man, had lost all faith in Americans and had given up hope of achieving a just peace until the Americans forced both the Utes and the New Mexicans to cease their attacks. Collins finally made the qualified admission that "bad-disposed Mexicans exercised an evil influence over both Utes and Navajos by offering an outlet for stolen property and captives." It was not an honest statement, for the Navajos—with the possible exception of the scoundrel Sandoval—were no longer interested in selling captives. For them, the conflict had become almost entirely a defensive war.

Bonneville held an opposite view. Nothing could convince him that the Navajos would abide by any peace pact, even one indisputably favorable to them. They were, in his estimation, hopelessly addicted to outlawry. There was only one hope of controlling them: by force of arms.

Throughout the year 1859 columns of troops crisscrossed the Navajo country, and red men and white would leave their blood on the red rocks and yellow sands. If Collins entertained any doubts about the justness of the Bonneville treaty, he suppressed them and threw his full support behind Bonneville's plan of operation. Alexander Baker had been named as a temporary successor to Yost, and when troops commanded by Major John S. Simonson were sent on a campaign in June, Collins ordered Baker to accompany them. He instructed Baker to cooperate with the military in demanding fulfillment of the treaty stipulations, and warned him that no deviation from a strict compliance would be tolerated by the Bureau of Indian Affairs.

Although Simonson had seven hundred soldiers in his command, the Navajos appeared to be only mildly impressed, and intimidated not at all. In three councils with headmen, Simonson and Baker pleaded with them to sign a new "article of agreement" for the restoration of property stolen from New Mexicans. They were wasting their time, but the chiefs did not propose to waste their own time. They would sign no more papers until the Americans demonstrated their intention to demand of Utes and New Mexicans what they were demanding of the Navajos.

Baker informed Collins of his conviction that the Navajos were much richer and stronger than previous reports had indicated. After a long trip through large sections of the country, he judged their population to be between twelve and fifteen thousand. Their prosperity was unquestionable and, despite the warfare, appeared to be steadily improving. He had observed immense herds and bountiful fields and orchards. For this reason he believed them fully able to "repay any debt."

He said nothing about Utes and New Mexicans repaying their debts to the Navajos, or about the restoration of Navajo captives, but some of the military officers brought up the subject. Not a few of them voiced the opinion "that demands being pressed against the Navajos were unjust; and that many reports of the New Mexican losses had been falsified or padded."

Baker was replaced by Silas F. Kendrick, and Major Simonson gave way to Major O. L. Shepherd, but the shuffling of personnel brought no changes in the thinking of either the Indian Bureau or the military. Kendrick's zeal apparently amused the Navajos. They responded to his summoning them to council in the manner of men hopeful of being entertained. His impassioned pleas to them to abide by the terms of the Bonneville treaty result in their surrendering to him nineteen bony horses and 130 sheep.

The remark of a veteran soldier that when Navajos give up any livestock they cull their herds for animals too poor to be of any use to them was not conducive to soothing Kendrick's feelings. He was chagrined by his failure, and angrily wrote Major Shepherd: "Having used every means within my power as agent for the Navajo Indians to obtain from them a compliance with the treaty stipulations, and these means having entirely failed . . . it now becomes my duty to bring officially to your knowledge the delinquency of the tribe, and to apply to you to enforce the provisions of that treaty." At the time, Kendrick had been at Fort Defiance less than two months.

Reports filed by his predecessors may not have been readily available to Kendrick, or, if they were, he had not taken the trouble to study them, for he believed he had made an alarming discovery when he learned from Navajos at Chinle that Mormons were offering to aid them in fighting American soldiers. The Mormons had been advising the Navajos, Kendrick dutifully reported, not to comply with the treaty, "as the Americans were cheating them out of their land, timber, grass and livestock."

This was not news. More than three years earlier, Henry Linn Dodge had informed the Indian Department that he had talked with Navajos who had attended Mormon meetings in Utah. These Navajos, said Dodge, told him the Mormons "had asked why the Navajos did not drive the American soldiers out of their country, for if they were permitted to stay they would take the entire land." Both Dodge and Major Garland had stated that they had seen "a few fine rifles silver mounted, tobacco, blankets, among Navajos near the Hopis, obtained from the Mormons." Garland had informed the War Department that "Latter Day Saints were trying to bring about a peaceful settlement between the Utes and Navajos in an attempt to turn the two tribes against the United States government."

Several detachments patrolling the Navajo frontier during the summer and fall had succeeded in "capturing" a number of horses, cattle, and sheep to be added to the few Kendrick had managed to obtain. In November a small contingent of cavalry was assigned to aid the agent in delivering the prizes to Albuquerque. On the first night after the company left Fort Defiance, Navajos stole all but a few of the horses. A passing Navajo was encountered the following morning and persuaded to take a letter to Major Shepherd at the fort. The Navajo performed the errand, but Shepherd, discovering that he had dawdled on the way, rewarded him with a severe flogging on his bare back.

The Navajo messenger was a relative of a powerful chief, Ganado Mucho, and the undeserved punishment destroyed forever all hope of maintaining an amicable relationship with that leader.

The growing fury of the Navajos was demonstrated shortly after the year 1860 began. At sunrise three hundred wildly screaming Navajo warriors sought to stampede the cattle at the fort, but were driven off with heavy losses. They struck again at two outlying camps, and although they were repulsed at both places they killed four soldiers.

A few days later a friendly Navajo leader, Agua Chiquito, appeared at Fort Defiance and asked to confer with Kendrick. Shepherd intervened and forbade the agent to speak with him. Chiquito, puzzled and frightened by the argument that ensued between Shepherd and Kendrick, decided he would depart without talking with anyone. As he rode away, Shepherd yelled to guards to fire on him. Either the guards who obeyed the order were poor shots or they had no wish to shoot an innocent and friendly man in the back, for, although bullets passed close to him, Chiquito dashed out of range unharmed.

Shepherd ordered agent Kendrick not to council with any Navajo leader without permission. Bristling with resentment, Kendrick returned to Santa Fe and resigned.

Bonneville was summoned to the East, and command of the New Mexico district was given to another experienced Indian fighter, Colonel Thomas T. Fauntleroy. Cautiousness was perhaps the dominant characteristic of Fauntleroy's nature. He had at his disposal twenty-two companies of infantry and cavalry, far more than had been available to any previous commander of the territory, but he wanted a greater number before he would agree to undertake an offensive against the Navajos.

Meanwhile, strong bands of Navajo raiders were sweeping through the country, burning ranches and stealing livestock. Indian Superintendent Collins adhered to his policy of urging Utes to send war parties against the Navajos, and the Ute agents, Albert W. Pheiffer and Christopher (Kit) Carson, assisted in organizing forays in which Ute warriors and New Mexicans would unite to attack their "common enemy." Collins professed to be opposed to the taking of Navajos to be sold as slaves, but he did nothing to halt the practice by either Utes or New Mexicans.

Still Fauntleroy refused to move. His actions were mysterious. He asked the War Department for authority to call upon Governor Abraham Rencher for a thousand civilian volunteers and to recruit several hundred Utes as the nucleus of a militia. At the same time he notified the commander at Fort Defiance that no offensive against the Navajos would be immediately undertaken. The inactivity of the American forces brought vigorous complaints from the public, and the territorial legislature authorized the formation of "irregular companies" to wage an independent campaign against the Navajos.

Confusion mounted and the controversy grew bitter. Governor Rencher, complying with the demands of the legislature, asked Fauntleroy to furnish arms and supplies to the proposed irregular force. Fauntleroy refused. At a mass meeting in Santa Fe a demand was made upon the governor to act independently of the army and raise a regiment of volunteers. He refused. Collins suspiciously wrote the Indian commissioner: "I fear Fauntleroy is influenced in making this call for volunteers by a party of men, some of whom are well known to you, who have been engaged in speculating in land warrants. These men have been constantly courting his favor."

Five hundred Navajos attacked the soldiers assigned to guard the beef herd at Fort Defiance, and were driven off only after a fierce fight lasting two hours. Several troopers and a score of Indians were killed. Other bands of Navajo marauders repeatedly struck at army supply caravans on the Albuquerque road that were conveying supplies to Fort Defiance. Fauntleroy reacted in a manner that stunned both officers and civilians. He ordered a company of infantry moved from Fort Defiance to Bear Springs to construct a new post, to be called Fort Fauntleroy.*

Aware of the weakened condition of the Fort Defiance garrison, more than a thousand Navajos attacked in predawn darkness. So swift and well organized was the assault that they had taken possession of the most exposed buildings, including the storehouse, before defenses could be properly mounted. For an hour the battle raged, and at

---

* *Bear Springs, a few miles east of the present Gallup, New Mexico, was the scene of numerous councils with the Navajos. The name of Fort Fauntleroy later would be changed to Fort Lyon and finally to Fort Wingate.*

one time troops were firing on troops, believing them Indians. The coming of daylight, when the soldiers were able to achieve strong defensive positions, saved the fort from falling. The garrison suffered heavy casualties, and the Navajos withdrew as the sun rose, leaving the parade ground and adjacent areas strewn with dead.

Still Fauntleroy did not retaliate. Reports of the assault were rushed by couriers to Washington, but summer had come before replies reached New Mexico. "Active operations will be instituted against the Navajos as soon as the necessary preparations can be made," ordered Secretary of War J. B. Floyd. "A winter campaign with infantry, if inaugurated with secrecy and prosecuted with vigor, will prove the shortest and most effectual plan of operations." Two regiments of infantry and several companies of cavalry were being transferred to Santa Fe from Utah. The Secretary of War was of the opinion that, in view of Colonel Fauntleroy's many administrative duties, he could not be spared to take command in the field. Therefore he would remain, at least temporarily, at his present desk. The commander of the campaign would be Colonel Edward R. S. Canby, who was en route from Fort Garland, Colorado, with three companies of infantry and cavalry.

In the twenty years since he had graduated from West Point, Canby had been in almost constant combat from the Florida Everglades to the western frontier. He had distinguished himself in the Mexican War, and his competence as a field strategist had been demonstrated in campaigns against Indians on the plains and in the mountains of the Southwest. Highly respected by officers serving with him, he was known as the "prudent soldier," a term intended to denote both wisdom and shrewdness in his conduct of practical affairs.

Canby moved with all rapidity possible to organize his

expedition against the Navajos. Hardly more than a month after he had reached Abiquiu his plans were being executed. Three powerful contingents, heavily armed and well supplied, were converging on the Navajo country. Canby's brother-in-law, Major Henry Hopkins Sibley, was moving westward from Albuquerque with four companies of cavalry, one of infantry, and Blas Lucero's Spies. Captain Lafayette McLaws was marching northwest on a route that would take him past the Zuñi pueblos. He had under him one company of dragoons and two of infantry. Canby himself would advance westward through the heart of the Navajo land. His guides would be agents Kit Carson and Pheiffer and a strong band of Utes and New Mexicans they had recruited. The three columns would rendezvous at Fort Defiance, then fan out to strike at the Navajos on separate fronts.

Column One (Canby) met the first resistance, which Canby termed a "trifling success—one Navajo warrior was killed by spies on October 1; six squaws in the melee could not be distinguished from warriors and were killed by the troops and spies in a conflict with a superior force of Navajos on the 2nd inst." A few score horses were captured. Column Two (Sibley) reported that on his march through the heavily populated Tunicha Valley he had found that the Navajos were fleeing westward toward Navajo Mountain, one of the most rugged and inaccessible areas of the country.

By mid-October Canby was admittedly disappointed and not a little frustrated. The enemy he had hoped to meet had all but vanished. Whole valleys, the floors of which were covered with unharvested fields, were deserted. Hundreds of hogans were unoccupied. Herds grazed unattended. It was an utterly amazing situation. Columns One and Two went beyond Canyon de Chelly, while Column Three scoured areas to the east in the hope of intercepting Navajos who might flee in that direction. The results of the operations were almost too few to mention. Sibley's men killed five Navajos in a skirmish. Canby's men exchanged shots with snipers. New Mexicans with Column Three came upon what they thought was the trail of a large group of Navajos. After a chase of five hours they saw ahead of them not a band of warriors, but two men, a squaw, thirty horses, and forty sheep. The two men vanished. The woman was captured. With a sweeping gesture toward the western horizon, she said that almost all Navajos had fled far beyond the Canyon de Chelly. Soldiers would find no one of importance.

But a group of New Mexican spies and Pueblo scouts did find someone of importance. On a rutted trail between Klagetoh and Ganado, south of Canyon de Chelly, they saw a lone horseman coming toward them. One of the Pueblos —some Navajo accounts say he was a Zuñi—recognized the rider and called out that he was the great leader and orator, the very aged Zarcillas Largo, a man who had always wanted peace between his people and white men, but the others

closed their ears to his words, and someone shot at Long Earrings, wounding him. Now Long Earrings drew an arrow and came on. He fired four arrows before he turned to escape, and one struck a man in the breast, and another man was shot through the mouth, and another in the ear, and one arrow went toward the sky. Then Long Earrings' horse plunged and threw him. He crawled into a small gulley under a rain of bullets, and shot the rest of his arrows. Then bullets riddled him. The New Mexicans and the Pueblos each threw a rock on his body, mashing it. They stripped him of his turquoise and his silver ornaments, and then they scalped him.*

The long rides, sometimes over terrain without adequate grass or water, the eternal red dust, the nights made sleepless by signal fires and snipers, had exhausted both horses and men. Canby was beginning to despair: "Our recent operations have shown that even when pressed to the extreme limits of their country, the Navajos still have the means of escape, and they will abandon their families and their flocks, rather than fight." Sibley stated that his horses were "completely exhausted" and that four cavalry companies were "entirely inefficient for any further active service."

In nearly two months of campaigning, only thirty-four Navajos had been killed and only eight thousand head of livestock had been confiscated. Most of the troopers, being without horses, were on foot with the infantry. Winter was at hand. Canby turned back and established his headquarters at Fort Fauntleroy. He was not as discouraged as might have been expected under the circumstances. On paper the expedition appeared to be nothing more than a fiasco, but Canby had learned a great deal about Navajos, and out of the failure of his operations had evolved strategy he believed would be successful.

As he kept his patrols scouring the eastern perimeter of the Navajo country, through the Zuñi Mountains, along the Rio Puerco, in the Chuska Valley, and in the area of the Hopi villages, he refined his new plans based on his conviction that the only way to control the Navajos was to keep them on the move, to harass them constantly, to break them

---

* Later, some Navajos said that Long Earrings had grown weary of life because of the great age weighing upon him, and that he had not fled to the safety of the Navajo Mountain wilderness because he had decided that it would be better to die fighting than waste away as a helpless old man. But no one really knew if this was the truth.

up into small groups, to station contingents of troops at strategic points, to make it impossible for them to maintain permanent farms. An offensive that kept them on the run would be disastrous to their economy.

Indeed, that was what he had achieved in a large measure during the fall.

As the year 1860 neared an end, several delegations appeared at Fort Fauntleroy under flags of truce to learn if Canby would be agreeable to negotiating a new peace agreement. Of course he wanted peace, Canby told them. That was the reason he was in their country. But he did not propose to rush into signing a treaty. It would have to be acceptable to the entire tribe, not to just a few headmen. Spread the word, and have the chiefs gather at Fort Fauntleroy for a preliminary council on January 12.

Unlike his predecessors who had negotiated treaties with the Navajos, Canby took a firm stand on one of the main issues that had made peace impossible: the refusal of the New Mexicans and the Pueblo Indians allied with them to halt their raids against the Navajos for booty and slaves. In the mild language he customarily used, he wrote Fauntleroy: "Those [raids] and other occurrences of minor importance indicate, I think, a settled disposition on the part of some of these people to protract the Navajo troubles indefinitely. For myself I shall have no hesitation in treating as enemies of the United States any parties of [New] Mexicans or Pueblo Indians who may be found in the country assigned to the Navajos."

The treaty Canby prepared was signed by thirty-two Navajo headmen on February 15, among them the most influential leaders of the tribe—Manuelito, Armijo, Barboncito, Herrero Grande, Ganado Mucho, Herrero Chiquito, El Barbon. Canby's efforts might have been fruitful, for the provisions of the treaty were reasonable and workable, but there was no opportunity to learn if they would bring peace to the Navajo country: as the Navajo leaders sat in solemn council at snowbound Fort Fauntleroy, southern states were seceding from the Union.

Within a few weeks it could not be said that an American army existed in New Mexico. Soldiers were there, but they were widely scattered, badly disorganized, and almost completely demoralized. Hundreds of privates and noncoms deserted and scores of officers left to take up arms for the Confederacy. Fauntleroy resigned, leaving the Ninth Military Department without a head. Canby's brother-in-law, Sibley, said farewell and told his troops: "Boys, if you only knew it, I am the worst enemy you ever had."

Orders came to Canby to abandon Fort Defiance. He was to leave a small garrison at Fort Fauntleroy (soon to be renamed Fort Lyon), and move the main body of his remaining force to the Rio Grande.

As spring advanced, New Mexican, Ute, and Pueblo raiders swept into the Navajo country, laying it waste, stealing livestock and anything else movable, and taking captives. Out of the Navajo country screaming bands of warriors swept down upon the villages of their Indian enemies. The beautiful country of blue mountains, yellow mesas, and red-rock canyons from Santa Fe to the Colorado River, was once more aflame with a terrible conflict.

Early in 1862 a colonel and a general faced each other in the Rio Grande Valley in New Mexico. The colonel was Edward R. S. Canby, commander of all Union forces in the territory. The general was his brother-in-law, Henry H. Sibley of the Confederate army. Hardly more than a year before they had been riding together against the Navajos. Now they were enemies, each charged with the duty of defeating the other in a deadly combat that would decide the political fate of the entire Southwest.

Canby had increased the garrisons at Forts Fillmore, Stanton, and Craig, any one of which might be expected to be attacked at the outset of hostilities, and strengthened the defenses at Albuquerque and Santa Fe. When word was received that Confederate forces were moving upon Fort Bliss, at El Paso, he appealed to Colorado for reinforcements and requested that troops be sent from California. The Colorado governor sent two companies of militia, and these Canby stationed at Fort Craig. More would come down from the north shortly afterward on a forced march through heavy snows. On the way from California was a brigade of volunteers commanded by General James H. Carleton, who had formerly served in Indian campaigns in the Southwest.

In an audience with Confederate President Jefferson Davis, Sibley had outlined a grandiose scheme of securing New Mexico, Arizona, and California for the Confederacy in one sweeping blow. These regions contained not only great mineral wealth, but countless thousands of Indians and Mexicans who might be enslaved. He had visions of vast new plantations reaching from the plains of Texas to the rich valleys of the Pacific coast. Davis thought well enough of the idea to commission Sibley a general and authorize him to raise a brigade of fighting men in Texas and start western gold flowing into the South's treasury. Within a few months Sibley had organized a force of 3,800 mounted Texans, who, he proudly reported, were "the best damn fighters that ever threw a leg over a horse."

Fort Bliss fell, and Canby moved down the Rio Grande to stop the invaders. The fighting began at Fort Craig on February 20 with an attack by Canby, but the Confederates held strong positions and the next morning the Union troops were forced to retreat to the post for ammunition and provisions. Within a matter of hours Canby moved them out again, and launched an assault at Valverde. Throughout the day the fighting was fierce. The turning point came when five companies of New Mexican militia refused to obey orders to advance, and Canby's strongest and best battery of field guns was captured by Confederate cavalry. The Union troops broke before a charge by Texans, "more like a herd of frightened mustangs than men." The Confederates were regrouping for a new advance when Canby sent out a truce party asking for a cease-fire to permit removal of dead and wounded. It was granted by Sibley, and the battle was over. Canby withdrew to Fort Craig in utter defeat, and Sibley moved north. Three days later he was outside Albuquerque.

After restocking at Fort Craig, the Union garrison burned the remaining supplies and fled toward Santa Fe, and Sibley and his men rode into Albuquerque without a shot being fired. Soon afterward Santa Fe fell to them in the same manner, the Union troops there destroying stores and retreating toward Fort Union. "It is needless to say that this country is in a critical condition," read a dispatch sent by a Union inspector general to army headquarters in St. Louis.

For two reasons, the situation was not as critical as the retreating inspector general had painted it: first, Canby's strategy and plans of battle; second, logistics.

Canby had well-armed cavalry and infantry, as well as several batteries of artillery, in strong positions between Fort Union and the mountains west of Las Vegas. These could be quickly shifted to meet contingencies. With his battered troops rested, reorganized, and well equipped from the stores he had prudently maintained at Fort Craig, he began a slow advance up the Rio Grande.

He knew that the Confederates would soon be desperately in need of supplies and ammunition. He could cut off any provision trains that attempted to reach them from El Paso and Fort Union, his strongest post, could delay, if not destroy, forces approaching from the east. He had burned all Union stores in Albuquerque and Santa Fe.

Canby not only knew the country, but also its resources. The Confederates might obtain enough food to keep them going, but Fort Union was the only remaining depot where they might obtain adequate quantities of munitions. Even the capture of supplies from Union troops in the field would not long sustain them.

Fort Union, as expected, became Sibley's objective, and Canby's scouts observed a picket column of six hundred Texans leave Santa Fe on March 22 and take a position at the western mouth of Apache Canyon. This force had orders to guard the approach to the capital until joined by the main Confederate force. Then the united troops would sweep on to Las Vegas and Fort Union. Their past victories had filled the Texans with confidence, and, as one of them wrote his wife, they all "felt like heroes . . . Fort Union was ours already; and then New Mexico would belong to the new government of the south and it would then be so easy to cut off all communication with California."

On March 28 scouts brought word to the Confederate picket that a small force of two hundred New Mexicans and two hundred regulars from Fort Union was moving up Apache Canyon. They raced forward to "dispose of the foolhardy Union troops." What they did not know was that the intelligence they had received was incomplete. They soon came in sight of the Union column, which was advancing in double time, and opened fire. The column halted and took a defensive position. The Texans continued to advance, and suddenly were caught in devastating fire that rained upon them from both slopes of the canyon. Union infantry, recorded one Texan, "were upon the hills on both mountains jumping from rock to rock like so many mountain sheep." The Texans were caught in a trap set for them by

Canby's Coloradans, "regular demons in the shape of Pike's Peakers from the gold mines." Fighting their way out of the canyon, they fled in disorder, leaving more than seventy dead and scores of wounded behind them.

Sibley rushed his full force—except for a few Texans who remained with him to hold Albuquerque—and his main supply train into the canyon. Union troops poured westward from Fort Union and Las Vegas. On March 28 the two armies met head-on in Glorietta Pass. Throughout the day the battle raged without either side gaining an appreciable advantage, but late in the afternoon the Confederate colonel commanding received news that made victory for him an utter impossibility. Union cavalry had circled the canyon without being discovered and had swept down on the supply train. They had captured the men guarding it, destroyed the wagons and all the munitions and foodstuffs in them, and killed the animals.

The Confederate leader asked for an armistice until the following noon to allow his dead to be buried and the wounded removed to safety. It was granted, but when the hour for its expiration arrived, the Confederates were gone.

Canby had come up to Albuquerque. His troops exchanged a few shots with the Confederates as Sibley led them in retreat, and then Canby ordered his men to fire no more. Leaving their sick and wounded behind, "without attendance, without medicine, and almost without food," the Confederates continued their retreat down the west bank of the river. Down the east bank moved Canby and several companies of Union troops. For a week the two forces were within gun range of each other, but there was no firing from either side. Officers urged Canby to cross the river and "wipe out the Texans, once and for all," and they wondered if his refusal was based more on personal than humane reasons. Through his glasses he could see his brother-in-law riding at the head of the Texans. There was no doubt that they were almost helpless, and there was no glory to be gained in attacking defenseless men. When Sibley and his weary column disappeared into the San Mateo Mountains, taking the hardest but shortest route to Texas, Canby turned back to Santa Fe.

For New Mexico the Civil War was over, but west of the Rio Grande another war was still raging, its deaths mounting, its fury rising, as Navajo and New Mexican raiders struck viciously at each other.

By the fall of 1862 the War Department somehow had found time to give its attention, if briefly, to the Indian problems in New Mexico and Arizona, and orders came from Washington to the Ninth Military District to take forceful measures, with the cooperation of Governor Henry Connelly and other civil officials, to resolve them. The arduous task fell to General Carleton, leader of the California column sent to help save New Mexico from falling to the Confederates. He had arrived several months too late to be of assistance in that respect but just in time to take over command of the district from Canby, who was being called East to receive a general's star and a new assignment.

It did not take Carleton long to prepare plans that would not only drastically alter the course of all southwestern history but bring utter disaster to the Navajos.

# 8

DURING THE Civil War only two companies of Union cavalry had remained in the Navajo country. They were stationed at Fort Fauntleroy, and they had virtually no duties to perform, except to keep open the military and trading road that ran along the Rio Puerco. Any attempt by such a small garrison to enforce the terms of the Canby treaty would have been an exercise in futility, and none was made. New Mexican and Navajo raiders operated with complete impunity. Disregarding the killing and plundering taking place in the vast land, the troops sought to relieve the heavy burden of monotony with various diversions.

A large number of Navajos lived and grazed their flocks in the immediate area—many of them having come there to gain the protection of the fort—and both officers and men were free to fraternize with them when off duty, which they were most of the time. The Navajo men came to the post to trade and to engage the soldiers in various sports. The soldiers attended the Navajo dances, and bid for the attentions of the women, which in most cases could be obtained for such trifles as shiny coins and buttons, small mirrors, cloth, and discarded uniforms. Most of the officers, having more resources than the enlisted men—including articles stolen from government stores—were able to maintain mistresses. Illegal traders kept everyone supplied with rotgut whisky.

The general camaraderie had ended abruptly on a bright afternoon in September 1861 with an argument over a horse race. Several hundred Indians had gathered to watch and betting was heavy. The soldiers backed a horse ridden by a Lieutenant Ortiz and owned by Dr. Kavenaugh, the post surgeon, which was being raced against an Indian horse. The bridle on the Indian horse broke shortly after the start and the horse ran off the track. Ortiz was declared the winner. Examination revealed that the bridle of the Indian horse had been partially cut, so that strain would snap it. The Indians demanded that the race be rerun, but the winner refused.

Because of the argument, the commanding officer, a Colonel Chavez, ordered that the Navajos should not be allowed to enter the post. A few minutes later, a Navajo who attempted to enter was shot by a guard. Soldiers quickly armed themselves and without orders attacked the crowd of Indians. Men, women, and children were shot and bayoneted. Before the Navajos could flee to safety, fifteen had been killed and many had been wounded. Colonel Chavez sought to keep the massacre a secret by forbidding private letters from being sent out in the mail.

Superintendent Collins informed the Indian Bureau that in 1862, while the Confederates were invading New Mexico, the Navajos had "driven off over one hundred thousand sheep, and not less than a thousand head of cattle besides horses and mules to a large amount." At the same time New Mexican raiding parties were ravaging the Navajo country, but if Collins made a report on the number of Navajos taken captive and sold on the slave market, it disappeared from the files of the Bureau of Indian Affairs.

However, a statement by Dr. Louis Kennon of Santa Fe, long a resident of the territory, has been preserved: "I think that the Navajos have been the most abused people on the continent, and that in all hostilities the [New] Mexicans have always taken the initiative with but one exception that I know of." With the sanction of the Indian Bureau and the military, "there was a pressure brought to bear to make war on the Navajo . . . if you asked the [New] Mexicans any reason for making war, they would give no other reason but that the Navajos had a great many sheep and horses and a great many children." Dr. Kennon believed

the number of captive Navajo Indians held as slaves to be underestimated. I think there are from five to six thousand. I know of no [New Mexican] family which can raise one hundred and fifty dollars but what purchases a Navajo slave, and many families own four or five, the trade in them being as regular as the trade in pigs and sheep. Previous to the [Civil] War their price was from seventy-five to one hundred dollars, but now they are worth about four hundred dollars.

A hundred and seventy-five miles southeast of Santa Fe the red muddy Rio Pecos twisted through the western reaches of the vast Llano Estacado, a dry barren land, treeless except for the ragged cottonwoods that lifted their tortured limbs along the edge of the alkaline stream. "It is impossible," Coronado's chronicler, Castaneda, had written, "to find tracks in this country, because the grass straightened up again as soon as it was trodden down. In 250 leagues was seen not a hillock which was three times as high as a man. The country is like a bowl, so that when a man sits down, the horizon surrounds him all around at the distance of a musket shot."

This land had changed not at all when General Carleton came to know it, more than three hundred years after Coronado's disastrous journey across the plains in search of Quivira. It suited in almost every particular the plan the general had in mind. It was isolated, far from any white settlement, a part of the public domain, and inhabited only by buffalo, wolves, coyotes, jack rabbits, and some wandering bands of Indian hunters. To his way of thinking, no better place could be found in which to resettle the Navajos—as well as the Apaches—and thereby end forever the terrible scourges these peoples had inflicted upon the territory of New Mexico.

Both the Department of War and the Bureau of Indian Affairs agreed to Carleton's proposal to set aside the required amount of agricultural lands as a reservation and to construct a fort so that troops could guard against depredations and prevent escapes. Carleton selected as a site for the new post a place known as Bosque Redondo, where groves of cottonwoods stretched for sixteen miles along the Pecos, and declared that it and the adjacent area would be ideal for his purposes.

A board of army officers assigned to inspect the place vociferously disagreed with Carleton, reporting that Bosque Redondo was "remote from the depot of supplies, Fort Union, and from the neighborhoods that supply forage. Building material will have to be brought from a great distance. The water of the Pecos contains much unhealthy mineral matter. A large part of the surrounding valley is subject to inundation by the spring floods." The board recommended another site, closer to Las Vegas and Fort Union, "where the supply of good timber for building and firewood is convenient, the water is pure and abundant, the grazing is very fine, and none of the neighboring country is subject to overflow."

Carleton overruled the inspectors, and was sustained by the War Department. Bosque Redondo would be the place, the new fort would be named in honor of General Edwin V. Sumner, and the Navajos would be collected "little by little" and sent there, "away from the haunts and hills and hiding-places of their country." And there the army would be "kind to them; there teach their children how to read and write; teach them the arts of peace; teach them the truths of Christianity."

Governor Henry Connelly gave his full support to Carleton's project, and "before many days had passed they had agreed on a plan to start a war against the Navajos." The military commander and the governor exchanged numerous letters, and these and other documents disclose that the campaign they had in mind had nothing to do with "teaching the Navajos the arts of peace and Christianity."

Both Carleton and Connelly were convinced that the Navajo country was rich in minerals. On May 10, 1863, Carleton wrote General Henry W. Halleck: "Among all my endeavors since my arrival here has been an effort to brush back the Indians, so that the people could get out of the valley of the Rio Grande, and not only possess themselves of the arable lands in other parts of the territory, but, if the country contained veins and deposits of precious metals, that they might be found." Shortly afterward he again wrote Halleck: "There is every evidence that a country as rich if not richer in mineral wealth than California, extends from the Rio Grande, northwestwardly, all the way across to Washoe [Nevada]."

In June 1863, on the eve of his Navajo campaign, Carleton wrote a Captain Walker, who was prospecting in Arizona: "If I can help others to a fortune, it will afford me not quite as much happiness as finding one myself, it is true— but nearly as much. My luck has always been not to be at the right place at the right time for fortunes."

Governor Connelly forcibly expressed his own reasoning by telling the New Mexican legislative assembly that "Navajos occupy the finest grazing districts within our limits" and "infest a mining region extending two hundred miles," and that therefore "an immense [white] pastoral and mining population is excluded from its occupations and the treasures of mineral wealth that are known to exist." Connelly thought that "public interest demands that this condition of things should cease to exist," for the Navajos "too long have . . . roamed lords of the soil over this extensive and valuable tract of country."

Although for three centuries searches for precious metals had been made in the Navajo country, no deposits had been found. Yet belief in their existence persisted. Carleton and Connelly were afflicted with the same fever that had burned in the *Conquistadores*. The only difference between them and their Spanish predecessors was in the method of operation to be employed. Carleton and Connelly did not propose to force the Indians to slave in the mines, but "simply remove or exterminate them."

In the summer of 1863 Carleton and Connelly set in motion the powerful machinery they had designed to destroy the Navajos. "I would respectfully recommend," Carleton wrote the War Department, "that the only peace that can ever be made with them must rest on the basis that they move onto the lands (at Fort Sumner) and, like the Pueblos, become an agricultural people and cease to be nomads." On the Pecos reservation, "old Navajos would soon die off, and carry with them all the latent longings for murdering and robbing; the young ones would take their places without these longings; and thus, little by little, the Navajos would become a happy and contented people, and Navajo wars would be remembered only as something that belongs entirely to the past."

Less reflective of humanitarian intentions were the orders Carleton issued to Kit Carson and other officers who would command the troops on the Navajo roundup. The Navajos would have until July 20, 1863, to surrender, and "after that date every Navajo seen will be considered as hostile and treated accordingly; after that day the door now open will be closed."

Connelly offered to raise several companies of civilian volunteers to aid the troops, but Carleton rejected the proposal. He preferred to rely on professional soldiers who were trained in Indian fighting, and wanted no unruly contingents in the field, for "troops must be kept after the Indians, not in big bodies, with military noises and smokes, and the gleam of arms by day, and fires, and talk, and comfortable sleep at night; but in small parties moving stealthily to their haunts and lying patiently in wait for them."

Carleton's rhetoric concealed his true feelings in the matter. He made no effort whatsoever to keep so-called unruly contingents out of the Navajo country, and through it raced numerous bands of New Mexicans and traders intent upon taking captives before the source of supply was closed to them. During the course of the campaign these groups of heavily armed slavers took hundreds of Navajo women and children to be sold as menials at very lucrative prices throughout the territory. In many instances women and children were taken from groups on their way to surrender at military posts, and men attempting to protect their families were wantonly shot down.

Kit Carson encouraged a Ute contingent he had recruited

to take Navajo prisoners for themselves. That was his way of rewarding them for "their continued zeal and activity." The captives, he thought, "would be better off than at Bosque Redondo, as the Utes would sell them to Mexican families who would care for them, thus they would cease to require any further attention on the part of the government." Carson thought also that selling Navajos as servants to New Mexican families would "break up that collectiveness of interest as a tribe which they will retain if kept together at Bosque Redondo."

Aware that his continued silence on the slave traffic might result in the accusation that he had willfully violated army practices, if not federal law, Carleton wrote Carson for the record that "all prisoners which are captured by the troops or employes of your command will be sent to Santa Fe, by the first practicable opportunity after they are, from time to time, brought in as prisoners. There must be no exception to this rule."

However, not until the Navajo roundup had been in progress for a year, and hundreds of men, women, and children had been driven over the "long walk" of four hundred miles to Bosque Redondo, did either Carson, Carleton, or Connelly take any official steps to halt the iniquitous slave trade. Moreover, they took action then only because the operations of New Mexican slavers had become so extensive that the troops were being hampered by them. Several Navajo leaders had notified army officers of their willingness to surrender but were fearful of falling into the hands of the New Mexicans before they could bring their groups to safety at the military posts.

Like the tentacles of a great octopus, columns of troops snaked through the canyons and the valleys and over the immense mesas from July until December 1863. Every hogan, every field, every storehouse they found was burned.

Carson reported that in the area of Bonito Canyon alone his men had destroyed more than two million pounds of Navajo grain. Devastating the country, however, was much easier than capturing Navajos. By late fall only a few hundred had voluntarily surrendered. Although accurate figures are not available, it is probable that as many had been taken captive by New Mexicans as had been sent to Bosque Redondo.

As the infiltration of troops began, hundreds of Navajos quickly disappeared. They fled to the north, west, and south, taking with them what livestock they could and abandoning the rest. Many crossed the San Juan to the inaccessible and unknown canyon country of southern Utah. Many went west of the Hopi villages and as far as the Grand Canyon. Many went into the vast wilderness south of Zuñi. Not a few reached the White Mountain Apache country in Arizona. But a far greater number remained, gathering in strongholds to defend themselves, expecting that the coming of winter would force a curtailment of military operations against them.

Deeply disappointed, Carleton ordered that an intensive campaign be continued through the winter. He rejected an appeal for a council made by several Navajo leaders. There would be no peace until every Navajo had gone to Fort Sumner. Those who refused would "feel the arm of the American military as never before." He ordered that soldiers be paid a bounty of twenty dollars for every Navajo horse and mule and one dollar for every sheep they confiscated and delivered to the army quartermaster. Despite his instructions that all Navajo prisoners were to be taken to Santa Fe, some soldiers found ways to abduct children and sell them to New Mexicans. Although these violations were reported, the soldiers who committed them were not punished.

No one understood better than the Navajos themselves

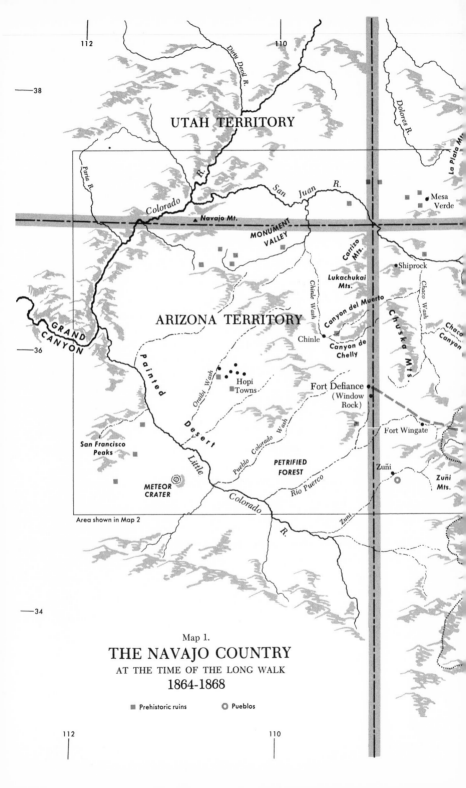

Map 1.
# THE NAVAJO COUNTRY
AT THE TIME OF THE LONG WALK
## 1864-1868

■ Prehistoric ruins   ◎ Pueblos

how desperate their situation was. Carson's holocaust had destroyed the greater part of their stores. There would be no opportunity to plant crops in the coming spring. Starvation rode with the soldiers against them, and it was an enemy far more formidable than the guns. Strong bands of warriors attempted to secure foodstuffs by attacking supply trains sent out from Albuquerque and other towns to the troops, but they met with little success.

In January 1864 the Rope Thrower, as the Navajos called Carson, was at Canyon de Chelly with four hundred men. They had traveled more than a hundred miles through deep snow and bitter cold. Navajos began to surrender, at first in groups of two or three families, but as Carson moved on through the country larger bands appeared under white flags. Many old people, women, and children had already died of hunger and exposure, and all were destitute and badly in need of sustenance.

By February 1 more than eight hundred Navajos were prisoners at Forts Canby and Wingate, waiting to be moved to Bosque Redondo. Before the month ended, this number had increased to nearly three thousand men, women, and children.

Carleton exuberantly wrote the War Department: "You have doubtless seen the last of the Navajo war. We now have over three thousand and will, without doubt, soon have the whole tribe. I do not believe they must number now much over five thousand, all told."

This was not the truth, and Carleton knew it. He was aware that several thousand Navajos had not yet surrendered and that hundreds had fled to remote areas where, as Carson had informed him, they were beyond the reach of troops. Carson also had estimated the Navajo population at twelve thousand, which included those who had vanished from the Navajo country. Carleton, seemingly with the intent of enhancing his own reputation, stubbornly disagreed with Carson and boasted to the War Department of his success in ending a war "that has been continued with but few intermissions for 180 years,* and which, during that time, has been marked by every shade of atrocity, brutality and ferocity which can be found in the annals of conflict between our own and the aboriginal race. . . . This formidable band of robbers and murderers have at last been made to succumb."

The shades of "atrocity, brutality and ferocity," however, were not all confined to the past. Carleton had not seen to it that adequate preparations had been made to care for the Navajos who were surrendering. Stores of food, clothing, and blankets at the posts were soon exhausted. Within a single week 126 died of dysentery and exposure at Fort Canby, and the death tolls at other installations were equally high in proportion to the numbers confined. The prisoners were started as rapidly as possible on the long walk to Fort Sumner. They were supplied chiefly with flour, a food totally strange to them, and given no instructions in its use. The starving Navajos mixed the flour with a little water and ate the cold paste. Many were stricken with cramps and fell to the roadside. Many collapsed from weakness. They could not be carried in vehicles, for the few army wagons available were crowded with the aged and crippled. The military escorts had only one alternative to leaving those who fell to die lingering deaths: they shot them and left their bodies to the wolves and vultures.

In the spring of 1864 Carleton found himself faced with two desperate situations. He had grossly underestimated the number of Navajos who would surrender, and as they continued to pour into military posts by the hundreds, he

* *That is, since the Pueblo Revolt against the Spanish, a date that had no significance at all to Americans.*

made frantic appeals to the army quartermaster for supplies. The other pressing problem was created by the New Mexicans. Bands of slavers stormed into the Navajo country, snatching helpless women and children seeking sanctuary at the forts. New Mexicans overpowered guards, usually only a handful of troops, and took captives from columns en route to Bosque Redondo.

Not unaware that he could be held wholly responsible for these monstrous conditions, Carleton set about establishing a written record that he hoped would give him the guise of a humane soldier deeply concerned with the welfare of the people he had conquered. He sent his friend, former Indian agent Collins, to Washington with explanatory dispatches and an itemization of foodstuffs and supplies most urgently needed at Bosque Redondo. On the ground that the Navajos had suffered a crushing defeat and that further punitive actions would be both unnecessary and unwarranted, he ordered an immediate cessation of the war against them.

"The exodus of this whole people from the land of their fathers is not only an interesting but a touching sight," he wrote Adjutant General Lorenzo Thomas in a deceptive but fervent plea for provisions with which to sustain his prisoners.

They have fought us gallantly for years on years. They have defended their mountains and their stupendous canyons with a heroism which any people might be proud to emulate; but when, at length, they found it was their destiny to give way to the insatiable progress of our race, they threw down their arms and, as brave men entitled to our admiration and respect, have come to us in confidence of our magnanimity, feeling that for having sacrificed to us their beautiful country, their homes, the associations of their lives, their scenes rendered classic in their traditions, we will not dole out to them a miser's pittance in return for what they know to be and what we know to be a princely realm.

Undoubtedly General Thomas was touched, but emotion seldom had the effect of accelerating the slow machinery of the War Department. Carleton had proceeded with an Indian policy quite his own, without official authorization, and no preparations had been made to meet the emergency that had resulted. His requests would receive due consideration, but not the priority for which he asked, not with every logistical channel clogged by urgent demands from the immense armies on the battlefields of the Civil War. Feeding Union soldiers was far more vital to the security of the nation than sending beans to a few Indians in a remote post in the western wilderness.

At Carleton's request Governor Connelly issued a civil proclamation stating that inasmuch as there existed "a suspension of arms against the Navajos, and the more hostile part of that tribe is now reduced,"

. . . hostile demonstrations on the part of our citizens . . . would frustrate the intentions and efforts of the government in the peaceable removal of the remainder of this tribe . . . to whom has been granted safety to life and property . . . and, therefore, all forays by our citizens of a hostile character into the country heretofore or now occupied by any part of the said Navajo Indians . . . shall cease . . . and are positively prohibited under the severest penalties . . . and any parties of armed men, with hostile intentions, hereafter found in the Navajo country will be arrested by United States troops. . . . It is proper in this connexion to warn the people against further traffic in captive Indians. The laws of the

country as well as those of justice and humanity positively forbid such a traffic. . . . Measures are now being
taken to have all Indians surrendered [restored] who
have been sold into slavery.

The proclamation brought little, if any, curtailment in the
slave traffic. Bands of citizens continued to roam through
the Navajo country, and post commanders made no attempt
to prevent them from taking captives. Indeed, several officers admitted that they had allowed slavers to retain prisoners, and Indian agents openly furnished both Utes and
New Mexicans with arms and encouraged them to prey on
Navajos.

Emissaries sent by Carleton to several western posts were
more successful than his appeals to Washington. Half a million pounds of flour, beans, shelled corn, and other commodities and more than two thousand head of cattle were
obtained. It was far from enough food to provide proper
sustenance for the six thousand Navajos, the four hundred
Apaches, and the troops then at Fort Sumner, but Carleton
believed that by doling it out carefully they would be able
to survive the winter. By that time, he felt sure, enough
additional supplies would have arrived to see them through
the summer until crops planted in the spring could be har-
vested. He ordered the troops put on half rations. The
Indians received even smaller food allotments, Carleton directing that they "be fed at the rate of one pound for each
man, woman and child per day, of fresh meat, or of corn,
or of wheat, or of wheat meal, or of corn meal, or of flour,
or of pickles." If none of these commodities was available,
the Indians were to be given "half a pound of beans or of
rice, or of peas, or of dried fruit."

Upon the advice of Secretary of the Interior John P.
Usher, President Abraham Lincoln in January 1864 had

signed an order creating a forty-square-mile reservation at Bosque Redondo. The President had been told that it was large enough to serve the needs of the three relatively small Apache bands inhabiting eastern New Mexico. Mr. Lincoln had not been informed, however, of Carleton's plan—which had been approved by the War Department and was already under way—to confine thousands of Navajos in the small area.

Thus, through no fault of the President, two cabinet departments became engaged in a bitter controversy over conflicting interpretations of regulations and policies. Compounded by political jealousies and personality clashes, it was a contest that could be ended only by political and administrative maneuvers, and, as long as it lasted, the persons who would suffer the most would be the Indians.

Stoutly defending his actions and the program he had devised, Carleton criticized the Indian Bureau for having recommended establishing the reservation and then failing to provide food, supplies, and tools for the Navajos. The Indian Bureau took the stand that since the War Department arbitrarily had driven the Navajos to Bosque Redondo it must assume the responsibility of supporting them. From the quartermaster department's western office came the complaint that stores were being depleted to dangerously low levels by Carleton's requisitions. Too bad, said the Indian department, but it was impoverished, all funds appropriated to it by Congress having been allotted to other projects.

Carleton stubbornly insisted that virtually the entire Navajo tribe had been captured, although no less an authority than Kit Carson had told him that many had eluded the troops. In the late fall of 1864, Indians at Bosque Redondo were run through a pen gate like sheep while soldiers counted them. The tally showed that 8,354 Navajos and 405 Apaches were on the reservation. Noticeably miss-

ing were two large bands known to be led by powerful
chiefs, Barboncito and Manuelito. A hunt was launched for
them, but not until the late summer of 1866 would Manuelito voluntarily surrender at Fort Wingate. He had been
badly wounded and was in dire need of medical attention.
Shortly thereafter, exhausted, hungry, and without means of
sustaining themselves longer, Barboncito and his followers
gave up the fight.

At Bosque Redondo hundreds of Navajos lived in holes
in the ground, sheltered only by pieces of discarded army
tents, cowhides, and brush. Many were dying of malnutrition. Many were almost naked, and most of them were barefoot. They were suffering from pneumonia, tuberculosis, and
venereal diseases. Navajo women sold themselves for food
to the four hundred soldiers stationed at Fort Sumner, with
the result that syphilis and gonorrhea spread rapidly among
both Indians and the troops.

Supplies trickled in, obtained largely through Carleton's
unceasing pleas, but the quantities were far from sufficient.
"I beg respectfully to call the serious attention of the government to the destitute condition of the captives, and beg
for authority to provide clothing for the women and children," Carleton said in one of his many letters to the War
Department.

Carleton never deviated from his determination to make
the Navajos self-supporting through agriculture. With the
arrival of the first Navajos at Bosque Redondo, he had
ordered that cultivation be begun, advising the post commander, Major Henry Wallen, that

every Indian—man, woman, or child—able to dig up the
ground for planting, should be kept at work every moment of the day preparing a patch, however small.
What with ploughing, spading and hoeing up ground,

with the labor of the troops and Indians, you must endeavor to get in at least three thousand acres. It will surprise you to see how much can be done if the bands are properly organized, and all the officers go out and set the example of industry. The very existence of the Indians will depend upon it, and they should understand that now.

The greatest problem was not organizing bands of laborers but obtaining implements. The tough virgin sod of the Llano Estacado could not be turned by ordinary plows. Carleton managed to acquire two large breaking plows in Colorado and arranged to have others constructed by blacksmiths at Fort Union, but he could secure only fifty spades and a small number of hoes. Having no implements, hundreds of Navajos used sharp pieces of wood, rocks, and their bare hands to tear out mesquite roots and dig several miles of irrigation ditches. In the spring of 1865 the quota of three thousand acres set by Carleton—he would increase it to six thousand the next year—had been planted. By early summer wide fields of corn, wheat, beans, melons, and pumpkins spread out in beautiful green relief against the barren monotony of the surrounding plains.

In a few more weeks every stalk of corn had been destroyed by cutworms, or, as they were popularly called, army worms. The wheat still stood, but as it began to head out, tornado-force winds flattened it and heavy rains completed the ruination. And so it would be in the summer of 1866, in the summer of 1867, and in the spring of 1868: drought, rains, snow, hail striking in turn to defeat all the superhuman efforts, and crush every hope.

Nearly all the Indians were garbed in rags, were barefoot, and suffering greatly from exposure. Carleton conceived a plan for sheltering them in large adobe buildings. Men with long experience among the Navajos informed him that because of the great fear they held of Chindi, the god of death, the plan would not succeed; that it was the way of the Navajos to abandon any dwelling in which a person had died, and not even the force of arms would keep them in a building, no matter how comfortable it was, through which death had stalked.

Carleton rejected the counsel with a curse, and ordered the construction of a pueblo town. He prepared the layout for it: "The buildings should be but one story high, and face to the placitas. By a proper arrangement—dead wall on the outside . . . a very handsome and strong place could be made." He selected a site close to the *acequía madre*, where every family was to be given a garden plot. The Indians would spend their spare time "in putting up their houses, and by next winter all can be comfortably sheltered. Then to have trees planted to make shade, and I fancy there would be no Indian village in the world to compare with it in point of beauty."

The Indian department dubbed the projected housing development "Fair Carletonia," but the decision only increased Carleton's determination to proceed, and work on the large adobe barracks was started. In a few days it was abruptly halted when the leading chiefs announced that under no circumstances would their people consent to live in them. If a death occurred, and surely it would, all the Navajos inhabiting the building would quickly abandon it and be forced once more to suffer from the elements. If Carleton wanted to provide dwellings for them, let him construct hogans.

All efforts to persuade the Navajos to forsake their superstition were futile, and Carleton capitulated. He insisted, however, that they be concentrated in villages, which he believed to be the only sensible solution to the housing problem. The Navajos would be "permitted to live in their traditional hogans, but these would be placed in uniform rows with good intervals and wide streets. One end of each row would be left open for those Indians desiring to move. Then when death struck, a family could immediately destroy their home and move to the end of their row, where a new building would be erected."

One of Carleton's strongest opponents was the New Mexico Superintendent of Indian Affairs, Dr. Michael Steck. Although Steck favored the reservation system in general, he thought the resources of Bosque Redondo sufficient to meet the needs of no more than a few hundred Apaches. Yet Carleton was proposing to confine there more than ten thousand Navajos as well. Steck advocated establishing an adequate reservation for the Navajos in their homeland.

Carleton brushed Steck aside as he would a fly. Steck retaliated by instructing all agents, including Lorenzo Lababie, Apache agent at Fort Sumner, to assume no responsibility until a "positive arrangement" had been made with the War Department to furnish enough supplies to sustain the Navajos. Then he went to Washington to confer on the matter with his superiors.

Burning with resentment, Carleton charged that Steck and his Indian Bureau cohorts were attempting to stifle all western progress, to stop the advance of civilization, and to frustrate him in his struggle to open the wilderness to development. "By the subjugation and colonization of the Navajo tribe," he contended, "we gain for civilization their whole country, which is much larger in extent than the state of Ohio; and besides being the best pastoral region between the two oceans, it is said to abound in precious as well as useful metals."

As early as the spring of 1864, the uproar over the reservation on the Pecos and reports on the plight of the Navajos had attracted the attention of some members of Congress. An emergency appropriation of $100,000 had been made "to aid in the settlement, subsistence and support of the Navajo Indians." Responsibility for the purchase and delivery of the needed goods was given to the Indian department.

After a hazardous crossing of the plains, the long-awaited supply train reached Fort Sumner as the year 1865 began. Three quartermaster officers were assigned to inventory the supplies and supervise their distribution. The elation that Carleton and his aides had harbored for months was suddenly dispersed by gloom. Wagons were loaded with nails, iron, blacksmith forges, and many types of tools of no use to Indians, even if they had known how to use them. Most of the provisions were of inferior quality, and some of them were spoiled to such an extent that they could not be saved. The inspecting officers found that, according to a manifest, the Indian Bureau buyers had paid $18.50 a pair for blankets of poorer quality than blankets supplied by the quartermaster department for $5.85 a pair, and that other goods had been purchased at similarly exorbitant prices.

The quartermaster estimated that the entire cargo of the supply train had a true value of approximately $30,000. Thus, $70,000 of the $100,000 appropriation had been either wasted or carried off in the channels of corruption that permeated the Bureau of Indian Affairs.

Shortly afterward, Carleton's own administration was rocked by a similar scandal. An investigation revealed that two captains had been selling government property, plows, shovels, pickaxes, hoes, cattle, and bags of grain, to Apache agent Lababie. Lababie had established himself on a sizable ranch, and in addition to the illegal purchases from the captains he had stolen cattle bearing a federal brand and driven off sheep owned by Navajos and Apaches. The captains received dishonorable discharges, and Carleton ordered the agent to leave the reservation. Lababie departed, but not far. Following orders from Steck, he re-established both his agency and his ranch headquarters only a short distance outside the reservation. It was Steck's contention, and he so reported to Indian Commissioner W. P. Dole, that the charges of malfeasance made by the quartermaster and the accusations against Lababie had been inspired by Carleton only for the purpose of embarrassing the Indian Bureau.

The defeat of the Confederacy brought into sharper focus the national questions arising out of the growing western turmoil, the most urgent of which was seen as the "Indian Barrier" impeding the development of agricultural and mineral resources. In 1865 Congress named Senator James R. Doolittle chairman of a joint special committee to study and report on conditions among the Indians. Hearings were conducted in various places, one of them New Mexico, and a vast amount of testimony was amassed.

Simultaneously Carleton was brought under scathing fire from numerous prominent citizens, civil officials, and editors, some of whom had only recently joined the ranks of his critics. While the attacks leveled against him differed in aspect, through most of them ran detectable threads suggestive of their common underlying motive.

A territorial judge charged that Carleton had refused to meet the Navajos in council to consider a peace pact, even though the Navajo delegation requesting the meeting was composed of headmen representing the entire tribe. Thus, Carleton had prevented a solution of the grave Navajo problem. The judge further accused him of admitting privately that the Navajos were not the "formidable nation of savages" that he "had been trying to make the government and the people believe them to be." Yet Carleton insisted on holding them on the brink of starvation in a disease-ridden concentration camp.

Glad of any opportunity to snipe at Carleton, Steck informed Indian Commissioner Dole that on a recent inspection trip to Bosque Redondo he had become "more than ever satisfied that the reservation will be a failure for so large a number of Indians. The Navajos are now leaving in small parties. They are all dissatisfied and can only be kept upon the Pecos by force."

Agent Steck also was pleased to report that Carleton was not only having troubles with runaways but with a new rationing system. In an effort to maintain strict control over provisions and at the same time facilitate distribution, Carleton had ordered the post quartermaster to make ration tickets of heavy cardboard and give one to each Indian. Within a few days the number of rations issued had soared greatly above normal. All cardboard tickets were withdrawn and counted, and it was found that hundreds were counterfeit. Carleton had then issued metal disks stamped with designs and the letters U.S. The forges and metal working tools sent out by the Indian Bureau were of some value to the Navajos, after all. Within a fortnight more than three thousand fraudulent ration disks were in circulation. Carleton had them collected, and appealed to Washington "for tickets of such intricate design as to be impossible to copy." He never received them.

From several sources came complaints about the immense cost of feeding degraded and lazy Indians who paid no taxes and for whose hands "no spade could be designed to fit." One report claimed—without supporting documentation—that $452,356.98 had been spent to feed Navajos from March to September 1865. "The cost for the previous year averaged higher than this, but exact figures cannot be given, on account of the large number of stores transferred to the War Department from other departments and not reported as to value. *All this time it was well known they could support themselves in their own country."* (italics added)

Some complainants estimated that the staggering sum of four million dollars a year would have to be appropriated to keep the Navajos at Bosque Redondo, and asserted that it would be more economical to turn them free and let whatever fate might befall them solve the dilemma. The Santa Fe *New Mexican* thought that the Navajos "cannot be subsisted on less than one pound of beef and one pound of flour per day each. The cost of these two articles alone, delivered at the reservation, will be about forty cents . . . about $2,-336,000 per year for the whole tribe." The *New Mexican's* editor also advocated removing the Navajos from Bosque Redondo, but not only because of the heavy burden on taxpayers: cattlemen were trailing immense herds onto the vast grassy plains of eastern New Mexico, and sheep raisers coveted the ranges of the Navajo country. Indians were a nuisance, and reservations took away from "civilized Americans" large areas that justifiably belonged to them and not to bands of savages. The stockmen were fearful that new reservations would be created.

At one time the *New Mexican* had given its unqualified support to Carleton's program, but now it suddenly reversed its policy. The attitude of the cattlemen, not a few of whom were members of the legislature, was graphically revealed in one of the paper's editorial columns:

The white man should not be overlooked or his rights ignored, nor should every interest of the territory be permitted to suffer because one man [General Carleton] in opposition to the almost unanimous will of the people, conceived the idea of bringing the curse to their prosperity into our midst; making one of our most fertile valleys [Bosque Redondo?] as asylum for the In-

dians of *another territory*; removing them from 300 to
400 miles east *against the current of immigration and
improvement.*

The italicized words are significant. The *New Mexican*
was endorsing the position taken by the stockmen and others
that inasmuch as most of the Navajos had dwelt in Arizona,
they should be removed to that territory and left to support
themselves as best they could in the deserts along the Little
Colorado and lower San Juan rivers.

# 9

LONG BEFORE THE final report of the Doolittle Commission was published, the nature of the recommendations it would make was known in Washington. Only a few weeks after the hearing in New Mexico the commission had requested the Interior Department to make a separate study of Bosque Redondo, preparatory to placing the Navajos under the control of civil authorities. Secretary of the Interior James Harlan delegated the duty to special Indian agent Julius K. Graves, who arrived at Fort Sumner in December 1865. A few months later he submitted a report.

The evidence gathered in these two investigations not only depicted with shocking force the miserable condition of the Navajos, but vividly recounted dangers to them originating outside the reservation:

- Both peonage and Indian slavery continued to exist.
- Peonage was authorized by a New Mexico statute, which provided that peons receive a wage of at least five

dollars a month, with which they had to support themselves. This, of course, was impossible. As peons were furnished necessities by their masters, their indebtedness constantly increased. The result was servitude from which they had no hope of escaping.

• Although the enslavement of Indians was illegal, it was widely practiced. Governors, military officers, members of the legislature, civil officials, businessmen, ranchers, Indian agents, and at least one justice of the highest court held Navajo slaves. The great majority of them were women and children taken in raids conducted by New Mexicans and itinerant traders. At least five hundred Navajo slaves were held in Santa Fe, and several thousand more throughout the territories of New Mexico and Arizona. As many of these Navajos had been captives for years, their children were born in bondage and were sold on the market like animals by owners who did not wish to keep them. Slave hunters continued to hunt through the Navajo country for more "merchandise."

• Slavery provoked the Navajos to continued acts of vengeance. Navajos were endowed, no less than other peoples, with the attributes of love and affection, and when robbed of their children experienced the deepest sorrow.

• The commissary of the War Department had ordered that provisions of poor quality that were unsuitable as food for soldiers should be sent to feed Indians at Bosque Redondo.

• Large quantities of supplies and equipment disappeared between the point of purchase and Fort Sumner.

• Carleton had stated that one of the reasons he had selected Bosque Redondo was that it would be a buffer zone between plains tribes and New Mexico settlements. This belief proved to be erroneous. For more than a year the reservation had suffered from raids by Comanches.

- Navajos who owned sheep, cattle, and horses had been encouraged to take them to Bosque Redondo. Most of these animals, as well as stock provided by the quartermaster, had been driven off by Comanches and not infrequently by New Mexicans.

- The Navajos, who had no arms or other means of protecting either their herds or themselves, lived in mortal terror of the Comanches. On one occasion, twenty Navajos attempting to recover stock stolen from them were murdered by a raiding party composed of Comanches and New Mexican rustlers.

- More than a thousand Navajos had slipped away. Numbers of them died of starvation while attempting to reach their homeland beyond the Chuska Mountains. Others survived only by stealing sheep and goats from ranches. Many more would have run away had horses been available to them. Carleton sent troops to recapture the runaways with orders to shoot any who refused to return.

- The Fort Sumner medical officer reported that cases of syphilis far outnumbered those of other afflictions, with the exception of malnutrition. The hospital provided for the Navajos consisted of nine small rooms, four of which were used as a surgery, kitchen, mess, and sleeping quarters for attendants. The entire building was on the verge of collapse. The roof leaked. Navajos feared to enter it, for people had died in it. Moreover, they were haunted by the memory of seeing sick men and women shot to death by soldiers on the Long Walk.

- The water of the Pecos was highly impregnated with alkali and other chemicals that made it unfit for human consumption, and it was the cause of dysentery, which weakened the Navajos and made them incapable of throwing off other ailments.

- All fuel adjacent to Fort Sumner had been used, and

Navajos were forced to travel as much as twenty miles for mesquite roots and bear them on galled and lacerated backs that distance to their homes. To obtain wood for the post, details were sent with wagons to the nearest groves, some fifty miles distant. The cost of supplying the garrison alone with adequate fuel was estimated at nearly $3,000 a month. Lumber and building materials had to be hauled more than a hundred miles, from Fort Union.

• Both soil and water were unsuitable for agriculture. The cultivation of large areas could not be achieved, and therefore the Navajos could not be sustained in this manner.

• The people of New Mexico, especially the stock raisers, were advocating the removal of all Indians from the territory. This would be neither feasible nor just. Reservations should be established for the various tribes, preferably in or adjacent to their homelands. The Navajo country should be examined with a view to establishing a reservation in an area of adequate fuel, water, and arable soil.

• The sum of $100,000 appropriated annually by Congress for the Navajos was enough to pay for only a small portion of their basic needs.

• The War Department had no acceptable excuse for failing to care properly for the Navajos. It was a fundamental of the American system that people restrained of their liberty or deprived of their civil rights for the purpose of being benefited should in fact be benefited, or at least not be subjected to further injury.

Even before the findings of the Doolittle Commission and agent Graves were made known, the subject of Indian slavery had come under fire from Senator Charles Sumner of Massachusetts in a speech in which he denounced Carleton and Governor Connelly for their failure to destroy the iniquitous system. President Andrew Johnson had been in office less than two months when he responded to the question with firm resolve:

> It has been represented to me in a communication from the Secretary of the Interior that Indians in New Mexico have been seized and reduced into slavery; and it is recommended that the authority of the Executive branch of the Government should be exercised for the effectual suppression of a practice which is alike in violation of the rights of the Indians, and the provisions of the Organic law of said Territory.
>
> Concurring in this recommendation I do hereby order that the heads of the several Executive Departments do enjoin upon their subordinates, agents and employes under their respective orders, or supervision of that Territory, to discontinue the practice aforesaid, and to take all lawful means to suppress the same.

That full compliance with Mr. Johnson's order had not occurred was made clear by both Doolittle and Graves. Their findings, however, gave stimulus to efforts to wipe out both peonage and Indian bondage. Because of the stubborn resistance of the citizens of New Mexico, three more years would pass before success was achieved. The territory's congressional delegate, José Francisco Chavez, owned numerous Indian slaves. A congressional act that prohibited slavery was largely ignored, the New Mexicans refusing to abandon a tradition that had endured since the time of Spanish colonization of the province. Attempts by the federal district attorney to enforce the law through legal procedures failed. Hundreds of people refused to answer summonses to appear before a grand jury. Had they appeared, nothing would have been accomplished, for the jurors themselves were slaveowners.

Not until authority to enforce the federal statutes prohibiting all forms of peonage or slavery had been placed in
the hands of General William Tecumseh Sherman were the
"barbarous and inhuman practices" halted. The methods he
employed were swift and effective:

(1) Persons holding Indian slaves would be arrested and
thrown into jail;

(2) Officers were instructed to inform all persons held in
bondage that they could be freed by appearing before a
federal court;

(3) Army funds would be provided to assist Indians in
locating relatives taken captive by New Mexicans or other
persons;

(4) All freed slaves would be escorted in safety to their
former homes at army expense.

Carleton made a strenuous attempt to defeat the move to
place the Navajos under civil authorities, writing the Adjutant General:

> I beg to express the opinion that the whole of this
> matter . . . be left in the hands of the War Department.
> I know and have so written, that to do this will impose
> a burden upon the military not properly belonging to
> them . . . but if this matter passes out of the hands
> which hold the power there will be complications, em-
> barrassment, misunderstanding, etc., which will result,
> I fear, in . . . the positive failure of the important mea-
> sure of fixing forever the Navajo tribe of Indians upon
> a reservation.

New Mexicans, especially the stockmen, had had all they
wanted of Carleton. In a memorial addressed to President
Johnson, the territorial assembly charged that Carleton had
accused New Mexicans of depredations committed by Nav-

ajos and had failed in his sworn duty to suppress the Indian menace. The assembly advocated that he be replaced by a commander who would protect the territory and uphold the rights of respectable white citizens.

Whether the memorial was effective in sealing Carleton's doom is not a matter of public record, but in September 1866 he was removed by Secretary of War Edwin M. Stanton and sent to Louisiana. With unconcealed elation the *New Mexican* informed its readers: "Our territory will be relieved from the presence of this man, who has so long lorded it amongst us."

The Washington machinery, festooned with red tape, laboriously turned out decisions. In 1866 General U. S. Grant, commander in chief of the army, directed the commander of the Department of Missouri, General Sherman, to "issue orders immediately" to the newly appointed commander of military forces in New Mexico, General G. W. Getty, to surrender control of the Navajo Indians to the Bureau of Indian Affairs of the Department of the Interior.

A. Baldwin Norton, a political appointee from Ohio, had taken over the duties of Indian Superintendent of New Mexico. If the only Indians with whom Norton was acquainted were of the wooden tobacco-store variety, the same thing was not true of Theodore H. Dodd, a former colonel in the frontier service, who would serve him as agent for the Navajos. Dodd would soon show himself to be an efficient administrator, a man of extraordinary energy, and a true friend of the Navajos.

After taking office at Bosque Redondo, Dodd compiled a list of equipment and personal articles most urgently needed by the Indians. Understanding the futility of attempting to obtain the goods promptly through regular channels, he went to Washington, and there demonstrated a rare ability to cut red tape. He obtained a letter of credit authorizing him to purchase the articles. The buying was done in St. Louis. With wagons drawn by yoked oxen and containing a cargo of agricultural implements, blankets, clothing, and utensils of various kinds, Dodd crossed the plains to Bosque Redondo. None of his purchases mysteriously disappeared en route, a calamity that customarily befell most Indian supply trains.

The War Department deliberately delayed execution of General Grant's orders, taking the position that it should conduct a final investigation at Bosque Redondo before relinquishing its control over the Navajos. The officer assigned to the task was a lieutenant, but if he lacked experience in such matters he believed what he saw with his own eyes. In a forthright report he reiterated many of the findings of special agent Graves and the Doolittle Commission, and recommended that the Navajos be moved as rapidly as possible from Bosque Redondo to a "suitable location" with sufficient natural resources for their needs.

The War Department seized on the words "suitable location" to invoke a further delay. What did the lieutenant mean by them? What was a suitable location? The lieutenant had no answer. The War Department pointed out that General Sherman had suggested the Navajos be removed to Oklahoma. The Interior Department announced that it favored a reservation in the Navajo country, and eventually won the argument. Congress, however, not knowing which proposal would prevail, had made only the customary annual appropriation of $100,000 for Bosque Redondo. Dodd saw the situation as opening the door to a terrible disaster, and angrily wrote the Indian Bureau that the "idea of trying to subsist them for one year for $100,000 is ridiculous." The government must either feed the Navajos properly "or turn them loose," and if they were turned loose to roam over the territory, "they will again commence stealing from the flocks of their old enemies." The result would be "another Navajo war which will cost the Government millions."

While Washington officials wrangled and dragged their feet, and Norton and Dodd waited helplessly in New Mexico for orders to assume responsibility for the Navajos, Congress appointed another commission to study western Indian problems and negotiate new peace treaties with the various tribes. The speed with which this group acted had few, if any, precedents in the annals of the government. Perhaps the reason was that almost everything the members found out had been found out before, and almost everything they elected to do had been done before. After a western trip in the summer of 1867, the commissioners recommended that a reservation be established for the Navajos in their own country.

Not until late in 1867 did General Getty, Superintendent Norton, and agent Dodd receive the instructions that would enable them to take the necessary preliminary steps for transferring jurisdiction over the Navajos from military to civil authorities. General Grant's orders had been held up nine months by the machinations of the War Department.

For nearly seven more months the chaos on the Pecos continued. In numerous councils held during the long winter Dodd reassured the Navajos that relief from their hunger and misery would come, but as they gazed across the frozen white plains their "eyes were empty." By the spring of 1868 the hope the Navajos had harbored in the previous fall was all but gone.

On May 29, 1868, a dozen army vehicles convoyed by cavalry came to a halt before the headquarters of Fort Sumner. As cannon roared in salute, the post commander hurried forward to greet General Sherman and Colonel Samuel F. Tappan. Sherman wasted no time in formalities. He was there for one purpose: to negotiate a peace treaty with the Navajos, remove them to a suitable reservation, close Fort Sumner as a military post, and abandon Bosque Redondo. He requested that Dodd submit a "status report" with recommendations and that Navajo leaders be summoned to a council. Neither order was difficult to carry out, for the agent and all the Navajo headmen were waiting almost within reach of his crisp voice.

Dodd was prepared. There were, he informed Sherman, according to a recent head count, 7,304 Navajo men, women, and children at Bosque Redondo. An estimated two thousand had died since the tribe had been confined there, and about nine hundred had escaped. Several hundred others had disappeared, and it had not been determined whether they had returned to their homeland or had perished from starvation or at the hands of human enemies.

The Navajos owned 21 mules, 940 sheep, about 1,000 goats, and approximately 1,500 horses, a thousand of which they had recently recovered from Comanches who had stolen them. Before being subdued, the Navajos had owned more than 200,000 sheep, thousands of goats, and hundreds of horses and mules.

In their own country they had managed to raise very good crops. "They are," said Dodd, "acquainted with the principles of irrigation and are quite skilfull in making *acequías.*"

Dodd was aware of Sherman's suggestion that the Navajos be removed to Oklahoma (Indian Territory), and bluntly stated his conviction that

> if they are not permitted to return to their own country . . . many will stealthily return and in doing so commit depredations upon the people of N.M. and thus keep up a state of insecurity. . . . It would be better for the Navajos and the people of N.M. and a saving to the Government & in the end more likely to succeed in

civilizing and making them self-sustaining to locate them on a good reservation west of the Rio Grande.

Dodd thought the Navajos "the best material in the country for rapid progress in agriculture" and described them as "far in advance of the other tribes in manufacturing blankets, bridles, saddles and other articles, yet they are Savages and extremely superstitious" and many of them were "lazy, indolent and thieving people who will have to be watched constantly, and if they commit depredations, punished."

He called Sherman's attention to an issue to which he thought the government had not given sufficient attention, stating: "The Utah Indians have been enemies of the Navajos for many years. It is very important that a treaty of peace be made between these tribes, otherwise the Utah Indians will constantly be making raids upon the settlements of the Navajos, stealing their children and stock."

Finally, Dodd proposed that the Navajos "be furnished at least with 40,000 head of sheep and goats . . . that one physician, one blacksmith and one carpenter be employed and shops be created" on their new reservation.

Sherman agreed in general with Dodd's recommendations, and stated he would make every effort to see that they were carried out.

With his aides and Colonel Tappan, post officers, and interpreters beside him, General Sherman told the assembled Navajo headmen: "We are here for the purpose of learning and knowing all about your condition and we wish to hear from you the truth and nothing but the truth."

The general heard what other investigators and agents had long heard.*

HEADMEN: We have done wrong but we have learned

* The following are excerpts from the proceedings of several councils, as recorded by interpreters.

better and if allowed to return to our mountain homes, we will behave ourselves well.

HEADMAN: Cage the badger and he will try to break from his prison and try to regain his native hole. Chain the eagle to the ground—he will strive to gain his freedom, and though he fails, he will lift his head and look up to the sky which is home—and we want to return to our mountains and plains.

HEADMAN: When the Navajos were first created, four mountains and four rivers were pointed out to us, inside of which we should live, that was to be our country and was given us by the First Woman of the Navajo tribe.

HEADMAN: Here at Bosque Redondo we never refused to do everything we were told to do. This ground is not productive. We plant but it does not yield. We have done all we could possibly do but found it to be labor in vain. We know how to irrigate and farm, still we cannot raise a crop here.

HEADMAN: There were a great many of us who were once well off. Now they have nothing in their houses to sleep on except gunny sacks.

Hour after hour the general listened to dignified men speaking with deadly seriousness, revealing only in their eyes the emotion surging within them, recounting the reasons why Bosque Redondo was a living hell to them, recounting their sufferings, pouring forth fact after fact about their condition, submitting plea after plea to be allowed to return to their homeland, delivering promise after promise that they would live in peace.

Barboncito was selected by the headmen to be the chief negotiator.

BARBONCITO: We have all declared that we do not want to remain here any longer. If we are taken back to our country, we will call you our father and mother. I am speaking for the whole tribe, for their animals from the horse to the dog, also the unborn. It appears to me that the General commands the whole thing as a god. I hope therefore he will do all he can for us. This hope goes in at my feet and out at my mouth. I am speaking to you now as if I were speaking to a spirit.

SHERMAN: The world is big enough for all the people it contains and all should live at peace with their neighbors. We want to do what is right, right to you, and right for us. If you will live at peace with your neighbor we will see that your neighbors will be at peace with you. We have a map here which if Barboncito can understand I would like to show him a few points on it, show him his own country, places inhabited by other Indians, the four mountains spoken of and old Fort Defiance. If you do not want to go to the Arkansas, where corn can be raised without irrigation and the land and grass are good, then we will discuss going back to your own country, and if we agree we will make a boundary line outside of which you must not go except for the purpose of trading. If people trouble you, you must go to the nearest military post and report to the Commanding Officer, who will punish those who trouble you. The Army will do the fighting. If the Utes come into your country with guns you of course can drive them out but you must not follow beyond the boundary line. You can come to the [New] Mexican towns to trade.

BARBONCITO: I hope to God you will not ask us to go to any other country except our own. It might turn out another Bosque Redondo. They told us this was a good place when we came here, but it is not.

SHERMAN: We merely made the proposition to send you to the Lower Arkansas country for you to think seriously over it. I want you to assemble again tomorrow, and I want the whole tribe to delegate ten men to come forward and settle about the boundary line of your own country, which will be reduced to writing and signed by those ten men.

BARBONCITO: We are very well pleased.

The ancient Ganado Mucho arose and spoke with emotion he was unable to conceal.

GANADO MUCHO: Let us go home to our mountains. Let us see our flocks feeding in the valleys, and let us ride again where we can smell the sage and know of hidden hogans by the smell of piñon smoke. Let us go where we can build our homes in solitude and privacy and live again as men, not animals. Let us be free to build a better way of life and learn to live in peace where the red buttes rise from the desert sands, and eagles sweep across the sky. Let us go home. We have learned not to kill and not to steal from the flocks of others. Here we have nothing. Our children grow up in ugliness and death. Let us go home.

KIT CARSON: General, I'm not so sure the Great Spirit means for us whites to take over Indian lands. I brought this proud people to this place because they would not listen to Washington. Now they have heard, and three thousand died here while they were hearing. Let me lead them back while they still have the will to live.

BARBONCITO: We are willing to abide by whatever orders are given us. After we get back to our country it will brighten up again, and the Navajos will be as happy and peaceful as the land.

SHERMAN: One has pity on you. Go slowly. I will help you.

The document signed on June 1, 1868, by representatives of the United States government and the Navajos was a form prepared by the Department of State. Several of its thirteen articles were standard provisions suitable for inclusion in any peace treaty consummated with a foreign nation of Indians.* Other articles contained blank spaces in which negotiators were to insert geographical, monetary, and other details specifically applicable to the case under consideration. Even these provisions, however, had been assigned a "range of acceptability" in Washington after being thoroughly discussed in the sanctums of the State, War, and Interior departments. The actual powers of federal negotiators, therefore, were invariably subject to previously established restrictions. Indeed, all they had to do at Bosque Redondo to complete the long paper—as the Navajos called the treaty—was to insert the name "Navajo" a total of five times and append certain numerals and the word "dollars" denoting the amounts of provisions and supplies to be furnished during a specified number of years by the Bureau of Indian Affairs.

Article II established a reservation

bounded on the north by the 37th degree of north latitude, south by an east and west line passing through the site of old Fort Defiance, in Cañon Bonito, east by the parallel of longitude which, if prolonged south, would pass through old Fort Lyon, or the Ojo-de-oso, Bear Spring, and west by a parallel of longitude about 109°30' west of Greenwich, provided it embraces the outlet of the Cañon-de-Chilly, which cañon is to be all included in this reservation.

This area contained approximately 3.5 million acres, but its water resources were sufficient for only a comparatively small number of people. It comprised only a fifth of the country in which the Navajos previously had found it neces-

* An 1871 act of Congress ended treaty making between the federal government and Indian tribes and removed the tribes from the category of sovereign nations.

sary to live in order to obtain enough irrigable land and grazing range to support themselves. Now, under the treaty, the entire tribe, with the exception of the Cebolletas, were to be confined in it. Sherman had agreed to allow the Cebolletas, or "Enemy Navajos"—the band of the traitor Sandoval—to remain in their old homes among the New Mexicans.

Article V provided that if any Navajo

> being the head of a family, shall desire to commence farming, he shall have the privilege to select . . . a tract of land within said reservation, not exceeding one hundred and sixty acres in extent. . . . Any person over eighteen years of age, not being the head of the family, may in like manner select . . . a quantity of land, not exceeding eighty acres in extent.

Obviously the treaty authors labored under the delusion that all of the reservation, or at least the greater part of it, was arable land. They were applying the principles of the Homestead Law, which made no differentiation between lands in areas of heavy precipitation and lands in areas of scant rainfall. In the Navajo country 160 acres of irrigable land comprised a veritable kingdom, and would supply twenty or more families with adequate grain, fruit, and vegetables. Few farms of this description were to be found, and if each of them was legally awarded to one person, hundreds of other people would be unable to grow the food they must have to survive. The understanding that in the arid Southwest *he who controlled the water controlled all* apparently had not seeped into the heads of the learned lawmakers who gazed from their office windows at the lush estates along the Potomac. Even when they were apprised of the facts in a case, they adamantly adhered to popular theorems—such as *free land for free men*, considered to be the mortar in the foundation of the republic. Communal

enterprises were an invention of foreign radicals—or Indians
—and could not be tolerated in a democratic system, no
matter what the circumstances.

When "a head of a family" had selected the land he
wished to farm and had convinced the Indian agent that
he would cultivate it "in good faith," he was entitled to receive "seeds and agricultural implements, for the first year,
not exceeding in value one hundred dollars," and for each
of the next two years seeds and implements "to the value
of twenty-five dollars."

Article VI, which was to be found in countless Indian
treaties, was contrived to illustrate the Great White Father's
profound desire to provide for his ignorant red wards an
opportunity to develop and progress. Within a few years it
would become a greater source of discord than any other
provision, except that which delineated the reservation
boundaries. Article VI said:

> In order to insure the civilization of the Indians en-
> tering into this treaty, the necessity of education is ad-
> mitted, especially of such of them as may be settled
> on said agricultural parts of this reservation, and they
> therefore pledge themselves to compel their children,
> male and female, between the ages of six and sixteen
> years, to attend school; *and it is hereby made the duty
> of the agent for said Indians to see that this stipulation
> is strictly complied with;* and the United States agrees
> that, *for every thirty children* between said ages who
> can be *induced* or *compelled* to attend school, *a house
> shall be provided,* and a teacher competent to teach
> the elementary branches of an *English education* shall
> be furnished, who will reside among said Indians, and
> faithfully discharge his or her duties as a teacher.

The provisions of this article to continue for *not less than ten years.* *

In Article VIII the United States agreed to deliver to the Navajos,

> on the first day of September of each year for ten years, the following articles, to wit:
>
> Such articles of clothing, goods, or raw materials in lieu thereof . . . not exceeding in value five dollars per Indian—each Indian being encouraged to manufacture their own clothing, blankets, etc., to be furnished with no article they can manufacture themselves.
>
> And in addition . . . the sum of ten dollars . . . for a period of ten years, for each person who engages in farming or mechanical pursuits, to be used by the Commissioner of Indian Affairs in the purchase of such articles as from time to time the condition and the necessities of the Indians may indicate to be proper. . . . If at any time within the ten years it shall appear that the money needed for clothing . . . can be appropriated to better uses . . . the Commissioner of Indian Affairs may change the appropriation to other purposes.

Perhaps no language could have been precise enough to prevent malfeasance on the part of Indian Bureau officials, but the loose phraseology of Article VIII was a standing invitation to almost everyone involved in Indian affairs to engage in dishonest practices. It effectively swept aside all barriers to corruption, with the exception of the variable characteristic called conscience, a force that was rarely exhibited during the ensuing two decades.

* *The words I have italicized would be the basis of numerous troubles in the future.*

The Navajos were to be supplied with fifteen thousand sheep and goats. Five hundred cattle and a million pounds of corn would be sent to Fort Defiance "for the relief of the needy during the coming winter." All costs of the return journey were to be borne by the government, and soldiers were to escort them to the new reservation headquarters.

Within a few days of the signing of the treaty, long columns of Navajos were moving westward from Bosque Redondo. The crippled, the ailing, and the old were carried in army wagons. Squaws with several children clinging to them rode on bony horses. More than seven thousand men, women, and children were on the dusty, rutted, hot trail that snaked through the red hills and yellow arroyos toward the Rio Grande. All were undernourished, all were ragged, but in their eyes was reflected the new hope and the new courage that filled their hearts.

In their desperate straits, the Navajos doubtlessly would have signed any piece of paper placed before them and would have agreed, as they did, to terms not only indisputably unfavorable to them but, in some instances, totally infeasible and absurd.

The twenty-nine headmen who made their marks on the last page of the Bosque Redondo treaty were thinking only of regaining freedom for themselves and their people. General Sherman, Colonel Tappan, and the other government signers were thinking only of achieving peace. None of the participants could have been aware that he was signing a document of transcending historical importance. But in the years to come that would be recognized as an unquestionable, unalterable truth.

The treaty of Bosque Redondo, ratified by the Senate and signed by President Andrew Johnson in the summer of 1868, would be the most enduring and most significant agreement of all the hundreds consummated between the United States and American Indians. Not only did it mark the beginning of the era of permanent peace in the Navajo country, but it opened the gate through which a destitute and dispirited people would pass to find new character, new unity, new strength—a new destiny.

# 10

THEY WENT BACK TO devastated fields and ruined hogans. The orchards were crooked rows of blackened stumps. Corn and fruits and vegetables could not reseed themselves, but that was not true of other valuable foods. Kit Carson's war machine had not been able to destroy native plants or control rainfall, and wild tubers, berries, and herbs were plentiful. Rabbits and squirrels and prairie dogs had enjoyed a prolific four years unmolested in the empty areas, except by their natural enemies, and deer were thick in the upland forests. On the ranges sweeping against the sky the grasses stood waiting in luxuriant growth for new herds to crop them.

To the Navajos it was a paradise on earth, and they spread out like a suddenly created stream of water finding myriad crevices through which to trickle and vanish. Man-made boundaries, lines on maps, meant little or nothing to them. Most of the families wanted to return to the places where they had dwelt before the Long Walk, but there were reasons why many of them were delayed for nearly two years in reaching their destinations. They needed rations, blankets, and clothing, and seeds and corn, both to eat and to plant, and these things could be obtained only at Fort Wingate, and later at the Navajo Agency at Bonito Canyon (Fort Defiance), and they were forced to remain near these posts if they were to get them. But they never stopped thinking about getting home, of living again in familiar places.

Others—a great many of them—did not wait at the posts to get anything. They disappeared, families and clans clinging together as best they could, putting the world of the soldiers behind them as rapidly as possible. On they pushed, north beyond Shiprock, by Teec Nos Pos, beyond Red Rock Valley and Sehlagaidesa Canyon. And they went west far beyond Canyon de Chelly and Beautiful Valley, past Ganada Mesa and Black Mountain, on beyond the Hopi country to Moenkopi. Some of them moved on as if they never intended to stop, northwestward toward Kayenta and Monument Valley and Navajo Mountain to the San Juan River. Or south to Klagetoh and the Painted Desert and on to Red Lake. Into a thousand canyons, big and little, into a thousand valleys, hidden and open, they moved, determined to survive somehow, preferring to suffer hunger and defy death than live under the domination of white men.

But not all the places they went were devoid of human life. In some places they were welcomed by Navajos who had slipped out of the noose Carson had thrown. He himself had estimated that at least three and perhaps four thousand had avoided capture. With small herds and their belongings they had disappeared into the wilderness beyond the reach of any soldiers, and there they had lived, and even prospered, for four years or more, planting new fields, carefully conserving and breeding their flocks, storing grain, never wavering in their belief that the others would come back. And when the others came back, clan members sought out their kin and gave them blankets and skins and corn to plant and helped them build new hogans or took them into their own.

Around piñon fires throughout a vast region, large parts of it unknown to white men, drums beat under the welling stars in the chants of the Enemy Way, the feather dance, the victory dance, the corn-grinding dance, and the Yeibe-chai. The squaws could cook again in their own ways, no longer struggling with the strange and tasteless food parceled out at Bosque Redondo, and there were substantial and delicious meals of mutton, wild roots and herbs, sliced wild potatoes, corn meal mixed with sheep's blood and boiled in intestines, and kneeling-down bread made of freshly ground corn and baked in shucks, truly a great delicacy. And medicine bundles, sand paintings, and melodious songs and tone poems drove the evil from racked bodies.

They were the fortunate ones, the people who received help from relatives. But there was a limit to these resources; there was far from enough for all. More than half of those who had returned from Bosque Redondo were forced to subsist on the rations handed out to them at Fort Defiance. Survival was a day-to-day matter for them, and to have been absent on "ration day"—which came once a week—would have driven them to the brink of starvation. As it was, they were often on that brink, through no fault of their own.

Supplies never exceeded dire needs. Orders were not filled on time, sometimes because the supplies requested were not in stock, but more often because they were not correctly dated, or a signature had been omitted, or arithmetic was in error. Not infrequently shipments had a way of disappearing before they were started toward their destinations.

Some weeks the big ox-drawn wagons that crawled out from Albuquerque were days late reaching Fort Defiance. Many weeks they did not bring enough, and Indians holding ration tickets were turned away with nothing. Some weeks they did not arrive at all. On such occasions, the unfortunate ones kept themselves barely alive on post garbage, rats, mice, rabbits, foxes, and badgers—if they were lucky enough to catch any—and the meat of beloved horses saved not a few lives.

Not until late in the fall of 1869, more than sixteen months after the signing of the treaty, did the sheep promised by the government begin to arrive. They had been driven as far as three hundred miles over plains, mountains, and deserts from ranches in the vicinity of Fort Union, where they were purchased, and they were bony and half starved. But they were hardy little animals, the prolific Spanish churros that for more than two centuries had thrived on the sparse grasses and brush of New Mexico. They could recover rapidly from almost any ordeal, put fat meat on their bones and wool on their backs—that is, if they were given a chance. In the beginning most of them were eaten as soon as they arrived, but later, when there was more of other kinds of food—goats, cattle, and wheat—families slipped away with a few ewes and a ram to begin building a herd of their own.

The Bureau of Indian Affairs informed Congress it had purchased more than thirty-five thousand sheep, more than double the number the government had agreed to supply under the treaty. If that was true, more than half of them mysteriously vanished somewhere between Fort Union and Fort Defiance.

The Navajos spoke of agent Dodd, their good friend, as

Big Gopher. The origin of the name was not explained in the accounts of the time, but it was recorded that, harassed and overworked and grieving at the continued failure of the Indian Bureau to furnish sufficient supplies, Dodd's health failed. Five months after leaving Bosque Redondo he was laid to rest in the shabby Fort Defiance cemetery.

A replacement, J. C. French, was sent out from Santa Fe, but his tenure was short. Someone in Washington decided that Navajo affairs could be more efficiently handled by a military man. There was justification for the decision, at least in the reasoning of officials considering the problems from a distance of more than two thousand miles. The Navajos obviously had no intention of obeying the edict that they live within reservation boundaries. Dodd had failed to enforce this treaty provision. Navajos were wandering far and wide, and there were reports that livestock had been stolen from New Mexican ranchers. A man vested with the authority of both a civilian agent and a military commander would be in a position to exercise the greatest control over them—or so it was hoped.

The man given the two posts was Captain F. T. Bennett, commanding officer of a cavalry company at Fort Wingate (forty-five miles southeast of Fort Defiance), where troops assigned to duty in the Navajo country were stationed. Bennett was big, genial, and soft-spoken, and possessed a genuine desire to aid the Navajos, whose name for him was Big Belly. He understood, as had Dodd, that the Navajos could not support themselves on the reservation, and he made no attempt to hold them within its confines. If they were to become self-sustaining, they had to be allowed to find adequate grazing ranges and irrigable farmlands, and that they could accomplish only by spreading out over a vast territory.

Throughout the winter of 1868–69 Bennett badgered the Indian Bureau offices in Santa Fe and Albuquerque for grain and vegetable seeds. The quantity he received was much less than he had hoped for. He apportioned them as equably as he could, but many requests remained unfulfilled. Every Navajo seemed to be eager to plant crops, but in the end those who had received no seeds were no less fortunate than those who had spent weeks hoeing, sowing, and nurturing the growing plants. In June unseasonable snow and hail destroyed them. "They were the most sorrowful, discouraged, downhearted people that could be imagined," Bennett wrote headquarters. "Send more seeds."

So it was in ensuing years, drought, grasshoppers, floods, sleet, and snows taking their toll, the evil cycle only occasionally broken. Yet, each spring hopes rose anew and the planting went on, as it had for centuries. It took more than adverse weather to break the spirit of the Navajos. Not even the unholy alliance of weather and the bumbling, corrupt, heartless Indian Bureau could achieve that.

Dodd had warned that unless adequate rations, clothing, and tools were furnished to the Navajos, trouble could be expected. Bennett reiterated the warning several times. The chiefs advocated peace at all costs. The words of Barboncito typified their admonitions: "We lost everything. Tell that to your children. See that they do not fight. See that they work. Take an old ram and tie it to a tree. Watch how it breaks its horns and bruises its head, trying to get free. That is what will happen to us again if we fight Washington. Stay at home and be at peace."

But not all the fires could be extinguished. Hunger could not be banished by words. Poverty could not be cured by promises. And there were other forces to drive men to violence. There were the memories of the affluence the Navajos had once enjoyed, memories of the days of glory, the days of great adventure, when they were the supreme lords, the incomparable plunderers. In 1869 bands of Navajos, most of them hot-headed young warriors, stole livestock from New Mexican herds east of the reservation. In the next year bands crossed the San Juan and raided Mormon communities in Utah. In 1871 and 1872 the thefts continued, the raiders vanishing with stolen sheep, cattle, and horses into the remote canyons. Bennett made urgent appeals for emergency supplies, but they remained unanswered.

The chiefs, the Indian agents, and the military would have been more successful in halting Navajo depredations had it not been for troubles for which non-Indians were responsible. Among New Mexicans, from the highest territorial officials down to the smallest farmers, hatred for the Navajos continued to smolder, and frequently broke into flame. They were bitter against the federal government for permitting the Navajos to return from Bosque Redondo instead of moving them to the lower Arkansas, or some other place equally remote from the Rio Grande. New Mexican stockmen encroached on reservation grazing lands, and if driven off by Navajo herdsmen reported that they had been attacked by war parties and that their stock had been stolen by Navajo raiders. In most instances their complaints were without foundation.

Navajos were murdered as they rode through the country. On one occasion five men, a woman, and a child were shot to death by New Mexican vaqueros employed by the McCarty Ranch, located near Cubero. This was not an isolated occurrence. Similar tragedies frequently took place. Ute raiders from western Colorado prevented the Navajos from developing the excellent farming lands near the San Juan River.

Bennett knew the truth of the matter: that many of the Navajo raids were made in retaliation for attacks on them. The Utes were beyond the jurisdiction of the Fort Wingate garrison and even if the New Mexican thieves and killers were apprehended—they seldom were—there was no hope of convicting them in local courts. "The Navajos," Bennett stated, "are obliged to fight in their own defense in many situations."

The Indian Bureau now decided that there were drawbacks to having a military man serve as agent to the Navajos. This reversal of policy was announced shortly after the inauguration of President Ulysses S. Grant. It coincided, as well, with the beginning of the era in which the entire Department of the Interior enjoyed its golden years of corruption. Although the Indian Bureau, on which the Secretary of the Interior kept a tight rein, did not become the largest cesspool in Washington during Grant's two administrations, it achieved the dual distinction of being the most vicious and most noisome. If Grant had an Indian policy, its essence was: *Take the easiest way out.* The easiest way more often than not meant the adoption of procedures that were brutal, unjust, and illegal. Indians were a damn nuisance, a barrier to progress. If they refused to adjust to a civilized way of life, then let them suffer the consequences. Grant left behind him a formidable spoils system that would endure for decades.

Some of the agents sent to the Navajos in these decades—more than twenty would hold the office between 1869 and 1900—were men of high intelligence and dedicated to performing their duties with the utmost efficiency and integrity. Others were scoundrels, bigots, intellectual bumpkins, and fanatics of various types. Yet, no matter what their qualifications and characters, assets and liabilities, each faced an almost insurmountable obstacle to success: maintaining adequate communications with the people for whose conduct and welfare he was responsible.

Few agents ventured far from the confines of their station unless escorted by a contingent of cavalry. They sat at a crude board desk in a little room at Fort Defiance, plagued by an endless chain of requests for itemizations of expenditures, inventories of rations, reports on everything from weather conditions to petty thefts, from the morals of their charges to the number of lambs born in the past year. They had neither the time nor the information, not to mention the energy, to prepare accurate responses. Their answers were necessarily guesswork, and the result was that facts seldom encumbered the accounts received in the Indian Bureau.

The Navajos could understand soldiers, for they knew what soldiers could and would do. That is, they understood force, and respected it. But the complicated political and administrative structure that they knew only under the all-embracing name of Washington completely baffled them. To them Washington was not Congress, not the Department of the Interior, not the appropriations committees. To them Washington was the Great White Father who held their destiny in his hands, and their only direct link with this supreme chief was the man who sat at the desk in Fort Defiance. To him they must look for their needs, for their protection, for justice. To him they must make their appeals and present their problems. In him they must place their faith and their hopes. If he failed them, they were lost and bewildered. Beyond the comprehension of the Navajos was a political machine that forced them to accept at frequent intervals a new and inexperienced agent who proclaimed policies different from those of his predecessors. In many instances the Navajos had no more than made the acquaintance of an agent before he was removed. Then they were obliged to await the arrival of his successor, a political appointee who in most cases knew no more about them and their problems than they knew of him and the life he had left behind him.

The Navajos knew only what they saw with their own eyes. They knew nothing of profiteering, of graft, of how In-

dian Bureau purchasing agents received kickbacks for helping manufacturers unload surpluses. They knew only that
instead of badly needed foodstuffs a wagonload of suspend-
ers would arrive at Fort Defiance or that the frenzied agent
would be obliged to sign a receipt for "five hundred silk hats
instead of the seed he had requested. He would receive
crates of overcoats with velvet collars instead of flour, or
several gross of lead furniture castors in boxes that should
have contained cloth from which squaws could make garments for themselves and their children, or crates of high-
buttoned women's shoes instead of canned fruits." They
knew these things, because they saw them, but they did not
understand them. They made what use they could of the
silk hats and the Chesterfields and the ladies' shoes. The buttons were removed and fastened to buckskin or strung on
thongs as decorations. There wasn't much they could do
with the castors, although the children made toys of them.

The quarters of the Navajo agent at Fort Defiance were
dilapidated, sparsely furnished, and provided little protection against inclement weather. Bennett had reported that
snakes crawled in and out of holes in the walls. Annual salary was $2,000. Pay vouchers rarely arrived on schedule, and
in the fiscal year 1870–71 none was received by any federal
employee at Fort Defiance. To these drawbacks were added
the burdens of loneliness, unending paper work, and constant frustration. The agents and the Navajos could not understand each other, and for several years this obstacle had
to be overcome by having Navajo translated into Spanish
and the Spanish translated into English, at best a laborious
and unsatisfactory process.

This was the discouraging situation in which J. A. Manley
found himself in 1870 when he was sent to replace Bennett.
He stayed only a few months. Next came James A. Miller,
a man of courage possessed of a profound desire to im-

prove the economy of the Navajos. His industriousness resulted in his death.

Miller had in mind a plan to develop farms in the San Juan country by building an irrigation system to bring water to the fertile lands adjacent to the river.* With several companions he went on an inspection trip of the region and was shot to death by a Ute horse thief.

In June 1871 J. H. Beadle, an Ohio journalist who had spent five years among western Indians, arrived in Fort Defiance. He thought the Navajos

> as much like a tribe of dark white men as it is possible to conceive . . . splendid specimens of physical humanity. . . . Their countenances are generally pleasing, even mild and benevolent. Wit, merriment and practical jokes enliven all their gatherings, and, quite contrary to our ideas of Indian character, they laugh loud and heartily at everything amusing. They are quite inquisitive, too, and seem vastly pleased to either see or hear something new.

Beadle's reports provide ample evidence to show why the Navajos would come to be called "the indestructibles." He wrote:

> In all their troubles the Navajos are lively, cheerful and looking for better times. To see ten thousand people able and willing to do almost any kind of work, with natural talents of no mean order, and most anxious to improve, to see such a people shut up on this barren plateau, and kept out of that part of their country in which they could live, literally perishing without a chance to help themselves, was enough to sadden even

---

\* *This is the area of the great Navajo Irrigation Project built by the federal government at a cost of hundreds of millions three-quarters of a century after Miller had proposed the development.*

a hard heart. What would a community of ten thousand whites do in such a case?

Beadle was somewhat at a loss in attempting to explain the moral code of the Navajos. He found it "extremely vague." He was more successful writing about their handiwork, which he thought "very ingenious."

> Their blankets are the wonder of all who see them. They are woven by the squaws in a rude frame, and are so compact that water can be carried in them four or five hours before it begins to leak through. . . . Two months are required to complete an ordinary blanket, five feet wide and eight long. . . . One will outlast a lifetime; and though rolled in the mud . . . until every vestige of the color seems gone, when washed with the soap weed—mole cactus—the bright native colors come out as beautiful as ever. They also manufacture, with beads and silk threads obtained from the traders, very beautiful neckties [scarves], garters, cuffs and other ornaments.

More interesting to Beadle than their handicrafts was "the unwearying patience they display in all their work, and their zeal and quickness to learn in everything which may improve their condition." He believed that "surely such a people are capable of civilization."

Beadle proved a keen observer of the Navajo squaws:

> They are treated well . . . and are very communicative, humorous and mirthful, and nothing seems to amuse them so much as my attempts at their language. . . . They are the only Indian girls who even approximate to the James Fennimore Cooper ideal. Their dress is picturesque, consisting of a separate waist and

skirt, the former leaves the arms bare, and is made loose above and neat at the waist; the skirt is of flowered calico, with a leaning to red and black, and terminates just below the knee in black border and frills. Neat moccasins complete the costume, the limbs being left bare generally in the summer. They are very shapely and graceful, and their strength is prodigious.

How these mountaineers, on the thin food they have, manage to produce such specimens of perfect physical womanhood is a mystery to me.

The Navajo Agency clerk, young Tom Keams, was appointed acting agent shortly after Miller's death. Practical, intelligent, and enterprising, he was thoroughly familiar with the problems of the Navajos. He recognized the dire necessity of enlarging the reservation westward and southward to embrace regions that were then, and long had been, occupied by them. The idea of dividing the land into 160-acre parcels was totally infeasible. The Navajos' own customs involving the occupancy and use of land were more sensible.*

Keams believed that if given the proper authority, the Navajos themselves could relieve agents and the military of much of the task of maintaining order in the country. He organized a police force. For a short period the experiment was highly beneficial. Congress, however, refused to appropriate funds for the wages of the policemen, and the force had to be disbanded.

Keams, an Englishman without a sponsor in Washington,

---

* *Every early agent, if he did not know it when he arrived, would quickly come to realize that the proposed program of awarding individuals legal title to reservation land was so completely foreign to Navajos as to be inconceivable to them. No agent would attempt to persuade them to adopt the system.*

was soon ousted and supplanted by a political appointee. He learned to speak the difficult Navajo language with fluency, married an attractive squaw, and took her and a growing brood to live in the beautiful canyon that would bear his name. In Keams Canyon he acquired land and for years operated a trading post.

In the first decade following the return of the Navajos from Bosque Redondo, the federal government failed in almost every respect to abide by its treaty obligations. True, a reservation, although ridiculously inadequate, was established, and the promised fifteen thousand sheep were distributed, but other commitments were at best only partially fulfilled and some were wantonly disregarded. The only school was in a small crumbling adobe structure at Fort Defiance. Few tools and agricultural implements had been sent to Navajo farmers, or if they had been sent, they had not reached their destination. Each year appropriations for the Navajo Agency had been insufficient to meet minimum requirements.

The promised protection against trespassers was not forthcoming. Although the reservation was surrounded on three sides by public domain, all proposals to provide the Navajos with the additional lands so vital to their progress were rejected. Congressmen from areas of heavy precipitation could not be convinced that 3.5 million acres were insufficient to sustain 10,000 people. Why, that was 350 acres for every man, woman, and child! Representatives from the Southwest were in the forefront of the struggle being waged by westerners to reserve public lands for white settlers and deprive Indians of all civil and legal rights. Navajos living by dire necessity outside the reservation were branded as lawbreakers. Violent clashes between them and New Mexican stockmen increased in frequency.

Manuelito led a delegation to Washington to plead with President Grant to solve the problem by ceding grazing and water rights to Navajos who were being driven from ranges on which their herds had grazed for nearly two centuries. He was turned away, although Mr. Grant offered to recommend that the Navajos be awarded some lands north of the San Juan River in exchange for those from which they were being excluded to the east and south of the reservation. The area immediately north of the river was virtually worthless for grazing and agricultural purposes, whereas the lands immediately south and east of the reservation were among the finest ranges in the entire Navajo country. It was not a fair exchange—or so it was believed at the time. Three-quarters of a century later, reservation lands north of the San Juan would pour vast revenues into the Navajo tribal treasury in the form of gas, oil, and mineral royalties.

Navajo leaders counseled the people to do no more than defend themselves to the best of their ability, and sternly warned that violent acts could bring only disastrous results. The great majority of the tribe heeded the advice. A few did not, and organized bands marauded the encroaching white stockmen. As the depredations increased, two of the most powerful chiefs, the aging Manuelito and Ganado Mucho, saw the necessity of taking forceful measures to halt them.

The weapon the two shrewd old men employed was the Navajos' universal fear of witchcraft. They spread word that the Navajos who were marauding white stockmen had fallen into the control of evil spirits. Next they prepared a list of those they believed were guilty of sorcery, and dispatched a band of warriors to seek them out. Within a few weeks more than forty Navajo "witches" had been slain along lonely trails in the Navajo country. Among them was Biwos, an unreconstructed headman from Chinle, who had signed the 1868 treaty under the name of Muerto de Hombre. The raiding stopped.

In 1873 W. F. M. Arny was appointed agent to the Navajos. A former territorial secretary under Governor Connelly, he had served as acting governor for a year after Connelly died in office. His brief tenure had been marked by bitter clashes with the War and Interior departments over Indian policies. He was a rabid moralist, an uncompromising bigot, and fanatically religious, although he did not always adhere to biblical teachings in his business dealings.

Arny sought to gain a monopoly on Navajo wool production. His plan was simple. He urged, and sometimes commanded, Navajos to deliver their wool to the post sutler at Fort Defiance. An arrangement was made with the sutler to pay for the wool in goods, charging the Indians an excessive rate of exchange. Arny then purchased the wool from the sutler at a considerably lower figure. The sutler made a profit, and Arny obtained the wool at or below its true market value. He hauled the wool to Albuquerque, and shipped it off to eastern carpet manufacturers.

Arny also gave his attention to Navajo blankets, for which there was a steadily rising demand. Concluding that this might be developed into a highly lucrative side line, he implemented a project to increase production by the use of modern high-speed looms. A number were brought out from the East to Fort Defiance.

However, not Arny's business acumen, but his fanaticism and inability to avoid controversies brought him into difficulties from which he was unable to extricate himself. He excoriated the Indian Bureau for failing to provide educational facilities on the reservation and declared that if given the funds, he could soon train two hundred Navajo women to be teachers. He accused the War Department of encouraging squaws to become prostitutes. He pried into the private lives of agency employees to such an extent that the women would not speak to him, and on one occasion almost his entire staff resigned and departed without notice. He sought to forbid marriages between Navajo women and white men, and branded squawmen as lost souls.

At the end of two years of continual turmoil and dissension at Fort Defiance, Arny was summarily removed. The modern looms were discarded, and the squaws continued to weave on the crude apparatus they had always used, and always would use. Yet the Arny ledger contained at least one entry in his favor: he had been the first to awaken the Navajos to the fact that the far-off strange world of the white man would pay for their wool, and they were not a people to overlook any opportunity to improve their economy.

In 1869 a census had been taken for the purpose of determining the quantities of rations and goods to be purchased for the Navajos—which did not mean that the quantities needed would be purchased, or that if purchased they would be delivered at Fort Defiance. The Navajo population was officially estimated to be 8,181. [It was at least 3,000 greater, as later studies would show.] Navajo sheep were believed to number about 30,000 head.

For 1872, government reports set the population at 9,114, the number of sheep at 130,000, and horses at 10,000.

For 1875: population 11,768; livestock: 175,000 sheep, 2,500 cattle, 30,000 goats, 14,000 horses.

For 1879: population approximately 14,000 (a new estimate made a few months later gave it as 16,000); livestock: 500,000 sheep, 22,500 horses, 40,000 goats, 1,600 cattle; wool sold to traders: 600,000 pounds.

Revised estimates for 1880: 700,000 sheep, 40,000 horses,

500 mules, and 1,000 burros; wool sold: 800,000 pounds; wool retained for weaving: 100,000 pounds; lands under cultivation, on and off reservation: 10,000 acres.

Far from cold and meaningless, these statistics tell an amazing story of a people's determination and courage that appalling adversities had failed to destroy.

# 11

IN 1870 PRESIDENT GRANT had approved a new plan purportedly designed to promote the welfare of the Indians. For reasons best known to himself and his advisers on Indian affairs, it was labeled a "peace policy." The announced objective was to civilize and Christianize the degraded, backward, red infidels, instead of exterminating them by the simpler means of starvation and warfare. This humane goal was to be achieved not by civil justice, not by large appropriations of federal funds, not by the creation of adequate reservations, not by rigid enforcement of statutes prohibiting the theft and exploitation of Indian resources, but by "the assignment of religious and education work (among the Indians) to the various religious denominations on a regional basis."

The Navajos drew the Presbyterians, but it would not be long before other sectarians would be active in the field.

Miss Charity Gaston was sent from the East by the Pres-

byterian Home Mission Board to be the first white teacher
of the Navajos. When she stood before the leaky mud-
walled hovel that was to be both classroom and home for
her, she was somewhat less enthusiastic about helping to lift
Indian youngsters out of the mire of ignorance than she had
been six weeks earlier as she set out on the wearying trip
across the plains and deserts. It was not only determination
to fulfill the obligation she had accepted that caused her to
remain: the pay was satisfactory, $600 a year; the country
was indescribably beautiful; and there were several attractive unattached men at the agency, especially the handsome
physician-minister, Dr. James Menaul.

The rough log benches of the school could have accom-
modated twenty-five pupils, but there were never that many
present, even during the most pleasant weather. Some morn-
ings three or four would arrive, clinging to one another on
a pony. On other days six or seven might appear. On many
days the classroom remained empty. Rarely did the same
children attend on two consecutive days, or even on any
two days in one month. Occasionally two or three squaws
would come to spend an hour staring incredulously at the
young woman with pompadour and combs, immaculate in
her neat white shirtwaist, long woolen skirt, and high shoes.
They would giggle and chatter unintelligibly, but with obvious appreciation, if she served them lunch.

A number of the children were noticeably retarded or
unwell. The agent said that some families sent sickly boys
and girls to the school in the hope that they would be cured
of their afflictions. If they were killed by exposure to "book
magic," the loss would not be great.

After a courtship of several months, Dr. Menaul and
Charity Gaston were married, and in 1872 they were sent to
establish a mission at the pueblo of Laguna. Other women
teachers came and went in the ensuing years at Fort De-

fiance, but the school was never more successful than it had been when Charity Gaston had presided in it. Nor were the facilities improved.

The little mud school at Fort Defiance comprised the sum total of the federal government's educational program for the Navajos during the first decade after the signing of the Bosque Redondo treaty and the inauguration of the "peace policy."

In 1879 Congress was persuaded by the Bureau of Indian Affairs, which enjoyed the support of societies dedicated to improving the Indians, to authorize a boarding school at the Navajo Agency. However, no money was made available for the project for another year, and then only $875 was appropriated in the fiscal budget for 1880. With this niggardly amount Captain Bennett—who had again become agent—began construction. Using Navajo laborers, he installed a small sawmill and quarried stone. Congressional parsimony did not discourage him: "When completed as per plan it will be both spacious and admirably arranged in all its appliances . . . and will accommodate from one hundred and fifty to two hundred pupils." He was soon relieved of the responsibility by the Presbyterian Home Mission Board, which assigned J. D. Perkins, described as a qualified teacher and practical builder, to direct the work. Funds continued to arrive in dribbles, and two more years elapsed before the structure could be completed. More instructors arrived, separate dormitories for boys and girls were furnished, desks were installed in classrooms, and a kitchen, laundry, and dining room were equipped.

Many Navajos came to admire the grandeur of the building's thick stone walls and modified mansard roof, then rode away in silence. In September 1884, several months after the school had opened, less than twenty pupils were enrolled. In October there were twenty-two, and in November twenty-four. But few of this number remained any length of time. Agent John H. Bowman reported that "they would come and stay a day or two, get some clothes, and then run away back to their hogans, but few of them attended regularly, consequently the school done little real good."

Bowman thought the situation was partially due to the incompetency of the staff, as the school's superintendent had informed him that he did not believe there "was one day when all the school employees were on speaking terms." Bowman "adopted the plan of having one of the police in attendance, and if any of the children leave without proper permission he promptly brings them back." He declared himself satisfied that in the coming year "we will have as large an attendance of children at school as we can accommodate." His hope was not to be realized, for in 1885 the attendance totaled thirty-three thoroughly frightened youngsters, although Bowman was happy to state that with a policeman at the door, few of these "so far attempted to run away."

In 1887 Congress passed the Compulsory Indian Education Law. Thereafter the Navajo educational program developed the aspects of a penal system. In the boarding schools subsequently built at Tuba City, Leupp, Tohatchi, Shiprock, Chinle, Crown Point, Toadlena, and Fort Wingate, pupils were in every sense prisoners, and discipline was enforced with the rigidity and brutality exercised in penitentiaries.

Agents accompanied by police moved through the country forcefully taking children from their homes and transporting them to the boarding schools. Many were taken to institutions that the federal government had established outside the Navajo country in New Mexico, Colorado, Nevada, Arizona, and in far-off California, Oklahoma, and Pennsylvania.

Between 1869 and 1897 Navajo educational programs remained almost entirely in the hands of mission groups, among them the Presbyterians, Methodists, Catholics, and the Christian Reformed Church, all of which received federal subsidies. It was the theory of Congress that through the churches "the dual objective of Christianization and acculturation of Indians" could be "promoted at minimum expense to the Government." However, in 1897 Congress took an opposing view of the matter, ordering that "it be the policy of the Government hereafter to make no appropriation whatever to subsidize sectarian schools serving Indian groups."

The church organizations were not to be thwarted by a mere congressional resolution. They found means of getting their hands on treaty and tribal funds. Thus the Indians themselves became the subsidizers of mission schools. This manipulating, in which the Bureau of Indian Affairs had connived with the mission organizations, was "adjudged to be contrary to the intent of Congress" as early as 1905, but not until 1917 was a statute enacted providing that "no appropriation whatever out of the Treasury of the United States may be used for education of Indian children in any sectarian school."

Although no federal funds were available to them, the mission schools continued to operate and the number steadily increased through the next three decades. To the original schools under the jurisdiction of the Presbyterian, Methodist, Catholic, and Christian Reformed churches would be added mission schools operated by the Mormons, Mennonites, Seventh-Day Adventists, Navajo Gospel Crusade, Church of the Brethren, Quakers, Plymouth Brethren Church, Global Gospel Fellowship, Inc., and Navajo Bible Academy. Other sectarian schools were opened by various groups in Bluff, Utah; Cortez, Colorado; Albuquerque and Sante Fe, New Mexico; Tucson, Glendale, and Cottonwood in Arizona.

The opening of the reservation to missionary organizations was one of the greatest injuries inflicted on the Navajos. Religious zealots were thereby given sanction by the federal government to force their beliefs on captive audiences by any means, intellectual or physical, they chose to employ, not excluding chicanery, bribery, and threats.

The Navajos suffered an emotional trauma from which they have never recovered, and which still appears to be irremediable.

Any sect can build a church on the reservation and freely invade the private lives and intrude upon the private thinking of the Navajo people. They can build mission schools, staff them with fiery-eyed fanatics, and hammer their creeds into the heads of the children they lure into their sanctums under the pretense of giving them an education. Yet any secular group or individual desiring to establish a medical clinic or an industrial plant that would contribute to the physical or economic well-being of the Navajos is subject to searching examination, must obtain numerous licenses, and must share profits with the tribe. That is as it should be. But churches are as free as the wind that blows through the great red canyons to do as they please, when they please, without any restrictions whatsoever. And that is not as it should be.

The Navajo language contains no word that can be translated as "religion." Yet no people on earth are more influenced by the supernatural, or more guided by spiritual beliefs, than the Navajos. Unlike white society, which tends to turn religion on and off as needs demand or moods please, the Navajo is never detached from it, day or night. It affects very nearly everything he does and everything he thinks.

In the Navajo pantheon there is no deity identifiable as the "Supreme Being." There is no clearly defined divine hierarchy. There are many supernatural beings, a few occupying pre-eminent positions. There are no

temples or cults associated with religious practice. Neither is there a priestly administrative hierarchy on the basis of which the religion is organized for practical purposes. There is a group known as Singers. Individually they acquire knowledge of one or more of the complex Chantways by dint of long apprenticeship, and thereafter become practitioners corresponding roughly to the priests of other religions.

The Navajos have no heaven or hell. Their religion "is a system of imitative and sympathetic magic aimed ritually at fulfillment of the requirements of life and living. It is not concerned with preparation for death and afterlife." Although, like any sane human being, he attempts to prolong his life, the Navajo does not live in morbid fear of dying. He considers death the normal end of a life cycle for man, just as it is for plants and animals. Religion helps a man in life, but it is not needed after death. When death comes, a person's breath and "that which stands within one" leaves his body, and he loses his identity and merely becomes one with the cosmos, a condition in which he is neither punished nor rewarded: water poured into a river is no longer identifiable.

Every Navajo ceremony is designed to accomplish a specific purpose. Some are prophylactic in nature, conducted to ward off evil or attract goodness. Others are meant to exorcise evil and restore the person for whose benefit they are held.

The legends, prayers, poems and songs that make up the immense body of Navajo Sacred Literature exhibit great beauty and imagination and are in no wise less

worthy of literary rank than the Homeric poems,
Hymns of the Rig-Veda and many other heritages from
our past. They are stories of adventure and magic, hero-
myths and travels. There is humor and suspense in
tales told with mimicry and great beauty in the Navajo
language. The poems form parts of chants; beautiful in
content, and chanted in a peculiar rhythm with vowel
lengths and tones of the words altered in a characteristic manner.

Today a few of the missions scattered through the Navajo
country operate modern schools and medical facilities, but
by far the larger number of them are exclusively concerned
with evangelization.

Some groups pursue a long-term policy of gradually
superimposing Christianity on the native religion to
ultimately supersede it; other groups maintain a short-
term policy and strive to extirpate native religion immediately to replace it with a form of Christianity. Re-
gardless of the policy, the Navajos continue to practice
the native religion and often find no inconsistency in
simultaneously participating in Christian practices.

What movement away from the traditional religion has
occurred has not been toward the usual forms of Christianity. An estimated twenty thousand Navajo adults have
been attracted to a denomination known as the Native
American Church, which uses peyote in its rituals. The
peyote is a cactus button containing mescaline and other
alkaloids capable of producing hallucinatory effects when
ingested in sufficient quantity.

Peyote has been used by some Indian groups for many
years, but its association with religion did not develop to
any extent among Navajos until after 1935. It is interesting
to note that this was the year when the federal stock-reduc-

tion program began, and the slaughter of the animals struck forcefully at Navajo beliefs associated with sheep and horses. Navajo religion and economy are inseparably woven together.

The picture of a God that is all-good is incomprehensible to the Navajos. Christianity speaks of lands far distant which they cannot visualize. From almost any place in the Navajo country at least one of the four sacred mountains can be seen. Christian ministers and priests talk only of a male God. Changing Woman is perhaps the principal Navajo deity. In the Christian doctrine, the Navajos miss the whole feeling for the position of woman that is embodied in both their social organization and their religious lore. These, perhaps, are the chief reasons why so few Navajos have converted to the Christian faith.

The Navajo looks upon wrongdoing as an action that produces disharmony within society. It must be averted or remedied to prevent chaos in human relationships. The Navajo credo is that a man should live and conduct himself in a manner assuring prosperity, personal enjoyment, and good health. To achieve these ends he must be industrious, generous, courteous, just, responsible, and, above all, moderate in his habits and actions. A Navajo does not live with a dream of eternal salvation in some "hereafter." To him the important thing is to live well and properly on earth, between the four sacred mountains.

The Navajo Tribal Council has not yet found a way to eradicate the turbulence that has been created in the minds of the Navajo people by the various creeds being shouted at them and the inane demands being made on them by the apostles of missions representing all manner of sects. Certainly no Congress and no administration, national or state, has been willing to incur the enmity of church leaders— much less the wrath of their blindly devout congregations, who cast a large number of votes—by restricting the operations of missionaries.

If relief for the Navajos from the damage being done by these sects is to be achieved, the Navajos themselves must take the first steps. The enlightened members of the Tribal Council are fully cognizant of the bewilderment of the Navajos as they struggle to reconcile the drastically conflicting tenets of the Christian faith with their own. Yet some members of the council are inclined to consider the problem unresolvable, and therefore treat it with indifference. "There is no legal means of closing the Navajo country to any religious crackpot who wants to come into it," a council member said to me. "Hell, anyway, I think most Navajos laugh at them inwardly, and some laugh openly at them."

A Navajo Agency official advanced the argument: "How are you going to keep them out? It's still a free country. If you can keep religious freedom out of the Navajo reservation, you can keep the other three freedoms out, can't you?"

The premise is fallacious. The Navajo reservation is not a "free" country in the sense that it is open to all groups and all promoters who wish to enter it. Commercial establishments operated by whites are subject to strict regulations. One may not open a store, a gas station, a motel, a hamburger stand, or any other type of business without the sanction of the Tribal Council, and often with the approval of the Commissioner of Indian Affairs and the Secretary of the Interior as well.

Nor is the contention that doctors and hospitals supported by church funds have greatly aided the Navajos sufficient reason for allowing rabid evangelists to wage campaigns against Navajo beliefs. That is analogous to maintaining that any public or private foundation that contributes money for a project to improve the economy of the Navajos automatically has the right to insist on their acceptance of a particular faith or moral code.

But certain truths are evident, and one who has the best interests of the Navajos at heart may find a measure of consolation. Despite the pressures brought to bear upon the Navajos in the name of religion, the missionaries have come nowhere near their goals. Traditional ceremonials are performed in every part of the Navajo country, often within hearing distance of the missions, and, in proportion to the population, the number of native rites and dances performed today is greater than at any time in the past.

From the day the Fort Defiance boarding school opened its doors until almost the middle of the twentieth century all Navajo schools—both those operated by mission organizations and by the Indian Bureau—had one supreme objective: to destroy Navajo culture.

As the most effective means of progressing toward this goal, school officials began by imprisoning children. If Navajo boys and girls were to be "fit to enter white society," the first thing to be done was to remove them from their environment. They must be prevented from having any contact with their families for at least four, and preferably six or eight, years. They must not be allowed to speak their own language. They must wear the clothes of white children. All heathen teachings must be driven from their minds. They must be made to forget the songs taught them by their mothers. They must attend Christian services. They must not play Navajo games. They must be made to forget everything they knew. They must be forced to think, act, and believe as white children. They must be taught to labor, to assume responsibilities, to behave like civilized persons. They must be disciplined, and severely punished for infractions of rules. They must be given new instincts. Above all, nothing must be permitted to enter their lives that might remind them of their homes, their parents, their brothers and sisters. The world of the Navajo must be forever closed to them.

A Navajo woman remembered:

The teacher wanted us to sing songs and some of us didn't sing. She said if we didn't sing we would have to stand up and sing alone. She made some of the boys do this, but I wouldn't. The song was "My Country 'Tis of Thee." She took me to her room and strapped me. Then she looked at me, she wanted me to cry but I wouldn't. She said: "Have you had enough?" I didn't say anything, so she strapped me again. [Did you sing?] Yes, I sang a little bit. She said, "If you haven't had enough I'll send you to the head missionary and he has a long heavy strap." . . .

Then once in the sixth grade, we had a man who brought the food to the dining room. He was always strapping the boys and when we worked in the kitchen the cooks always strapped us. Once I was hit very hard and my nose bled because I peeled the potatoes too thick. But when this man came around he strapped a boy and the boy jumped up. He was going to fight . . . He knocked that boy down and sat on his stomach and then he kept hitting him in the face and one of the cooks ran in and she was crying but she couldn't stop the man. That boy's face was all red and swollen, and his sister swore at that man and he came over to our table and said to me, "Did you say that?" I said I didn't say anything but he made me come in the kitchen and he took some thin pieces of wood from a box and he hit my hands until he broke the wood but I wouldn't cry, so he got a piece of pinyon from the wood-box. . . . He

kept on beating my hands. They got cut and swollen
and I couldn't close them. . . . He said: "Why did you
say those things?" . . . I think of that man lots of times.
I hate him. Sometimes I see him even now and I get so
mad I want to get even with him. [But you were there
eight years and you only got punished twice.] Oh, no,
lots of times we had to hold out our hands so they could
hit them with a ruler. Generally they did this twelve
times. Then we got demerits. Most of them got them
for talking Navajo. When I got a few they made me eat
standing up. Sometimes they made us stand on a stool
while everyone ate supper. [Did everyone laugh at
you?] Yes, that's what they did. And after supper when
we could sometimes play they made us stand in a
corner. But if you had more demerits the worst thing
was on Sunday afternoon, they made us stand in the
sun all afternoon out by those posts . . . from one
o'clock to five.

In 1892 agent Dana Shipley went to Round Rock with
two policemen to "recruit" Navajo children. He soon found
himself besieged in a trading post by a group of thoroughly
angry and well-armed fathers led by a headman named
Black Horse. After spending two days barricaded behind
bags of flour and wool, Shipley and the policemen were
rescued by a squadron of cavalry. Military officers warned
that unless Shipley ceased his unreasonable and stupid attempts to capture children he would start a Navajo war. The
commander at Fort Wingate refused to act on the agent's
request that Black Horse be arrested and punished.

Several Navajos who had participated in the violence tes-
tified in a hearing held at Fort Defiance.

Said a father:

When we put our children in school it is like giving

our hearts up, and when the superintendent abuses our children it hurts us very much. The name we have given this superintendent is Billy Goat. A billy goat is always butting all the rest of the sheep and imposing on them, and we think this is a good name for him. We make this complaint to you white people who want to see children well treated.

A mother whose son had been taken to the school said:

He was confined as a prisoner in the belfry of the school building for two days without food. After this period the boy was allowed to go out in the schoolyard with manacles on his ankles. In this condition the boy attempted to reach his home by crawling on his hands and knees. When within a short distance of home, the boy sank to the ground, exhausted, where I found him and carried him home.

Said a father:

When I brought my boy to school he had two eyes. The next time I saw him he had only one.

Said an agency carpenter:

The superintendent is guilty of vile and inhuman treatment of the Navajo boys in school, by placing them with handcuffs on their hands in the dark and poorly ventilated cellar.

Before being enrolled in the boarding schools, whether through voluntary submission or by force, the Navajo boys and girls had never known anything but life in the mesa and canyon country, unbridled freedom in wind and sunlight and stillness, kindness and security in a quiet home environment. Since they were toddlers they had been taught the

traditional techniques of agriculture and stock raising and
the legends, practices, and tabus of Navajo culture. Few of
them either spoke or understood a word of English. They had
absorbed the myths and legends and history taught them by
their elders, and knew only the customs and rites of their
own people.

> [They] had been patients in the curing chants . . . had
> gone with their families to all-night public exhibitions
> (sings and ceremonies) where dancers, masked to imi-
> tate the Navajo divinities, sang, danced, and shouted in
> the light of large fires.
>
> This imagery and the excitement and fears accom-
> panying it were stored away in the unconscious long
> before the youngsters could reason or objectify what
> they saw. All this conditioned them fundamentally, so
> that subsequent Christian imagery could not supplant
> or alter it. Anything which affected them from white
> culture in later years was a veneer which readily
> cracked when they had occasion to reexperience their
> own tribal religious emotions.

It was a long way from the world of the hogan, with its
small, tightly knit family group, to the stern and cold military world of the boarding school. Very small was the number of students who made the transition without suffering
some psychological or physical injury. Most of them were
never able to identify in any sense with the strange and
conflicting cultural values. Upon being released from con-
finement, all but a very few—actually rare exceptions—returned to their people and re-established themselves as
members of Navajo society. Some had become so emotion-
ally disturbed that they remained hopelessly maladjusted
throughout their lives.

As late as 1926 the daily food allowance established by Congress for Navajo schools was eleven cents per student. For the boarding schools the appropriation was set at $225 a year for each pupil. Out of this sum had to be paid the wages of teachers and employees, maintenance costs, and all expenditures for equipment, books, clothing, and other supplies.

For several years numerous scientific and civic organizations, among them the Advisory Council on Indian Affairs, had been strenuously urging Congress to appropriate adequate funds to resolve educational, health, and welfare problems on Indian reservations. In 1927 Secretary of the Interior Hubert Work had complained about the "poverty of the Indian Service." He requested that a special committee be appointed to study the situation and submit a report that could be used as a guide in the enactment of progressive programs and for determining the amount of funds required to alleviate adverse conditions.

The expenditure was authorized, and a special committee, under the auspices of the Institute for Government Research and headed by Lewis Meriam, spent two years visiting Indian schools and observing reservation facilities. In June 1928 the committee issued its report.

"Malnutrition was evident," Merriam and his colleagues wrote. "The pupils were indolent, and when they had a chance to play, they merely sat about on the ground, showing no exuberance of healthy youth."

A heartless and miserly Congress was slowly starving America's Indian children to such a degree that, unless the barbaric practice was halted, they would be deprived of living normal lives. Because of the paltry appropriations, schools were forced to produce much of their own food. Under the euphemism "vocational training," the Indian school children were obliged to perform all the hard, menial labor required to raise food, produce milk and butter, repair shoes, launder clothing and perform other functions necessary to the operation of the institution. Discipline was severe and the use of police remained necessary to enforce the enrollment and continued attendance of the reluctant scholars. Dressed in uniforms, the children "stood formation," and marched from place to place.

Stricter regulations could not be found in a prison, as the Indian child

must maintain a pathetic degree of quietness. In fact, several matrons and disciplinarians said that they did not allow the children to talk in the dining rooms. Despite the fact that the children were faced with the problem of learning English, they were denied the privilege of conversation at the table as one informal opportunity to practice, and the use of their mother tongue was prohibited.

Several dairies have milking machines, but the bulk of this work is done by hand and, in some instances, the same detail of boys is kept on for the entire school year, although this work requires very early rising. Almost all dairy details include a few very small boys.

Every available space that will accommodate beds is often pressed into service. The children are frequently quartered on attic floors, in close placed beds, with the same lack of light and air. Not infrequently in these attic dormitories the fire hazard is serious.

In some places two children slept in a single bed, "not because they preferred it to keep warm during the cold nights, but because there were no other beds for them."

The use of child labor in the Indian schools appalled the committee members:

The laundry is an important feature of every government school. It is one of the chief sources of labor for the pupils. The superintendent of one school said he can get more work out of the children if he keeps large piles of laundry before them. An inspection of the plant verified his statement. A number of small children were literally hidden behind great piles of wet laundry in a greatly overcrowded room filled with steam.

If the labor of the boarding schools is to be done by the pupils, it is essential that the pupils be old enough and strong enough to do institutional work.

Under existing conditions, this work had to be done "by very small children—children, moreover, who according to competent medical opinion, are malnourished."

The committee found that in "nearly every boarding school there were children of eleven or twelve spending four hours a day in more or less heavy industrial work—dairying, kitchen work, laundry and shop. The work is bad for children of this age, especially children not physically well-nourished; most of it is in no sense educational."

School employees "followed disciplinary methods which are now regarded as antiquated, even in a reform school."

The committee unequivocally blamed Congress for the conditions, declaring that "the small amount of money allowed for food and clothes makes it necessary to use child labor."

The competence of teachers and superintendents was below desirable levels. "Nearly every boarding school visited furnished disquieting illustrations of failure to understand the underlying principles of human behavior. Punishments of the most harmful sort are bestowed in sheer ignorance."

Beneficial changes in the Navajo educational system began to take place in the mid-1930s. The Meriam report had sent a wave of indignation sweeping across the nation, but it alone was not responsible for opening the gate to improvements. New Navajo leaders, some of them veterans of World War I, had arisen who understood the advantages to be gained by adopting some of the methods of the white world. These enlightened headmen inspired a social and economic revolution. One of its most significant aspects was a change in the attitude of the Navajo people toward education.

By 1936 the Indian Bureau had opened fifty day schools in areas of heaviest population. The pupils lived at home, and buses were provided to transport them to and from their classes. Under this program parents could keep in close touch with educational processes. They could assure themselves that their children were being properly treated. They could attend school functions, hear talks delivered in their own tongue, and consult with teachers. These opportunities brought understanding and stimulated their interest in both school and community matters.

Unfortunately, the day-school plan was not combined with a road-building program. The deeply rutted dirt roads on the reservation were easily obliterated by storms—only a few gravel roads existed—and there were times when the buses could not move for days and the little schoolhouses were isolated in seas of mud. With the outbreak of World War II, all road work was halted and the buses were removed. Some of the day schools that pupils could reach by horseback or in wagons continued to operate. The others were deserted. However, a start had been made, and a steadily growing number of Navajos began to demand that this sensible system of "paper learning" be continued.

The off-reservation boarding-school system which takes children away from their families for years will never be acceptable to the Navajos. If facilities are improved today in these schools, the atmosphere is little better than it was in the past. The children are lonely prisoners. Defiance and spirit, strongly inherent in them, is still countered with re-form-school methods. Most of the students dream only of escaping, and once they do, few of them seek further educa-tion. They have had all they want of "Washington *beolta*" (Indian Bureau schools). The same bitter attitude is har-bored by girls and boys taken away to mission boarding schools.

The curriculum of Indian elementary and secondary schools, with rare exceptions, is designed to turn out la-borers and mechanics. Little thought is given to graduating students qualified to attend institutions of higher learning. This is demonstrated by the fact that 90 percent of Navajo students who start college flunk out in their first semester. Yet the intellect and capability of the average young Navajo are not surpassed by students of any other race.

At long last the Navajos themselves are making an at-tempt to correct this situation, to accomplish what the Indian Bureau has failed, or refused, to do. They have estab-lished the Navajo Community College on the reservation near Many Farms. It is the belief of the college's first presi-dent, Robert A. Roessel, Jr., that "education has cheated the Navajo, cheated them badly. For years the white man's schools have educated the Indianness out of these people. The result is a group of bleached Indian youth, who are miserable on the reservation, but rarely learn to adjust when they leave for the big city. They are neither Anglo nor Indian, but just full of self-hatred."

Roessel, a white man who holds a Ph.D., has taught Nav-ajos for many years. A full-blood Navajo is slated to succeed him as president, but Roessel will remain to teach. The col-lege doors are open to any serious man or woman over the age of eighteen. There are no other requirements for admission. The pupils range in age from eighteen to sixty. Land for the campus was donated by the Navajo tribe and individual donors. The original financing was supplied by the Tribal Council from oil royalties, and later supplemented by funds from the Office of Economic Opportunity and private contributors. The Board of Regents are all Navajos. The college has been swamped with applications from white teachers.

Numerous educators scoffed at the idea of the Navajo tribe attempting to operate a college, but they have been proved wrong. The college is crowded. The teachers are fully qualified. Accreditation has been awarded by educational associations, and many colleges have offered to accept transfer credits from Navajo Community College.

Hundreds of Navajo servicemen and wartime production workers returned to the reservation at the end of World War II with a new appreciation of education and a clearer understanding of its value to younger generations. In May 1946 a delegation of Navajo leaders went to Washington to testify before congressional committees. Formal education, they declared, was considered by the Navajo people to be their primary need. Their statements were publicized, forcefully bringing to the attention of Americans "that there was a group of some seventy thousand Navajos for whom not even necessary school plants existed and who, lacking an education, could not even speak, read and write the national language."

A loud public protest followed, but Congress reacted slowly to demands for adequate Navajo schools, and not until the 1950s were laws enacted to improve the situation. Then much of the money appropriated was spent on facilities at existing schools. Few seats were added for Navajo pupils.

Angered by the slow rate of progress, the Navajo leaders

again raised their voices and demanded a crash program. They got it. Funds were reallocated, and within a year more than eight thousand new seats were provided. Eager to do its share, the Tribal Council appropriated $350,000 to supply school clothing to needy youngsters.

Reared in the reservation environment, nearly all Navajo six-year-olds still enter school knowing little if any English. Thus the Navajo child is seriously handicapped at the beginning of his school career. Time must be taken to teach him a basic speaking knowledge of the language of instruction. The establishment of kindergartens—a project barely underway—would help alleviate this problem, but the handicap will never be eliminated until the cultural environment of the reservation becomes more closely assimilated with the national norm. And that day may be far in the future, for Navajos cherish their culture and are determined to preserve it to the greatest possible extent, while at the same time accepting non-Indian concepts.

"You will learn paper," General Sherman had told the Navajos at Bosque Redondo. It was not his own promise. It was contained in the empty political mouthings sent to him from Washington, and being a dutiful soldier, he had repeated it. After the passage of a century the pledge is not yet fulfilled.

If there is enlightenment in the announced policies of the Division of Indian Education, that does not mean that those policies will be successfully carried out in the near future. Many social, economic, and political barriers must first be removed. If young Navajos are successfully to counter the inescapable pressures of the modern world, they must first be assured of these things:

(1) A standard of living equal to that of the country as a whole;

(2) Freedom of choice: an opportunity to remain in their homeland without surrendering their dignity, or to move to the towns and cities equipped with the skills to live in equality and dignity;

(3) Full participation in the life of America, with a full share of economic opportunity and social justice.

Congress is at fault for making the job more difficult than necessary. Now the task is formidable. The Navajo population will continue to soar. More and better roads must be constructed. Jobs must be created, both on and off the reservation, to absorb the steadily growing number of young people. Knowledge is of little value unless it can be beneficially applied. Education is more a liability than an asset if it frustrates, if it causes hopelessness and bitterness in the individual. A Navajo who has spent years in school can hardly be expected to be content to dig ditches for a living. Much more than "learning paper" is involved in the problem.

In 1880 the Indian Bureau estimated that at least eight thousand Navajos were residing outside reservation boundaries on federal lands. Bitter quarrels between them and New Mexican and Arizona stockmen over waterholes and grass were increasing, and several men on both sides had been slain. With the hope of halting these clashes, President Rutherford B. Hayes agreed to an Indian Bureau recommendation to extend the reservation on its eastern, southern, and western sides. In January 1880 he issued an Executive Order giving the Navajos an additional 1.2 million acres. Two years later President Chester Arthur established a rectangular area of 2.4 million acres "for Moki [Hopi] and other Indians" on the west of the Navajo reservation. As many Navajos long had occupied parts of this region, they considered themselves as the "other Indians." The loose phraseology of the order was one cause of a dispute between Hopis and Navajos that would not be resolved for three-quarters of a century.

As the steel rails moved westward across New Mexico and Arizona, hordes of unsavory characters poured into the bleak little shanty settlements that sprang up overnight along the line. Law-enforcement officers made few attempts to protect Navajos from the white rabble, and they were beaten, robbed, and killed. Numerous official reports of their brutal treatment were sent to Washington.

Navajo agent Galen Eastman informed the Indian Bureau that Navajo leaders were pleading with him to stop the sale of whisky to the tribe. He had no means of enforcing such a regulation, and white law officers would not cooperate with him, even to the extent of attempting to keep whisky peddlers off the reservation.

In September 1883, General S. C. Armstrong wrote:

The Navajo Reservation has never been surveyed;

they are utterly ignorant of any change of their ancient limits, and to them their native land is the great tract they occupy, upon which civilization is advancing with irresistable force. The agent in charge cannot drive off white squatters when the lines are not fixed, and appeals to Washington have been fruitless.

Migrations from the east, pushing up through New Mexico and Arizona, down from Colorado, from Utah on the northwest—Mormons—from California and Nevada on the west and the railroad on the south taking alternate sections on both sides, sweeping along in a belt 80 miles in width, taking up the finest valley lands, create, altogether, an aggressive movement that will before very long drive the Navajos back to their undefined limits. There may be trouble . . .

Their million sheep and goats, their fifteen thousand horses, their cattle cannot find food enough in this barren waste. Secretary of the Interior Henry M. Teller sent the Navajos a superior man as agent, D. M. Riordan, who soon resigned in disgust, not because of the Indians but because of the Government's failure to do what it had promised . . . Next to nothing has been done.

General Armstrong's report brought widespread demands that the government live up to its commitments. An inquiry by newspaper correspondents disclosed that only $5,000 had been appropriated for relief of the Navajos in the fiscal year 1883, and that more than $150,000 due them under treaty guarantees was mysteriously being held in the Treasury.

Agent Riordan was induced to return, and it was largely through his efforts that more than 2.4 million acres were added to the reservation by Executive Order in 1884. These lands were bordered on the north by the San Juan River, and lay in both Utah and Arizona. The reservation now contained more than 8 million acres, but as immense parts of the seemingly generous addition were worthless for farming and grazing purposes, it was still far too small for the swiftly increasing Navajo population.

Violence between Navajos and white settlers and stockmen continued to increase, and in 1885 Interior Secretary Lucius Q. C. Lamar ordered the Land Office to "close all entries to non-Navajos wishing to homestead on the public domain adjoining the established Navajo Reservation." It was Lamar's intention to give Navajos living in these areas an opportunity to file for homesteads, but the plan failed. Not a Navajo filed. They didn't see any reason to homestead land that already belonged to the tribe.

For more than six years the status quo was maintained, but what General Armstrong had termed "the pressures of civilization" continued to mount. Mining companies became interested in the lands that had been allotted to the Navajos in 1884, which were known as the Utah Strip. In November 1892, President Benjamin Harrison, knowing on which side his political bread was buttered, ordered "all Navajo lands lying west of 100 degrees west longitude and within the Territory of Utah" restored to the public domain. Although Navajos were permitted to use it for grazing, not until 1933 was the tribe able to regain title to it through an act of Congress.

In 1894 a Navajo sheepowner killed a Mormon stockman in a fight over water rights on the Moenkopi Wash. Navajos had farmed and grazed their herds in this well-watered area since early in the century. In 1875 a group of Mormons had moved down from Utah and settled in it. They had established a town, Tuba City, named after a Hopi chief, Toovi. From that time disputes between them and the Navajos were frequent. The killing of the Mormon focused attention on the situation, but no official action was taken for several years.

In the winter of 1897 the Board of Supervisors of Coconino County (Arizona) ordered the eviction of a score of Navajo families living west of the Little Colorado River. Their herds were destroyed when deputy sheriffs drove the animals into the icy waters of the stream. Incidents such as this and the trouble along the Moenkopi Wash prompted a missionary, William R. Johnston, to take a Navajo delegation to Washington in 1901 in the hope of obtaining relief for all Navajos living west of the reservation.

President Theodore Roosevelt was a sympathetic listener to their pleas. He arranged to have allotments made to some Navajos living in the area, and solved the Moenkopi problem by purchasing for $40,000 the Mormon holdings of the Tuba City community and turning them over to the Navajos. Roosevelt also issued two Executive Orders that added 1.5 million acres to the reservation west of the 1882 extentension and approximately 500,000 acres in the vicinity of Leupp. Another 56,000 acres in the Four Corners area, known as the Aneth Extension, was added in May 1905. Half a century later this would be the Aneth oil field, which would bring a fortune to the Navajo tribe.

In 1907 President Roosevelt sought to halt conflicts between Navajo and white stockmen by awarding to the Navajos more than 3 million acres east of the 1868 treaty line. At once there arose what a government report termed "a growing clamor of protest brought to bear by non-Indian stockmen and politicians who were determined to force restoration to the public domain of this portion of the old Navajo Country [Dinetah]. Since there were rumors of oil deposits in the area after 1907, the demand was especially great."

Anticipating that the white protesters would be victorious,

the Bureau of Indian Affairs sent allotment agents to the region and succeeded in making some two thousand allotments among four thousand Navajos living in it. The bureau's fears were justified. In January 1911, President William Howard Taft revoked Roosevelt's order and restored to the public domain all unallotted lands in the area in New Mexico known as the Pueblo Bonito section. Here the Hospah oil fields would be developed.

For another six years no changes were made in the size of the reservation. In January 1918, President Woodrow Wilson gave the Navajos 94,000 acres along the Little Colorado. Suspecting that Wilson might be considering restoring to the Navajos some of the valuable lands taken from them by President Taft, New Mexico secured enactment of congressional legislation prohibiting enlargement of the reservation by Executive Order. Large numbers of Navajos were still living on the public domain, and the Indian Bureau renewed its efforts to protect them through allotments. More than 4,600 individual allotments were made, but it was not a successful method of aiding the Navajos, for most of them seemed to fear signing any legal document, while others took the position that papers were not necessary, that the land on which their homes stood and their sheep grazed was part of the Navajo homeland and thus theirs by right of occupation. White stockmen aligned with water, land, and mining corporations, and in 1930 were able to influence Congress to discontinue the allotment system.

About 135,000 acres were added to the Arizona portion of the reservation in 1930 and 1931. In 1933 nearly 50,000 acres in Utah were brought within reservation boundaries, but the state of Utah got its fingers into this pie by persuading Congress to include in the legislation a provision that should oil or gas be discovered in the area, the state would receive 37.5 percent of all royalties "for payment of the tuition of Indian children in white schools, and/or in the building or maintenance of roads across the lands described." Utah also was granted the privilege of "relinquishing such school tracts as it might wish to relinquish within the area, and select lieu tracts of equal acreage outside the area." This had the effect of freeing Utah from the responsibility of providing schools for Navajos living in the state. Also, it placed the state in a position to harvest millions of dollars from oil and gas produced on Navajo lands.

The last major legislation that increased Navajo lands was enacted in 1934 and signed by President Franklin D. Roosevelt. It established boundaries in Arizona that gave the Navajos an additional 800,000 acres. Interior Secretary Harold Ickes sought similar action to protect Navajo interests in New Mexico, for, as a government report stated: "Friction between Navajos and non-Navajos had continued unabated since President Taft's recission [sic] of the Executive Order of 1907 returning a large part of the Pueblo Bonito Reservation to the public domain. This action constituted a victory and a gain in land ownership for non-Indian residents of this portion of the Old Navajo country, while for the Navajo population it was a serious economic blow." A bill to carry out Ickes' intentions died in a Senate pigeonhole.

Using mineral royalties, the Tribal Council purchased three ranches containing 250,000 acres adjacent to the reservation, and through exchange or purchase obtained other tracts in disputed areas. They succeeded in holding on to more than 600,000 acres of federally owned lands.

The present Navajo reservation contains approximately 16 million acres.

In the higher altitudes on the reservation, generally above 7,000 feet, excellent stands of marketable timber are spread over more than half a million acres. These immense forests contain little undergrowth and cover the mountain slopes like great open parklands. Commercial exploitation of Navajo timber is a comparatively recent development. In 1958 the Tribal Council appropriated $7.5 million to finance the Navajo Forest Products Industries. Forest and lumber specialists employed by the tribe now recommend an annual production of 50 million board feet. The lumber industry is wholly owned and operated by the tribe. It brings to the Navajo treasury an annual net profit in excess of half a million dollars.

In a normal year about 80 percent of days in the Navajo country are at least partially clear. A high rate of evaporation is one of the most important causes of water loss, particularly from reservoirs and natural lakes. Thus irrigation projects are costly.

Nearly a fifth of the Navajo country cannot be used for grazing or farming, being barren of edible vegetation and unadaptable to irrigation. Ecological studies show that another 48 percent contains soils rated poor to fair. The soils of 10 percent of the land are rated as excellent.

Two extensive coal fields lie partly within the reservation, but the income from them is negligible, due to the use of other fuels by railroads and industry. Comparatively small amounts of gold, silver, and copper exist, but the amounts do not warrant commercial production. Other minerals found on the reservation include bentonite, asphalt rock, clays, gypsum, lime, and alum.

During World War II a small amount of uranium was mined. The advent of the atomic age sent demands soaring, and prospectors combing the region made substantial discoveries on Navajo lands. Tribal leases to mining companies jumped from $66,000 in 1950 to $152,000 the next year. In the next three years the income to the tribe from leases averaged more than $650,000. It now averages more than $1.2 million a year.

In 1907 a lone well pumped small amounts of oil in Monument Valley. The region was a remote wilderness, it contained no dependable roads, and the deposit was not believed large enough to justify a greater investment and the expense of transporting the oil to refineries hundreds of miles away.

By 1950 there were only fifty-one oil wells in the entire Navajo country, producing a total of 133,000 barrels a year. The tribe's income from oil royalties amounted to $42,000. During the next five years the number of wells increased very little.

On March 1, 1933, Congress had added a tract of marginal grazing land in southeastern Utah to the reservation. It was called the Aneth Strip, and it was inaccessible and exceedingly rough country. Even white stockmen were willing to let the Navajos have it, for it could be of little use to them. The Aneth Strip covered a large part of one of the richest oil and gas deposits in the United States.

In February 1956 the Texas Company, drilling under a lease from the Navajo tribe, brought in a gusher. Other companies rushed to obtain leases in the Aneth Strip area, now known as the Four Corners oil field. Before the year ended the tribe had received lease-bonus, rental, and royalty payments totaling $35 million. In the next year another $30 million had accrued from these sources.

The flood of black gold continues, and more than $200 million has poured into tribal coffers since 1956. New oil and gas leases negotiated in 1968 paid revenues of more than $11 million. The prospecting goes on, and new oil and gas wells have been brought into production, but not in the great quantities of the Aneth–Four Corners strike.

Geologists maintain that large new fields will be discovered.

The federal government holds title to all reservation lands in trust for the Navajo tribe, as well as lands purchased by the tribe outside reservation boundaries, and therefore is responsible for the protection and management of all the tribe's vested interests. A federal agency, the Navajo Branch of Realty, executes this responsibility. Its functions include the sale, exchange, partitioning, patenting, and leasing of Navajo lands; securing of bids for mineral, oil, and gas leases; negotiations for rights-of-way; and issuing of exploration permits. The reservation proper has never been allotted in severalty, but is held in common by all tribal members. The 1969 royalties of approximately $1 million a month are expected to increase substantially in the next few years. To this large income must be added the benefits that the general Navajo economy has enjoyed since the oil and gas boom began. Thousands of Navajos have been employed in drilling and in constructing pipelines, booster stations, power plants, access roads, bridges, buildings and homes, and a large number hold permanent jobs with oil, gas, pipeline, construction, and public utility companies.

The Navajo tribe is the largest and the richest in the United States, but from an analysis of this fact emerges a picture quite in contrast to that portrayed at first glance. If all the oil and gas money credited to the Navajo account in the federal treasury between 1950 and 1960 had been distributed on a per capita basis, each Navajo would have received about $123 a year. The Navajo population in 1969 was approximately 125,000. If the oil and gas royalties accrued in that year had been equally distributed, each Navajo would have received approximately $10 a month. This system was tried for a time by other tribes that were deriving incomes from natural-resource leases. The results were disastrous. The money was quickly wasted on baubles and luxuries, drunkenness and absenteeism soared, and hundreds of battered cars and pickup trucks, for which owners had no cash to purchase parts or make repairs, were abandoned in the countryside.

Navajo leaders were too shrewd to make the same mistake. The royalties went into banks and drew interest. Any funds withdrawn, with the approval of the Secretary of the Interior, were used by the Tribal Council to finance programs to improve the living conditions of all Navajos, provide individuals with opportunities to progress, and bolster the overall economy of the tribe.

The Navajo birth rate is almost double that of the country as a whole. There is nothing to indicate that it will not maintain this high level. Indeed, improvements in home sanitation and a steadily growing number of clinics and medical services are reasons for anticipating a rise.

The infant mortality rate, although it decreased sharply in the last two decades, remains distressingly high, more than 40 percent above the national rate. This problem is being given major attention by the U.S. Public Health Service's Division of Indian Health, and progress toward lowering the rate is steadily achieved. Each year the number of babies born in hospitals increases, and prenatal and postnatal treatment is available to Navajo mothers in a growing number of field health centers.

From an estimated rate of 2 percent in 1900, the annual population increase has risen to an estimated 4 percent in 1970. This has occurred despite extremely poor sanitary conditions, a high mortality rate, a high incidence of tuberculosis and other diseases, improper and inadequate food for many Navajos, and an abiding distrust harbored by many elders toward modern medical practices and government doctors. The day of the medicine man has not ended. That will not happen for a long time, for faith in the singer and the healer is too deeply ingrained in Navajo culture to be easily obliterated.

The determinants of the Navajo population increase are many, and it may be, as eminent scientists suggest, that their "varied origins, so heterogeneous from both biological and cultural sources, have resulted in an outstanding manifestation of that phenomenon known to biologists as 'hybrid vigor.' At all events, there can be no doubt that the fecundity of the tribe is but one symptom of a generally radiant vitality. They want to live. They want children, many children."

To this may be added the remark that they are not only having many children but more of them are surviving than ever before in Navajo history.

# 13

BEFORE THEIR INCARCERATION at Bosque Redondo the Navajos, spread over an enormous territory, had enough cultivatable land, grazing ranges, and water to support themselves. Widespread hunger seldom occurred, even during periods of drought. After Bosque Redondo a reverse situation began to emerge, and it grew steadily more acute. Today agriculture and stock raising cannot sustain half the population.

Any alleviation of this dire condition depends entirely upon the development of scientific ways to increase production. This is not a dawning realization. It is what experts engaged by the federal government have been working to accomplish for nearly four decades. They have achieved considerable success in the face of severe difficulties arising not only from technical or physical problems, but from forceful opposition by the Navajos themselves.

Long before the first government agriculturist was sent

to the Navajos, attempts were made to improve farm and range conditions on the reservation. As early as 1880 Navajo agent Bennett had sought to develop new water supplies. He managed to extract the insignificant sum of $3,500 for the work from the Interior Department. "With this generous appropriation," he wrote sarcastically, "we have begun a system of irrigation by means of wind engines (windmills) and putting down stock pumps." If the program could be continued, it would "lessen the nomadic character of a large number of Navajos as they will not be required to move from one locality to another in search of water for their herds."

Navajos had practiced various types of irrigation since their first contacts with the Pueblos. In some locations plants were watered by hand, the farmers carrying the water from adjacent sources in pots or skins. The principal crops raised were corn, melons, squash, and beans. Corn was by far the most important, for around it "were clustered the rites, tabus and observances associated with agriculture. Likewise, in ceremony, myth and agricultural education, corn played a more important role than any of the three other products."

In the 1890s agent Edwin H. Plummer repeatedly informed Washington that the heavy dependence of the Navajos on stock raising was causing soil erosion and a steady reduction in range food. The result was that poorer animals were being produced. Overgrazing was destroying ground cover. In vain Plummer pleaded for funds to be spent on land-improvement projects, noting that the "annual appropriation for the support and civilization of the Navajos is only $6,500. Out of this comes all running expenses of the agency."

White stockmen and other commercial interests in New Mexico and Arizona were unrelenting in their efforts to take from all Indians in the two states enormous parts of the reservations awarded to them. By 1912 it was apparent that they had won strong support in Congress. In the case of the Navajos, the scheme they proposed was to allot each member of the tribe a small piece of land and to throw open the "surplus" to settlement by non-Indians. It was their claim—which their congressional representatives placed in the *Congressional Record*—that each Navajo on the reservation "owned" 1,100 acres, comprising a total amount "greatly excessive to the needs of the tribe." This, of course, was a falsehood. Nor did the covetous white men mention that enormous parts of the reservation were high mountains, rugged mesas, and barren deserts unusable for agriculture and that due to overgrazing, erosion, and destruction of water supplies, large areas had been virtually ruined. Nor did they reveal that the remaining ranges and farmlands could not produce enough animals and crops to sustain the reservation Navajos.

The machinations of the stockmen and corporations were thwarted largely through the efforts of Father Anselm Weber, a missionary at St. Michaels, Arizona, whose lone voice was more effective than those of Indian agents and organizations striving to improve reservation conditions. In a flaming diatribe, entitled simply "A Statement of Facts," which was printed in newspapers in Washington and other cities, Father Weber declared:

For several years past, there has been agitated the question of alloting lands in Arizona and New Mexico to the Navajos and other Indians [160 acres to each adult] and throwing open to settlement and entry under the public land laws the unallotted balance of lands now embraced in Indian reservations. The cry has been loud that these reservations are too large and are not needed by the Indians. Unfortunately some members of the delegations from these states have appeared to be influenced by exaggerated and untrue statements upon this question. . . .

The Navajo Reservation is stocked heavier and its range is more overgrazed and run down than the range in other parts of Arizona and New Mexico. The Navajos have 1,800,000 head of sheep and goats, and if other classes of livestock (horses, cattle, mules and burros) were converted to sheep units there are 2,328,000.

As a result the soil is eroding badly in many places. . . . Over considerable areas very little plant life is left, except sagebrush, scrub juniper and piñon. The former heavy stand of gramma grass over much of this region is nearly extinct.

Great gashes, deep arroyos, shifting sands, hummocks, and invasive types of vegetation signaled the quickening erosion, yet "the proponents of opening the reservation point to the provision of the 1868 treaty that offered 160-acre assignments to individual Navajos. A hundred and sixty acres could not possibly sustain a Navajo or a Navajo family." As a matter of fact, Father Weber pointed out, there was

little grazing land in the Western and Southwestern States with such a stock-carrying capacity that even four sections of it, 2,560 acres, would maintain a family in ordinary comfortable circumstances.

In the face of all this, what do you think of people who urge the allotment of 160 acres of such grazing lands to the person and then opening the balance to settlement? In Arizona the State Land Commission and the cattlemen and others have insisted on the Government doing that because they want the surplus Indian lands restored to the public domain so they can use them for grazing ground.

The clamor of these two vast, undeveloped States for the opening of the overstocked and overgrazed Navajo Reservation seems rather ludicrous. If it is absolutely necessary for the salvation of New Mexico and Arizona to open the Navajo Reservation, let it be done after adequate homestead and leasing and grazing laws have been passed . . . and after the United States has educated the Navajos to cope with their white neighbors.

The pressure on Congress to open the "surplus" lands on the Navajo reservation died away, but the problems of overgrazing and soil erosion rapidly became more urgent.

In 1927 Indian Commissioner Charles H. Burke reported: "The number of livestock belonging to the Navajos is increasing considerably, and it seems to be desirable that consideration be given to plans for regulating the grazing of stock on the range in such manner as to afford protection to the individual members of the tribe in the development of their stock interests."

A livestock census taken earlier had shown that more than 24 percent of the Navajos owned no sheep at all; 42 percent owned a hundred head or less; 32 percent had from 100 to 1,200 head; and 2 percent had more than 1,200 head. Thus, there were many *pobres* and few *ricos*. A large number of the poor Navajos worked as herders and laborers for the large stock owners, and others subsisted entirely on farming.

Burke's suggestion, if long overdue, was well taken, but he made it clear that the cause of the imbalance in the livestock economy of the Navajos had escaped his understanding. "Each individual member of the Tribe," he said, "is entitled to the use of his proportionate share of the lands belonging to the Reservation, and no one individual is en-

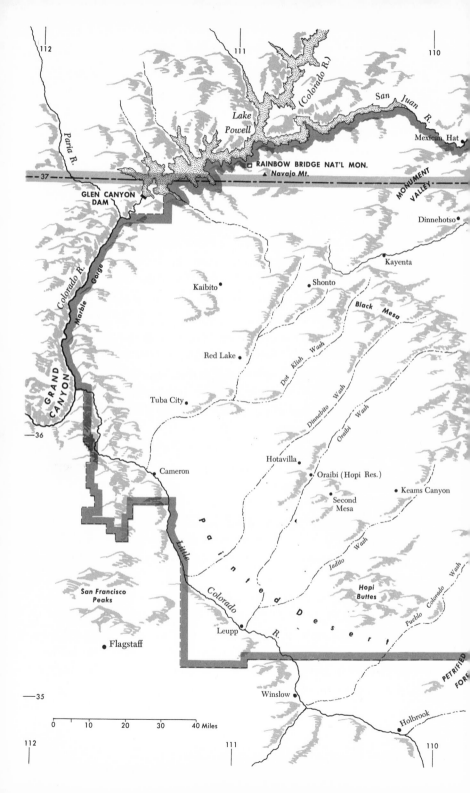

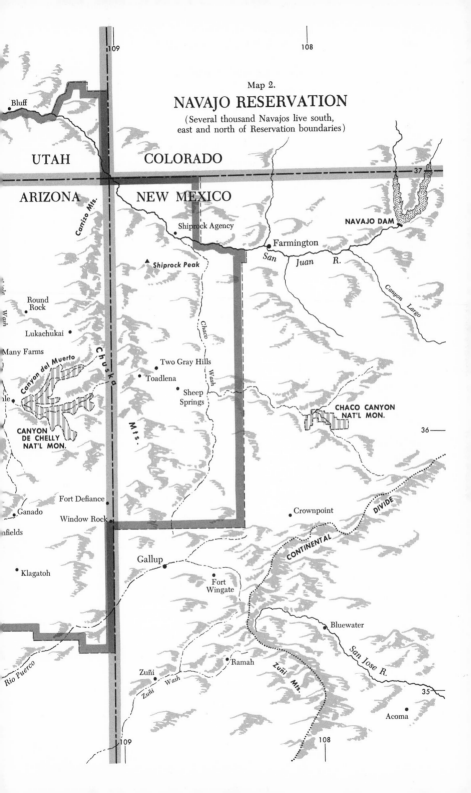

Map 2.

# NAVAJO RESERVATION

(Several thousand Navajos live south,
east and north of Reservation boundaries)

UTAH          COLORADO                                                    37

ARIZONA       NEW MEXICO

Bluff

Carrizo Mts.

Shiprock Agency                              NAVAJO DAM

▲ Shiprock Peak          Farmington

San    Juan    R.

Round                                                      Canyon Largo
Rock

Lukachukai                                    Chaco

Many Farms                                     Wash

Canyon del Muerto          Two Gray Hills

Chuska          Toadlena

Sheep                        CHACO CANYON
Springs                      NAT'L MON.

CANYON          Mts.                                            36
DE CHELLY
NAT'L MON.

Fort Defiance                                CONTINENTAL    DIVIDE

Ganado
Crownpoint
Window Rock

nfields

Gallup

Klagatoh          Fort
Wingate
Bluewater

San  Jose  R.

Ramah          Zuñi
Zuñi          Mts.

Zuñi   Wash                                         35

Acoma

Rio Puerco

109                              108

titled to increase his livestock holdings to the exclusion of other members of the tribe."

The source of this erroneous conception can be traced to the reasoning of officials in Washington that because title to the reservation land was vested in the tribe, each member of the tribe possessed an equal right to use it. This was a premise inconceivable to Navajos. The actual use pattern to which they had always adhered was based on the principle that a family, or group of families, was justified in claiming the right to use certain lands, more or less well defined, and surrounding residents were obligated to respect this claim. They considered mutual consent tantamount to a legal title.

Under pressure from the Indian Bureau, the Navajo Tribal Council placed on the agenda of its November 1928 meeting "The Question of Eventually Limiting the Number of Sheep, Horses, Goats and Cattle for Any One Indian, So that Benefits of the Range May Be more equitably distributed Among All Navajos." It was not a subject which the council members looked forward to considering, and for nearly two days they deferred it while deliberating on other matters, such as oil and gas developments, schools, and women's suffrage. At last Assistant Indian Commissioner A. B. Merritt and District Superintendent Chester E. Faris, both of whom had come out to Fort Defiance especially for the meeting, were able to gain the floor.

"You have more sheep per capita," said Merritt, "than any other people on earth. Some families have three, four and even five thousand head." These *ricos* were "the Fords, Morgans and Rothschilds" of the Navajos, yet a man owning two thousand sheep required a township to support his herds, and the entire Navajo tribe "had only about six hundred townships."

The council members absorbed this information behind

expressionless faces. Merritt persisted. Men with large herds should be required to pay a grazing fee to the tribe. The owner of a thousand sheep that were rightly bred and fed would have an income from their sale of $3,000 to $5,000 a year. A man who owned stock in excess of that number of sheep, or the equivalent in horses and cattle, should pay fifteen cents tax per head each year.

"The grazing area of the Navajo Reservation is your greatest asset," Merritt told the council. "It produced an income of more than $2,500,000 in 1927, in contrast to only $70,000 from oil. Each Navajo has an equal share in that asset. Our plan is to equalize your share in the great grazing asset."

Councilman Little Silversmith spoke: "You say every Navajo should be entitled to own one thousand sheep. I have two thousand sheep, seven children, three grandchildren, a family of twelve, including my wife and myself. No one member of a family owns the family's sheep. If I distribute them equally, each of us owns less than two hundred."

"Then you would not have to pay an excess grazing tax," said Merritt.

"No," said Little Silversmith, "but you say that every Navajo is to be limited to a thousand sheep. In that case, me and my family would have the right to own twelve thousand sheep without paying no tax."

"No," said Merritt. "Each family, the husband, wife and minor children, will be entitled to one thousand sheep without paying an excess grazing fee."

The shrewd and influential Navajo headman, Chee Dodge, had been figuring on a small pad of paper. He put his pencil away and remarked in his quiet voice that there were between ten and twelve thousand Navajo families, a husband and wife being considered a family whether or not they had children, and the population was rapidly growing.

"My boys and girls will soon all be married and will be families," Little Silversmith interjected.

Chee Dodge nodded. "If we say there are ten thousand families of mother and father and two children, and they each can own one thousand sheep, that would be ten million sheep. Even if there were only five thousand families, that would make five million sheep, more than twice as many as the Navajos own now. How can that solve the problem of overgrazing?"

"It is well and all right for Washington to say that we should have one thousand sheep for each family," said councilman Lee Bradley. "We don't have, and we won't ever have, so why talk about it?"

More for the purpose of ending the argument than for any other reason, a majority of the council voted to place a tax of eleven cents a head on all sheep in excess of one thousand owned by a family.

Merritt and Faris hadn't done their homework before meeting with the council. Their plan was not only foolish because it would have increased the number of sheep on the reservation, but it was totally impractical for two other reasons: large stock owners, the *ricos*, could well afford to pay the eleven-cent grazing tax, and therefore would not have to decrease the size of their herds; and there was no means of imposing the excessive grazing tax. The council had no power to enforce it, and if the Indian Bureau was to accomplish the task it would have to keep a small army of tax collectors on the reservation, an expense that would have been greater than the amounts collected—if, indeed, there was any tax to be collected.

In 1933 John Collier was appointed Commissioner of Indian Affairs by President Franklin D. Roosevelt. An eminent sociologist and author who had written extensively on Indian problems, Collier had long been in the forefront of the struggle to secure civil rights for Indians equal to those enjoyed by the white population. No greater champion of minorities had ever occupied the commissioner's office, and as the federal machinery was now geared to support the programs he had long wanted to see undertaken, he arrived at a most auspicious time. The nation was in the depths of the most disastrous depression in its history. The New Deal had been created. Treasury doors stood open to any plan that could alleviate the national distress and bolster the staggering economy.

Hundreds of Navajo families were completely destitute, and carloads of food and clothing were being sent to them by federal relief agencies and the Red Cross. The Navajo Agency reported in 1933:

> Depression for the last three years throughout the country has perhaps hit the Navajo people more severely than it has the average white person. The Navajo is almost entirely dependent upon his income from the livestock industry—principally the sale of wool and lambs. This income has been greatly reduced. In fact, it is almost reduced to the vanishing point since there has been practically no market for lambs and wool. During the past winter the Navajo was forced to feed his corn, which is ordinarily sold to the trader, to his sheep. This again reduced his income.

The day when the Navajos could live independent of outside commerce and trade had ended. They were rapidly becoming as dependent on the products and commodities of the white world as the rural population in most other sections of the nation. Collier saw that the two major problems in the Navajo country could be attacked simultaneously. Poverty and suffering could be alleviated by funds made available for public works, which included conservation projects. Therefore, an unprecedented opportunity existed to inaugurate desperately needed stock-reduction and range-management programs for the Navajos.

Collier wasted no time. A few months after taking office he was in council with Navajo headmen at Fort Wingate. He had been preceded by agricultural and livestock experts, soil scientists, hydrologists, and civil engineers. Their reports were ready for him, and they left no doubt that both the Navajos and their land were in desperate straits.

Collier understood Indians. He knew the necessity for proceeding with deliberateness. His first move was to authorize work projects that would provide destitute Navajos with daily wages with which they could support their families. Next he secured permission from the Tribal Council to construct a federal experiment station at Mexican Springs. Then he went away, but in November he was back again, accompanied by a staff of specialists. He called a council in Tuba City, and placed before the Navajos the plan he and his associates had devised.

If he had destroyed Tuba City with a bomb he would not have caused more excitement throughout the Navajo country.

A horse consumed four to five times as much grass as a sheep, he told the council. The immense bands of horses running wild on the reservation had to be removed, either through sale or outright destruction.

Cattle were not such a problem, as there were comparatively few of them, but a cow also consumed four to five times as much grass as a sheep. Perhaps many could be retained, but only if the necessary supplies of fodder were obtained by irrigation of new lands.

It was estimated that with proper range management and

intensified conservation, the Navajo country could support 560,000 head of sheep. At least an equal number would have to be sold.

Fifty new schools would be built, and more conservation and work programs would be launched. The federal funds appropriated for these projects would compensate for losses in livestock income. Improvements in breeding practices would increase the income from the remaining livestock.

This was the most practical and sensible plan ever devised for saving the natural resources of the Navajos from complete destruction, but few Navajos saw it in that light. They could not comprehend the objectives of the program, and could not equate money received in wages with livestock as constituting wealth and security. The effect on them was one of shock, a reaction that stemmed from a traditional respect for the right of all life to exist, combined with a profound aversion to what seemed a willful waste of a resource that for centuries had been a cornerstone of their economy. Moreover, to them large herds were not simply sources of meat, wool, and money, but status symbols, symbols of a life that was right and proper. Most important of all, animals, especially sheep and horses, were significantly symbolic in their culture and religious beliefs.

Following the "Emergence of the Navajos from the Underworlds" and the "Establishing of Surface World Features," according to the creation myth, "life was given to that which is called sheep . . . the sheep were set free to go in the four directions. They ate and then they shook themselves, whereupon black clouds came together in a mass overhead and on the same day hail fell. And on the same day the plants that had been placed with their mates on the world began to multiply and grow. With our sheep we were created."

In four hundred years the order of events can be forgotten, and the true origin of living things to which a people have grown accustomed can be obscured by myth. When the Southwest became American territory the Navajos had possessed livestock for nearly three centuries, and for many years animal husbandry had been an institution in their culture. Almost a century had passed after General Kearney marched into New Mexico before John Collier arrived, but the cultural and religious values that the Navajos associated with stock raising had lost none of their strength. If there were no horses, they said, there would be no Navajos. If you take away our sheep, they said, you take away our food. This cannot be right, they said, for without our sheep we die.

Every meeting between Collier's scientists and the Navajos was disrupted by emotional outbursts from enraged stock raisers. The women were especially bitter, and displayed their wrath in fiery verbal assaults on the "Washington" that was trying to impoverish their people and destroy their sanctified mode of existence. "An Indian war is one thing," a mild-mannered agronomist wrote his wife. "A squaw war is something else. I don't want to be here if it comes."

Collier understood the reactions, for he understood the Navajos and was thoroughly versed in their history. In the face of the storm he announced that arrangements had been made through the Works Progress Administration to launch the stock-reduction plan by purchasing 100,000 sheep at $1 to $1.50 a head for ewes and $2.25 to $3 a head for wethers. The eminent and brilliant Chee Dodge, one of the few Navajo leaders who believed the program was in the best interests of his people, suggested that a premium price be paid for good breeding ewes because, at the prices offered, Navajo stockmen would sell only cull animals. Government relief officials rejected the proposal. Prices could not be changed.

As might have been expected, Washington bureaucrats allowed the program to become bogged down in red tape and conflicting regulations. The Navajo country was divided into "jurisdictions," and a reduction quota was set for each subdivision. No consideration was given to the matter of individual ownership. Some Navajos owned thousands of sheep. Others owned a few hundred. Many families owned no more than twenty-five. The large owners flatly refused to bear the brunt of the reduction. The small owners refused to sell any animals, claiming their very life depended on the income derived from them.

After prolonged wrangling, the Washington desk generals proposed that each sheep owner be required to sell 10 percent of his stock, of which 75 percent should be ewes and 25 percent wethers. The plan was grossly unfair to the small stock raiser. By providing a market for culls, the government enabled the large stock owner to maintain his herds at the highest production level.

Next, the reduction planners turned their attention to the goats. An agreement was finally reached under which the Navajos were committed to sell 150,000 goats to the Relief Administration at $1 a head. The goats were to be delivered in small bands in the late fall of 1934 to various shipping points from which they would be transported to packing plants. Bitter cold and snow disrupted the schedule. The Navajos were given permission to slaughter as many of the goats as they could consume. A hundred and fifty thousand goats easily could have been eaten in the Navajo country before spring arrived, but government officials decided this sensible idea might establish a bad precedent, and retracted it. Agents were sent through the country, and thousands of goats were shot and left to rot. In one place, Navajo Canyon, more than 3,500 goats were shot in a single day. In time, thousands of horses would be destroyed in the same manner.

Wiser heads prevailed in the reduction program in ensuing years. They devised a policy under which the brunt of the reduction was placed on large owners, and persons owning one hundred sheep units or less—a horse was five sheep units and a cow, four—would not be required to sell any of their stock. Practical and just as this plan was, it was not well received. Large owners complained that small owners were benefiting more than they by daily wages from government projects. Small owners, the great majority of Navajo stock raisers, were too frightened, suspicious, and angry to recognize benefits in any government proposal.

Although the opposition of the Navajos to the stock-reduction, soil-conservation, and restricted-grazing programs would not subside with the passage of years—the controversy continues as these words are written—it is indisputable that many benefits have been derived from them. Large herds of useless horses no longer consume valuable forage. Through breeding experiments conducted at government stations a sheep has been developed that is vastly superior in every way to the animal grazed in the past. Wool production has been increased at least 40 percent. Lambs are heavier. Meat is high grade. Detention and diversion dams dot the Navajo country. Conservation programs include protection of the land against erosion and soil deterioration, restoration of depleted areas, stabilization of runoff and sediment production, improvement of cover on pastures and ranges, retention of water for farm and domestic use, and water management, pond construction, brush control, and the planting of trees.

Except for the San Juan River on the north there are few dependable streams in the Navajo country, yet modern engineering methods have brought under cultivation some forty thousand acres in small projects by ensuring an adequate water supply. The dream agent Bennett harbored in

1881 of constructing a canal from the San Juan has come true. The immense Navajo Dam stands on the river near the north border of Dinetah. The enormous reservoir behind it is the source of water for the Navajo Irrigation Project, comprising more than 110,000 acres. The cost of these developments was fantastic. In legislation authorizing Navajo Dam its cost was estimated at nearly $23 million and that for the irrigation project at $135 million. That was in 1958. Rising construction costs in the next few years significantly increased these figures as the dam and irrigation works were being built.

Squaws no longer scream epithets at agricultural experts, and stock raisers no longer attempt to conceal their sheep, cattle, and horses from inspectors, but the independence so deeply ingrained in the Navajo character sometimes prevents complete submission to control. Navajos still detest the quotas, grazing permits, and other restrictions that affect their traditional way of life. Their opposition is decreasing, but it is far from gone. Communications between them and government specialists have greatly improved in recent years. Proposed programs and new regulations are thoroughly discussed in meetings at the grass-roots level, not simply arbitrarily dictated by armchair strategists two thousand miles away.

Complete restoration of the health formerly enjoyed by the Navajo country is impossible. The cure was begun too late. At least a million acres of land once profitably used for grazing can never be restored. It will forever remain barren and totally useless. The fight to save another 5 million acres is still touch-and-go. Drought, high winds, and flooding rains cannot be halted by conservation practices. They are still the formidable enemies they were in the past. In 1943 the carrying capacity of the grazing lands for sheep units was set at 512,000. It is now more than a third less than that figure. Six or seven of the seventeen Land Management Districts into which the reservation has been divided are still overgrazed. Emergency feeding operations are necessary in most years. The cost of them, running into many millions, far exceeds the value of all the livestock on the reservation. Tribal funds must be used for emergency livestock-purchase programs designed to create an artificial market for lambs and thereby relieve the burden on the range.

The extent to which the Navajos depend upon livestock has declined drastically during the last thirty years. Perhaps no more than 40 percent of the total number of families possess grazing permits. Families who own no stock and those owning too few to provide them with an adequate income must look for wage work on and off the reservation. Employment of this type is difficult to obtain, and many families endure a precarious existence on the borderline of serious want.

A Navajo Agency report paints the situation in true, if somewhat gloomy, colors:

> The course of events since the 1930's emphasizes the fact that cultural change is usually a gradual process, especially where necessary adaptation requires changes which are revolutionary in their scope and effect. The spread of education and the broadening of work experience among the Navajo people will some day soon ring down the final curtain on the traditional economy of the Tribe, but the people must be trained and other sources of livelihood must enter the scene to supplant stockraising before The People will voluntarily exchange their pastoral life for one based on new and different pursuits.

Yet that is what they are being forced to do to survive,

and the outlook is not encouraging, for even "seasonal labor, tribally sponsored Reservation public works and construction programs, the livestock industry, and other economic media are all limited in their scope, their duration, and their adequacy to provide a livelihood, at acceptable standards, for the Navajo people."

The old way of life is disappearing, but it will never be forgotten until the chants of the creation myths are no longer heard in the light of ceremonial fires.

# 14

ALTHOUGH THE NAVAJO social structure was based on fundamental democratic principles, it had no resemblance whatsoever to the United States system of government. In a political sense a Navajo tribe did not exist at the time of the American occupation of the Southwest. The people shared a common language and culture, but their political organization did not extend beyond bands, or families, led by headmen called *naat'aanii*, literally "speech makers." These local leaders were respected and often revered, but they held no powers of coercion. They could persuade but not command. They were appointed by group decisions, and they could be removed by the same means. They were controlled by the voice of their respective followers.

Not until 1921 did this age-old political system undergo its first drastic change. In that year oil was discovered in substantial quantities on the northeastern part of the reservation, and the Bureau of Indian Affairs authorized a refining company to negotiate a development lease with Navajos residing in the area. Immediately a legal barrier was encountered. The treaty of 1868 stated that no part of the reservation "could thereafter be ceded without the consent of three-fourths of the Indians who resided on it or had an interest in it." As some lawyers saw the situation, the only avenue open was to obtain drilling permission from a general council of all adult Navajos living on the treaty reservation. Meetings were held at various places, and the necessary consent was obtained. Some opinions, however, declared this action to be legally insufficient because thousands of other Navajos inhabited official additions to the original reservation and "therefore retained an interest in the matter." A general assembly of all Navajos was impracticable, if not impossible, as many were scattered over immense and remote regions. The only feasible approach to the problem appeared to be the appointment of a "representative group to act in behalf of all Navajos."

This was the beginning of the Navajo tribal government. A "Business Council" composed of three influential Navajos was established in 1922. The members were Chee Dodge, Charlie Mitchell, and Dugal Chee Bekiss, and they were authorized to negotiate oil leases. Undoubtedly this was stretching the authority of the Commissioner of Indian Affairs beyond legal limits, and attorneys, fearing repercussions, pointed out that the Business Council did not, in fact, represent all sectors of the Navajo domain, nor could it represent all Navajo people since it had not been chosen by popular vote.

To resolve the issue, and to protect his own neck, Indian Commissioner Burke issued a new set of "regulations and procedures," which provided for the "establishment of a Navajo Tribal Council, and the office of Commissioner of the Navajos," who would be an Indian Bureau appointee with supervisory authority over Navajo affairs. The Tribal Council was to be composed of one delegate and one alternate from six districts, as well as a chairman and vice-chairman. The Burke regulations were soon revised to permit Navajo women to vote for their representatives, and the number of delegates was governed by district populations.

July 27, 1923, was the birth date of the Navajo Tribal Council. On that day the delegates and alternates assembled at Toadlena, New Mexico. Navajos think of them as their founding fathers and revere their memory. The Burke regulation required that a chairman be chosen outside the council membership, and the delegates accorded the honor to a man who fully merited it, Henry Chee Dodge.

The chapter system, designed for the purpose of bringing people of a community together to discuss common problems, had been introduced in some western reservations as early as 1922, but was not undertaken in the Navajo country until five years later. Superintendent John Hunter organized the first Navajo chapter at Leupp. Thereafter the program rapidly developed, and was enthusiastically supported by the Navajos. They willingly donated labor and materials to build meetinghouses.

Five years after it was launched, however, the chapter movement came close to being completely destroyed by a mandatory stock-reduction program to halt overgrazing of Navajo ranges. For twenty years no new chapters were organized, and few continued to function. A revival began in 1952, and by 1970 more than a hundred chapters were operating.

The first Tribal Council possessed no actual governmental powers. Many Navajos did not know it existed. Its actions had little direct effect on the lives of the people. It was an innovation, the function of which the Navajos did not understand, and the real leadership still remained at the local level in the hands of the leaders of bands and families.

In 1933 the council advocated a reorganization of its structure along constitutional lines so that it would be more truly representative of the people. The Indian Bureau endorsed the proposal, but most Navajos opposed it in the erroneous belief that it would ensure the Secretary of the Interior greater autocratic powers.

After enduring several stormy years, in November 1936, at the urging of Indian Commissioner Collier, the Tribal Council appointed an Executive Committee, headed by Henry Tallman, "to call a constitutional assembly for the purpose of considering and adopting a constitution and by-laws for the Navajo people." This was the final action of the council as it was originally formed. The resolution was without precedent in American Indian history. It opened the door to the creation of a genuinely representative form of government, with its functions prescribed, its powers delineated by statutes, and its members elected by popular vote.

A Navajo constitution was drafted, but Secretary Ickes refused to approve it on the ground that the drafting committee was no more than a "provisional council" and was "not empowered to exercise all the residual quasi-sovereign powers of the Tribe." This was legal mumbo-jumbo. The real reason for Ickes' action was that the controversy between the Interior Department and the Navajos over the stock-reduction program was bitter, and Ickes did not want to provide the Navajos with new weapons that could be used to fight him.

The Navajo constitution died aborning, but under regulations issued by Ickes an election was held on September 24, 1938. For the first time, it was conducted by secret ballot.

As the great majority of Navajos could neither read nor write, photographs and colors were employed to identify candidates running for the seventy-four seats to be filled— a number that gave equal representation to the residents of each election community into which the Navajo country had been divided.

The powers and functions of the Tribal Council have steadily increased through the years. In structure it is a miniature Congress. Various committees hold hearings on specific issues and proposals and send recommendations to the floor for consideration by the full membership. Officers receive substantial annual salaries. The Secretary of the Interior retains statutory authority to veto council programs and expenditures, but few have been rejected in recent years. The desire of the Navajos to operate reservation programs independent of the federal government is stronger than in the past, and they are looking to the day when it will be possible to take full advantage of the sovereign powers vested in the tribe.

For an unknown number of centuries Tseghahodzani, the great Window Rock near Fort Defiance, had been a Navajo shrine. Navajo historians say it was "very important in the rites of the Tohee, the Water Way Ceremony. It was one of four places where Navajo medicine men came with their woven water bottles to get water for the ceremony, which was held to bring abundant rain."

In 1936 Indian Commissioner Collier selected Window Rock as the site for the new Navajo Central Agency. The large buildings and residences are uniform in design and constructed of russet sandstone quarried in the vicinity. The complex, spread over spacious grounds shaded by cottonwoods, contains the administration officers of both the Bureau of Indian Affairs and the Navajo Council Chamber. It is an immense hogan.

In Window Rock it would be easy to imagine oneself in the civic center of a progressive American town—until one paused to think of the size of the territory under the jurisdiction of the Navajo government. Twelve states have less area than the Navajo country.

The Navajo government operates its own utility companies, supplying electric power, gas, and fuel to all consumers, industrial and domestic, in the region. It has its own legal staff, its own accountants and auditors. It maintains an insurance department, a bureau handling oil, gas, and mineral leases, a budget bureau, a realty department, and Tribal Council committees on administration, community services, engineering, resources, health, sanitation, water supply development, grazing permits, highways, and land management.

The first period of Navajo acculturation developed after their first contacts with the Pueblos. The second began with Spanish colonization of the Southwest. The third began in 1871, when the first trading post was opened on the reservation by Charles Crary.

It was in the trading posts that the Navajos became acquainted with many of the wonders of the outside world. There they could see yards of bright cloth, ready-made clothing, utensils, tools, knives, nails—everything from a bottle of soda pop to a farm wagon—and, most wonderful of all, canned and packaged foods, coffee, sugar, pork and beans, and especially canned peaches.

Business was conducted almost entirely by barter. A Navajo man or woman delivered wool, hides, blankets, or jewelry to the trader. The value of the articles was agreed upon, usually after long discussion and bargaining, and the amount was credited to the Navajo's account. Traders were bankers and pawn-shop operators as well as merchants, and they advanced credit to customers considered reliable.

A Navajo in urgent need could obtain foodstuffs or other commodities by depositing jewelry or rugs as collateral. If the debt was paid within a specified time, the valuables were restored to their owner; otherwise they could be sold by the trader as unredeemed pawn.

The traders created commercial outlets for Navajo rugs. Before 1890 a Navajo woman was obliged to spin her wool thread, make vegetable dyes, and unravel old cloth before she could weave. Usually she could make no more than one or two blankets a year. Traders supplied weavers with yarn in a variety of colors, and cotton string for warp threads. A good market developed throughout the nation, but many of the Navajo designs did not appeal to American buyers. The traders supplied the weavers with designs in colors that were popular, and thereafter the Navajo economy enjoyed one of its greatest boosts.

A trader operating on the reservation was required to have a license from the Commissioner of Indian Affairs. Usually a senator could get one for a political friend. As a result, unscrupulous traders opened posts, but most of them did not survive long. Licenses could be revoked without warning. The Navajos were not easily fooled. More than one dishonest trader found that the sacks of wool he had obtained at a bargain contained rocks cleverly concealed in them.

To be successful, a trader had to please his customers, and his post had to serve as more than just a general store. To the Navajos a post was a gathering place, a place they visited not only to buy and sell, but to meet friends and relatives, to exchange news and gossip, to learn of things new and exciting in the strange world of the white man beyond the far horizons. The trader, talking to them in their own language, was their chief link to the outside.

Since 1955 trading in the Navajo country has been controlled by the Tribal Council. In addition to licensing, Navajo Reservation Regulations provide for a rental based on 1.5 percent of a trader's gross annual receipts, or a minimum of $300 a year, and inspection of traders' books. The regulations prohibit ownership of multiple posts so as to assure free competition and to prevent monopoly. The council also provides funds for a system of tribal trading cooperatives.

The extent to which the Navajo Tribal Council has adopted modern methods is demonstrated each morning when a dapper young man enters a room at Window Rock. He is there to operate an electronic computer, which is used to "manage" well over a hundred tribal projects.

# 15

CURRENTLY THE FEDERAL government is spending approximately $125 million each year in the Navajo reservation. To this enormous sum must be added the millions expended by the Navajos' own treasury. Only in a few respects have the results of this outlay been encouraging.

As this is written, more than twenty thousand Navajos, almost a fifth of their population, are unable to obtain gainful employment, and more than three thousand young men and women enter the labor market each year. A majority of the unemployed can read and write to a limited extent and are under thirty years of age.

The mean annual income of Navajos (1970) is less than $700.

In 1940 more than 58 percent of the total income of the Navajos was derived from farming and stock raising. In 1970 approximately 7 percent of their income came from these sources. Agricultural production on lands now in use cannot be increased. Indeed, it may have to be decreased if the lands are not to be destroyed. The ranges and arable lands are utilized to their limits, and in some places beyond practical limits.

The recent construction of several surfaced roads, which opened large parts of the reservation to tourists, has been a boon of no small dimensions to the Navajo economy. More than half a million people travel through the beautiful country each year. Besides granting leases for a number of motels, service stations, and restaurants, all of which employ Navajos, the Tribal Council has set aside seven large tracts as recreational areas for visitors where they can enjoy camp grounds, fishing, swimming, and hiking amid surpassing scenery. A Navajo leader remarked that "tourists are easier to shear than sheep," and then added dolefully, "but they will never be a solution to the tribe's difficulties."

Computer analysis of projects, helpful as it may be, will not resolve the dilemma of the Navajos, nor will increased expenditures by welfare agencies. Greater expenditures to develop natural resources will not resolve it for not only can these wellsprings of revenue be depleted, but distribution of this income on a per capita basis would be no more effective than throwing it to the winds that sweep through the Window Rock.

The only means of building a sound and prosperous Navajo economy is to enact two fundamental programs for which the Navajos themselves long have pleaded.

The first is the establishment of schools and colleges on the reservation in which students can be trained to fill the many posts now occupied by hundreds of white employees of federal agencies who are stumbling over one another in the crowded reservation offices. Given the opportunity, the tribe would produce all the doctors, lawyers, teachers, scientists, technicians, business executives, mechanics, and laborers needed in the Navajo country.

This accomplishment would be futile, however, without the simultaneous development of industry *on the reservation* by both the federal government and private industry. Land is not a problem. Labor is not a problem. Money is not a problem. Fuel is not a problem, for the region contains enormous coal, gas, and oil deposits. Housing is not a problem, for the housing required could be quickly constructed. Transportation is not a problem, for trucklines, airlines, and a major transcontinental railroad serve the area. Although there is a shortage of water, acquiring an adequate supply is not an insurmountable problem. If oil and gas pipelines can be built, pipelines to transport water can be built. Lines from the existing reservoirs on the Colorado and San Juan rivers could deliver all the industrial and domestic water that would be required for years to come. The cost of building them would be much less than the amount that will be spent by welfare agencies in the next few years.

The progress already achieved by the Navajos is nothing less than phenomenal. They have repeatedly demonstrated that they are able learners and adapters. They display extraordinary perspicacity, remarkable physical stamina, and superior intellect. The symphonic functioning of their inherent aggressiveness, determination, and self-faith has made it possible for them to advance, against overwhelming odds, far beyond the progress attained by other Indian tribes.

As individuals the Navajos are fiercely independent, yet more than ever before in their history they are conscious of their common need to stand together against white men who would destroy their proud heritage. If they are unable to preserve that vital unity, it will not be their fault.

Unlike some other minority groups, Navajos are not burning down buildings, rioting, destroying property, defying authority, and killing to gain their rights. Their restraint does not stem from fear; that is not one of their weaknesses. It stems from an indestructible and profound desire to maintain harmony, to improve themselves, and to live in peace.

It would be a national tragedy if Americans force them to adopt the methods of the modern-day warpath.

# Selected Bibliography

MOST OF THE WORKS listed below contain extensive bibliographies which will guide students and other interested readers to the hundreds of books and scientific papers dealing with the history and culture of the Navajos.

ALEXANDER, C. I. *An Introduction to Navajo Sandpaintings.* Museum of Navajo Ceremonial Art. Santa Fe, 1967.

AMSDEN, CHARLES AVERY. *Navajo Weaving.* Santa Ana, Calif., 1934.

———. "Navajo Origins," *New Mexico Historical Review.* Santa Fe, 1932.

BAILEY, L. R., ed. *The Navajo Reconnaissance—A Military Exploration in 1859.* Los Angeles, 1964.

———. *The Long Walk.* Los Angeles, 1964.

———. *Indian Slave Trade in the Southwest.* Los Angeles, 1966.

BANCROFT, HUBERT HOWE. *History of Arizona and New Mexico.* San Francisco, 1889.

BANDELIER, A. F. and FANNY. *Historical Documents Relating to New Mexico.* Carnegie Institution. Washington, D.C., 1937.

BARTOS, LAVERNE. *The Navajo Tribal Utility Story.* Window Rock, N.Mex., 1968.

BEADLE, J. H. *The Undeveloped West, Or Five Years in the Territories, 1868–1873.* Philadelphia, 1873.

BENAVIDES, FRAY ALONSO DE. *Memorial.* Translated by Mrs. Edward E. Ayer; F. W. Hodge and Charles F. Lummis, eds. Albuquerque, N.Mex., 1965.

BLOOM, LANSING B., ed. "Bourke on the Southwest," *New Mexico Historical Review,* Vols. VIII–XIII. Albuquerque, N.Mex., 1933–38.

BOLTON, HUBERT E. *Coronado, Knight of Pueblos and Plains.* New York, 1949.

BRUGGE, DAVID M. *Long Ago in Navajoland.* Window Rock, Ariz., 1965.

———. *Navajo Pottery and Ethnohistory.* Window Rock, Ariz., 1963.

———. "Causes of the Navajo Wars," *Navajo Times,* Vol. VI. Window Rock, Ariz., 1965.

BUCARELY Y URSUA, ANTONIO. *Correspondence of 1772–1777.* Archivo General de Indias. (See Thomas, 1932.)

CALHOUN, JAMES S. *Official Correspondence of James S. Calhoun, White Indian Agent at Santa Fe and Superintendent of Indian Affairs in New Mexico.* Annie H. Abel, ed. Washington, D.C., 1915.

CHAVES, AMADO. *The Defeat of the Comanches in 1716.* New Mexico Historical Society. Santa Fe, N.Mex., 1906.

CHITTENDEN, HIRAM MARTIN. *History of the American Fur Trade of the Far West.* 3 vols. New York, 1902.

COHEN, FELIX S. *Federal Indian Law.* Washington, D.C., 1940.

COONS, CARLTON S. *The Story of Man.* New York, 1962.

CREMONY, JOHN C. *Life Among the Apaches.* San Francisco, 1868.

CROIX, TEODORO DE. Correspondence of, 1777–1783. Archivo General de Indias and Spanish Archives of New Mexico. (See Thomas, 1932; and Twitchell, 1914.)

CURTIS, E. S. *The North American Indian.* 20 vols. Cambridge, Mass., 1907–30.

DALE, EDWARD E. *The Indians of the Southwest.* Norman, Okla., 1949.

DAVIS, W. H. *El Gringo, Or New Mexico and Her People.* New York, 1857.

DITTERT, ALFRED E., JR., JIM J. HESTER, and FRANK W. EDDY. *An Archeological Survey of the Navajo Reservoir District.* School of American Research and Museum of New Mexico. Santa Fe, N.Mex., 1961.

DOUGLAS, A. E., "Dating Pueblo Bonito and Other Ruins in the Southwest," *National Geographic.* Washington, D.C., June 1935.

DUNN, J. P., JR. *Massacres of the Mountains.* New York, 1886.

FORBES, J. D. *Apache, Navajo and Spaniard.* Norman, Okla., 1960.

FOSTER, KENNETH E. *Navajo Sandpaintings.* Window Rock, Ariz., 1964.

HACKETT, CHARLES WILSON. *The Revolt of the Pueblo Indians of New Mexico and Otermin's Attempted Reconquest, 1680–1682.* 2 vols. Albuquerque, N.Mex., 1942.

HALL, E. T. "Recent Clues to Athapascan Pre-history in the Southwest," *American Anthropologist,* Vol. 46. Menasha, Wis., 1944.

HAMMOND, GEORGE P. *Don Juan de Oñate and the Founding of New Mexico.* Santa Fe, N.Mex., 1927.

—— and AGAPITO REY. *Narratives of the Coronado Expedition.* Albuquerque, N.Mex., 1940.

HAMMOND and REY, eds. and trs. *Don Juan de Oñate, Colonizer of New Mexico.* 2 vols. Albuquerque, N.Mex., 1953.

——. *Obregon's History of 16th Century Exploration in Western America.* Los Angeles, 1928.

——. *Gallegos Relation of the Rodriguez Expedition to New Mexico.* Historical Society of New Mexico. Albuquerque, N.Mex., 1927.

——. *Expedition into New Mexico Made by Antonio de Espejo, 1582–1583.* Quivira Society. Los Angeles, 1929.

HESTER, J. J. *Navajo Migrations and Acculturation.* Museum of New Mexico. Santa Fe, N.Mex., 1962.

HEYMAN, MAX L. *Prudent Soldier: A Biography of Edward R. S. Canby.* Glendale, Calif., 1959.

HILL, WILLARD W. *Navajo Warfare.* New Haven, Conn., 1936.

——. *Agricultural and Hunting Methods of the Navajo Indians.* Albuquerque, N.Mex., 1937.

HODGE, FREDERICK W., ed. *Handbook of American Indians North of Mexico.* 2 vols. Bureau of American Ethnology. Washington, D.C., 1906.

——. "The Early Navajos and Apaches," *American Anthropologist,* Vol. 8. Washington, D.C., 1895.

——. *Spanish Explorers in the Southern United States.*

HORGAN, PAUL. *Great River: The Rio Grande in North American History.* New York, 1954.

HRDLICKA, A. "Physical and Physiological Observations on the Navajo," *American Anthropologist,* Vol. 12. New York, 1900.

HUBBELL, JUAN LORENZO. "Fifty Years an Indian Trader," *Touring Topics* magazine. Los Angeles, May 1939.

HUGHES, JOHN T. *Doniphan's Expedition: Containing an Account of the Conquest of New Mexico.* Cincinnati, O., 1847.

IRVING, WASHINGTON. *The Adventures of Captain Bonneville, U.S.A., in the Rocky Mountains and the Far West.* New York, 1850.

KELEHER, WILLIAM A. *Turmoil in New Mexico, 1846–68.* Santa Fe, N.Mex., 1952.

KEUR, D. L. "A Chapter in Navajo-Pueblo Relationships," *American Antiquity.* Menasha, Wis., June 1944.

KLUCKHOHN, CLYDE, and DOROTHEA LEIGHTON. *The Navaho.* Cambridge, Mass., 1946.

KRUG, J. A. *Report on the Navajos.* U.S. Government.

KUPPER, WINIFRED. *The Golden Hoof.* New York, 1945.

LANGLEY, DAMA. "The Indestructibles," *Arizona Highways* magazine, August 1968. Phoenix, Ariz.

LETTERMAN, JONATHAN. "Sketch of the Navajo Tribe of Indians," *Smithsonian Report.* Washington, D.C., 1855.

LEUPP, FRANCIS E. *The Indian and His Problem.* New York, 1910.

LINK, MARTIN A., ed. *Navajo—A Century of Progress 1868–1968.* Window Rock, Ariz., 1968.

LUMMIS, CHARLES F. "Fray Zarate Salmeron's Relation," *Land of Sunshine* magazine, Vol. 12. Los Angeles, 1900.

LUXAN, DIEGO PEREZ DE (See Hammond and Rey, *Espejo Expedition.*)

MCCALL, GEORGE A. *Letters from the Frontier.* Philadelphia, 1868.

MARTIN, PAUL S., GEORGE I. QUIMBY, and DONALD COLLIER. *Indians Before Columbus.* Chicago, 1947.

MATHEWS, LINDA. Los Angeles *Times,* June 1, 1969.

MATTHEWS, WASHINGTON. *The Mountain Chant.* Bureau of American Ethnology. Washington, D.C., 1887.

———. *The Night Chant.* American Museum of Natural History. New York, 1902.

MERIAM, LEWIS, and others. *The Problem of Indian Administration.* Baltimore, 1928.

*Navajo Agency Letter Book.* Unpublished office records.

*Navajo Business Frontier,* Window Rock, Ariz., 1968.

*Navajo Centennial—A Century of Progress.* Window Rock, Ariz., 1968.

*Navajo Forest Products Industries.* 8th Annual Report. Navajo, N.Mex., 1968.

*Navajo Nation.* Window Rock, Ariz., 1968.

*Navajo Times.* Window Rock, Ariz.

*Navajo Treaty of 1868.* Flagstaff, Ariz., 1968.

NEWCOMB, FRANC J., and GLADYS A. REICHARD. *Sandpaintings of the Navajo Shooting Chant.* New York, 1937.

O'BRYAN, A. *The Dine: Origin Myths of the Navajo Indians.* Bureau of American Ethnology. Washington, D.C., 1956.

PHILLIPS, PAUL. *General Statement on Conditions in the Navajo Area.* Window Rock, Ariz., 1941.

POWELL, JOHN WESLEY. *Indian Linguistic Families.* Bureau of American Ethnology. Washington, D.C., 1891.

REEVE, FRANK D. "Federal Indian Policy in New Mexico, 1858–1880," *New Mexico Historical Review.* Santa Fe, N.Mex., Dec. 1937–Jan. 1938.

———. "Navajo-Spanish Wars 1680–1720," *New Mexico Historical Review.* Albuquerque, N.Mex., June 1958.

REICHARD, GLADYS A. *Social Life of the Navajo Indians.* New York, 1928.

———. *Navajo Religion.* 2 vols. New York, 1950.

RENGEL, JOSEPH ANTONIO. Correspondence of, 1785–1786. Archivo General de Indias (See Thomas, 1932.)

RUXTON, GEORGE F. *Adventures in Mexico and the Rocky Mountains.* New York, 1848.

Santa Fe *New Mexican,* December 12, 1863.

SAPIR, E. "Internal Linguistic Evidence Suggestive of the Northern Origin of the Navajo," *American Anthropologist,* Vol. 38. Menasha, Wis., 1936.

SAPIR, EDWARD, and HARRY HOYER. *Navajo Texts.* Iowa City, Iowa, 1942.

SCHAAFSMA, POLLY. *Rock Art.* Museum of New Mexico. Santa Fe, N.Mex., 1963.

SCHOOLCRAFT, HENRY R., ed. *Indian Tribes of the United States.* Philadelphia, 1856.

SIMPSON, JAMES H. *Navajo Expedition.* Norman, Okla., 1964.

SMITH, HOMER W. *Man and His Gods.* Boston, 1955.

SPICER, E. H. "Spanish-Indian Acculturation in the Southwest," *American Anthropologist,* Vol. 56. Menasha, Wis., 1954.

STALLINGS, W. S. *Dating Prehistoric Ruins by Tree Rings.* Laboratory of Anthropology. Santa Fe, N.Mex., 1939.

TERRELL, JOHN UPTON. *Traders of the Western Morning: Aboriginal Commerce in Precolumbian North America.* Southwest Museum. Los Angeles, 1967.

———. *Journey Into Darkness: The Story of Cabeza de Vaca.* New York, 1963.

———. *The Man Who Rediscovered America: A Biography of John Wesley Powell.* New York, 1969.

———. *Estevanico the Black.* Los Angeles, 1968.

THOMAS, ALFRED BARNABY. *After Coronado.* Norman, Okla., 1935.

———. *Forgotten Frontiers.* Norman, Okla., 1932.

TITIEV, MISCHA. *Old Oraibo: A Study of the Hopi Indians of the Third Mesa.* Peabody Museum Papers, Vol. XXII. Cambridge, Mass., 1944.

TWITCHELL, RALPH E. *Colonel Juan Bautista de Anza: Diary of His Expedition to the Moquis.* Papers of the Historical Society of New Mexico, No. 21. Santa Fe, N.Mex.

———. *The Leading Facts of New Mexican History.* 2 vols. Cedar Rapids, Iowa, 1911–12.

———. *Spanish Archives of New Mexico.* 2 vols. Cedar Rapids, Iowa, 1914.

UGARTE Y LOYOLA, JACOBO. Correspondence of, 1785–1787. Spanish Archives of New Mexico, Archivo General of Mexico, Archivo General de Indias. (See Thomas, 1932.)

UNDERHILL, RUTH M. *The Navajos.* Norman, Okla., 1956.

———. *Red Man's Religion.* Chicago, 1965.

U.S. DOCUMENTS:

Report of Secretary of War, 35th Congress, 2nd Session, 1858.

Report of Joint Special Commission on Indian Affairs, 1867.

Statistics Concerning Indian Education, Fiscal Year 1968, Bureau of Indian Affairs, 1968.

Federal Indian Law, 1958.

First Annual Report, Bureau of American Ethnology, 1879.

New Mexico Indian Affairs, 1849–1880. National Archives.

Records of United States Army, Department of New Mexico, Groups 92 and 98, National Archives.

Annual Reports of the Commissioner of Indian Affairs, 1846–1960.

Indian Record, September 1968, Bureau of Indian Affairs.

Navajo Progress. Window Rock, Ariz., 1967.

VAN VALKENBURGH, R. F. "Captain Red Shirt," New Mexico magazine, July 1941. Albuquerque, N.Mex.

―― and J. C. MC FEE. A Short History of the Navajo People. Window Rock, Ariz., 1938.

WALL, LEON. Navajo-English Dictionary. Window Rock, Ariz., 1958.

WATSON, EDITHA L. Navajo Sacred Places. Window Rock, Ariz., 1964.

WEBER, ANSELM. The Navajo Indians—A Statement of Facts. St. Michaels, Ariz., 1914.

WEDEL, W. R. Prehistoric Man on the Great Plains. Smithsonian Institution. Washington, D.C., 1940.

WILSON, JOHN P. Military Campaigns in the Navajo Country 1800–1846. Museum of New Mexico. Santa Fe, N.Mex., 1967.

WINSHIP, GEORGE P. Narrative of the Expedition of Coronado. Bureau of American Ethnology. Washington, D.C., 1896.

WOODWARD, ARTHUR. A Brief History of Navajo Silversmithing. Flagstaff, Ariz., 1946.

YOUNG, ROBERT W., ed. The Navajo Yearbook. Bureau of Indian Affairs. Window Rock, Ariz., 1961.

――. "The Role of the Navajo in the Southwestern Drama," Gallup (N.Mex.) Independent, June 1968.

# Sources

ALL REFERENCES are to books listed in the Bibliography.

PAGE

2      "its regeneration": Young, *Navajo Yearbook.*

11     Four towns banded together: Martin et al.

15     "although with some loss of form": Hester.

18     Estevanico's mission to the Zuñis: Hodge, *Spanish Explorers.*

25–27   Quotations from Oñate: Hammond and Rey, *Don Juan de Oñate.*

43     "a Portuguese and mestizos and sambahigos": Forbes.

43     "under the pretext that the Navajos were doing it": Hackett.

50–51   Concept of relatives: Kluckhohn and Leighton.

53     "framework of theology and ceremony": Underhill, *Navajos.*

58     "gathered to trade and barter with Indians": Bandelier.

66–67   "It is not presumable": Rengel.

73     "were debating how to divide the booty": Bailey, *Indian Slave Trade.*

74     Number of Navajo baptisms: Bailey, *Ibid.*

76     Patton's report: Underhill, *Navajos.*

PAGE

77      "a certain people are going to come": Sapir.
87      "You have a strange reason," paraphrased from the exchange between Largo and Doniphan as recorded by a Doniphan aide: Hughes.
90      "were overbearing": Bancroft.
93      "The Colonel Commanding": Bancroft.
96–99   Simpson's journal entries: Simpson.
104     Price of Navajo slaves: Bailey, *Indian Slave Trade.*
109     "Why can't the Americans understand": Bailey, *Ibid.*
115     "acquired a Navajo belle": Van Valkenburgh.
120     "designated by the President": Bailey, *Navajo Reconnaissance.*
120     Meriwether's orders: Report of Secretary of War, 1858.
121     Dodge's report: Report of Commissioner of Indian Affairs, 1855.
124     Meriwether to Manypenny: *Ibid.*
131     "to appease his wrath": Bailey, *Long Walk.*
134     "an arrogant presumption": Chittendon.
140     "that demands being pressed": Bailey, *Reconnaissance.*
142     "Latter Day Saints": Report of the Secretary of War, 1858.
147     "closed their ears": Underhill, *Navajos.*
152     Description of Union troops: Horgan.
153     "felt like heroes": *Ibid.*
158     Account of Fort Fauntleroy horse race massacre: Report of Joint Special Commission on Indian Affairs.
159     Kennon statement: Young, *Navajo Yearbook.*
160–61  Establishment of Bosque Redondo: Young, "Role of the Navajo."
161     Carleton's letters to Halleck: Bailey, *Reconnaissance.*
162     Carleton's letter to Walker: Young, "The Role of the Navajo."
162     Connelly's speech: Santa Fe *New Mexican,* May 20, 1863.
162     "simply remove or exterminate them": Young, "Role of the Navajo."
162–63  Carleton's report to War Department: Report of Joint Special Commission on Indian Affairs.
164     Kit Carson's plans for the Navajos: Bailey, *Indian Slave Trade.*
171–72  Connelly's proclamation: Bancroft.
174     "I beg respectfully": U.S. Report of Joint Special Commission on Indian Affairs.
176     Carleton's hogan town: Bailey.
177     "By the subjugation": Young, "The Role of the Navajo."
180     Carleton and rationing problems: Bailey, *Long Walk.*

PAGE

188 Carleton to Adjutant General: U.S. Documents, U.S. Army.

192–93 Dodd's convictions: U.S. Documents, N.M. Indian Affairs.

193–96 Council proceedings: Langley.

212 "five hundred silk hats": Bloom.

213–15 Beadle quotes: Beadle.

221 "The assignment of work": Young, "Role of the Navajo."

227 "temples or cults": Young, *Navajo Yearbook.*

227–28 "The legends, prayers, poems and songs": *Ibid.*

232–3 "the teacher wanted us": Kluckhohn and Leighton.

233–34 Fort Defiance testimony: *Navajo Agency Letter Book* and Young, "Role of the Navajo."

235 "had been patients": Kluckhohn and Leighton.

236–38 Report of Meriam committee: Meriam.

240 "education has cheated the Navajo": Mathews.

247–48 General Armstrong's report: Boston *Daily Advertiser,* September 13, 1883, in Young, "Role of the Navajo."

250 "a growing clamor of protest": Young, *Ibid.*

252 "Friction between Navajos and non-Navajos": Young, *Ibid.*

257 "varied origins": Kluckhohn and Leighton.

260 "were clustered the rites": Hill, "Agricultural."

261–63 Weber's "Statement of Fact": Young, "Role of the Navajo."

266–68 Dialog at Navajo Tribal Council: Young, *Ibid.*

269 1933 report of Navajo Agency: U.S. Documents, Report of the Commissioner of Indian Affairs, 1933.

276 Report of Navajo Agency: Young, "Role of the Navajo."

280–81 Developments leading to formation of Navajo tribal government: Young, *Ibid.*

283 "very important in the rites of the Tohee": Young, *Ibid.*

# Index

301

Indian Bureau (Bureau of Indian Affairs), 189, 200, 206, 210–12, 230, 285 (see also specific agents); Bennett and, 207–8; Carleton and, 173, 176, 177, 179, 180; Collins and, 139, 140, 158, 159; Dodge and, 118; and Navajo Reservation, 246, 247, 251, 266, 279ff.; and Tribal Council, 280ff.; schools, 223, 239, 240
Industry, 289
Infant mortality rate, 256
Institute for Government Research, 236
Interior Department, 197, 210, 230, 260, 282; and additions to reservation, 246; Army surrenders control to, 189; favors reservation, 190; and oil and gas royalties, 256; studies Bosque Redondo, 183; and Tribal Council, 283
Irigoyan, Padre, 62
Irrigation (see also Agriculture and farming): Navajo Irrigation Project, 213n., 275
Irving, Washington, 133
Isleta, 44

Jackson, Andrew, 134
Jackson, Congreve, 84–85, 88
Jaramillo, Pablo, 91
Jasin, 111
Jémez (and Jémez Indians), 25, 28, 40–45 passim, 56, 72, 74, 96, 111, 135; Baird special agent at, 109, 110–11; Sumner and Calhoun parley at, 107–8
Jicarilla Apaches, 118
Jobs, vi, vii, 287ff.
Johnson, Andrew, 186–87, 188, 201

Johnston, William R., 250
Jumanos, 17

Kavenaugh, Dr., 158
Keams, Tom, 215–16
Keams Canyon, 216
Kearney, Stephen Watts, 82, 83, 84
Kendrick, Henry L., 112–13, 114, 119, 127
Kendrick, Silas F., 140–41, 142, 143
Keshgoli, Hastin, 85
Kennon, Louis, 159
Keres, 26–27, 43
Kern, Edward M. and Richard H., 98

Labadie, Lorenzo, 177, 178–79
Laguna, 63
Laguna Negra, 121–23
Lamar, Lucius Q. C., 249
Land, 51, 52, 63–64, 119–20, 125ff., 215, 260–66ff. (see also Agriculture and farming; Livestock); and enlargement of reservation, 245ff.; and establishment of reservation, 198–99
Lane, William Carr, 110–11ff.
Language, vii, 1, 3, 34, 212, 242
La Purgarita, 99
Largo, Jon, 126
Largo, José, 97
Largo, Zarcillas, 87, 88, 115, 131; death of, 147–48; made head chief, 116–17; resigns as head chief, 122
Largo Canyon, 13
Lea, Luke, 106
Leal, James W., 91
Lee, Stephen, 91
Leupp, 224, 250, 281
Lincoln, Abraham, 172–73